Courting the Community

CHRISTINE ZOZULA

COURTING THE COMMUNITY

Legitimacy and Punishment in a Community Court

TEMPLE UNIVERSITY PRESS
Philadelphia • *Rome* • *Tokyo*

TEMPLE UNIVERSITY PRESS
Philadelphia, Pennsylvania 19122
tupress.temple.edu

Library of Congress Cataloging-in-Publication Data

Names: Zozula, Christine, 1983– author.
Title: Courting the community : legitimacy and punishment in a community
    court / Christine Zozula.
Description: Philadelphia : Temple University Press, 2019. | Includes
    bibliographical references and index. |
Identifiers: LCCN 2018044540 (print) | LCCN 2018045809 (ebook) |
    ISBN 9781439917411 (E-book) | ISBN 9781439917398 (cloth) |
    ISBN 9781439917404 (pbk.)
Subjects: LCSH: Neighborhood justice centers—United States. |
    Community-based corrections—Law and legislation—United States. |
    Punishment—United States. | Courts—United States. | Justice,
    Administration of—United States. | Dispute resolution (Law)—United States.
Classification: LCC KF9084 (ebook) | LCC KF9084 .Z69 2019 (print) | DDC
    345.73/01—dc23
LC record available at https://lccn.loc.gov/2018044540

To my parents

Contents

Preface

was introduced to community courts in 2004 as an undergraduate at Fordham College Lincoln Center. My anthropology professor, Benjamin Chesluk, suggested that I intern at Midtown Community Court, piquing my curiosity by making the vague statement that "interesting things" were afoot.

My experiences at Midtown Community Court helped me unpack a transitional moment in New York City and, in doing so, better forged my desire to become a social scientist. The September 11 attacks occurred during the first week of my freshman year. Makeshift memorials erected immediately afterward were soon replaced by more ominous and permanent fixtures: national guardsmen standing post with AK-47s on subway platforms, ubiquitous signs urging New Yorkers to exercise vigilance and to "say something" if we "see something." Years later, September 11 discourses leaked into Midtown Community Court. I listened as residents chastised a defendant for running to catch a train in Penn Station. Despite the defendant's claims, residents assured him that his "victimless crime" action was harmful—people might have thought he had a bomb or was fleeing from another terrorist attack. Toward more local concerns, every day I walked the six short blocks to Midtown Community Court, and I thought about quality-of-life crimes and Hell's Kitchen's increasingly corporatist cartography. Those thoughts remained when I arrived at court, where I listened to long-term residents celebrate a safer and cleaner neighborhood while also wondering aloud how much longer they could afford their sky-rocketing rents. Though I had been in the area only since 2001, I had already witnessed the rapid growth of high-end stores, the shuttering of small businesses, and the erection of the AOL Time Warner Center. Making sense of Midtown Community Court helped me make sense of myself and my temporary home during college.

While I was in graduate school, now an avowed social scientist, I continued to learn about community courts, this time in Greenville. My understanding of community courts shifted as I approached them with greater theoretical and methodological training. During my research in Greenville, I came to understand that community courts do not merely reflect community concerns and trends but, instead, actively shape and legitimize community concerns. Big-picture anxieties are filtered through community courts and given merit by the very performative justice that community courts practice. This book is thus about how community courts build legitimacy by actively "courting" the communities they serve. Training my focus on organizational identity, I argue that ambivalent and flexible punishment is central to community courts' legitimacy-building strategies.

As I wrote this book, phantom critics nagged me. (Thankfully, critiques raised by mentors, colleagues, my editor, and reviewers were much less withering.) One imagined critic questioned my book's lack of attention to race and racialization in community courts. The other specter asked why I invested my time and energy toward a critique of community courts—why criticize a criminal justice organization with noble goals and small stakes when ignoble goals and more urgent matters abound? I struggled to answer these phantom critics for many years. (The pat answer, that faculty members must publish to retain their jobs, while true, never satisfied.) In March 2018, I attended a lecture by Mariame Kaba, a prison abolitionist, at Brown University. Her ideas ignited answers that quelled my anxieties; I share my resolutions below.

The criminalization of incivility, which community courts encourage, legitimize, and proliferate, is important. In very recent memory, white women have called police officers for myriad "incivilities" perpetrated by people of color: a family barbecuing with charcoal, women failing to wave to a neighbor upon leaving an Airbnb, a student napping in a dorm's common area, and a child selling water. The line between order and disorder maps onto racial boundaries. Relatedly, this book emphasizes the importance of questioning "progressive" criminal justice reforms, especially those that operate in tandem with legitimacy-building strategies. Drug courts have been around since 1989, yet the criminal justice system continues to be overrun with drug-related cases. "Progressive" police forces now use body cams, in part to respond to demands by Black Lives Matter and Say Her Name campaigns. Despite the touted transparency of the technology, I have yet to see evidence that body cams prevent unnecessary use of force, much less hold officers accountable for harming or even killing unarmed civilians. Finally, while newly "woke" Americans rail against separating families at the border, journalists, activists, and scholars gently remind us of the persistent connections among white supremacy, colonialism, juvenile detention, and definitions of crime. Reminders of these trends are ignored or dismissed outright, as they detract from the horror of our immediate circumstances.

In my view, the criminal justice system is a glass shattered across the kitchen floor. Debating whether to first glue together the largest pieces or the smallest shards is fruitless—the glass is broken. Community courts are a shard amid this mess. I hope that instead of trying to cobble together something usable from the jagged pieces, thirsty readers close this book and demand a new glass.

Acknowledgments

've always believed that acknowledgments skew toward the self-congrat-ulatory—flowery compliments to others who helped the author be so *accomplished* and *brilliant*, a way to thank others overtly, while mostly patting oneself on the back. I am neither accomplished nor brilliant. But I have written this book, which is something, and many people helped me do that. Any insight, provocative observation, or interesting connection in this book is likely due to the people I name below. While I do not adhere to the overly sentimental conventions of most acknowledgments sections, know that I am deeply humbled and incredibly grateful for the help, sup-port, and friendship of everyone involved in this project.

To my undergraduate mentors at Fordham—Ben Chesluk, Pat Moyni-han, and, most dearly, Ayala Fader—who encouraged my interest in social science: Sometimes, I think I pursued this career in the hope that I could be as smart and cool as you all. (Impossible!) You have remained an inspi-ration and a resource far beyond my time at Fordham.

Faculty members at the University of Connecticut provided encourage-ment, critical feedback, and excellent training. In particular, I thank An-drew Deener, Brad Wright, Bandana Purkayastha, Clint Sanders, and Gaye Tuchman. My friends and peers from graduate school helped shape my thinking. I especially thank Melissa Lavin and Miho Iwata for providing feedback on sections of this book, including Chapter 6 (portions of which were originally published in my article "Courting the Community: Organizational Flexibility and Community Courts," *Criminology and Criminal Justice* 18, no. 2 [2018]: 226–244 [Copyright © 2018 by SAGE Publications. Reprinted by permission of SAGE Publications. http://journals.sagepub .com/doi/full/10.1177/1748895817709864]). As I stumbled through the publishing process, Barb Gurr and Katie Acosta were kind enough to share their book proposals with me.

My colleagues in the Department of Sociology and Anthropology at the University of Rhode Island have been incredibly supportive, and I feel very lucky to work with such smart and generous people. I especially thank Julie Keller and Melanie Brasher for reading and reviewing portions of this book and for creating/maintaining our writing accountability group (along with Heather Rackin, Kristin Johnson, Lehua Ledbetter, Sara Gundersen, and Smita Ramnarain).

To the librarians at Holy Cross, Providence College, Rhode Island College, North Providence Public Library, and the Marian J. Mohr Memorial Library (where I wrote the majority of this book): I am forever indebted to you for always smiling at me but never talking to me.

It has been a dream to work with Temple University Press, and I thank everyone at Temple for the guidance and work. My editor, Ryan Mulligan, has been exceptionally supportive from the very early stages of this book, and he provided incisive feedback throughout the writing process. James Nolan and an anonymous reviewer commented on an earlier version of the manuscript, and their insights greatly improved the book. I appreciate the keen editing of Heather Wilcox and Joan Vidal.

I somehow managed to convince (or perhaps trick?) friends from outside academia to help me. Laurie Gallagher was a taskmaster extraordinaire. Fran Harrington designed the concept for the cover illustration. I am very lucky to have such excellent friends.

To the people at "Greenville Community Court": Thank you for welcoming me into your workplace and sharing your insights and thoughts with me. I am especially grateful to "Nick," "Tom," and "Becca," who were remarkably kind to me.

Some people helped in capacities far too great to adequately capture here. To Breck Peters, Claudio Benzecry, Jim Wilson, Stacy Misarri, and Yaran Drawbridge: Your support has meant the world to me. And most of all, thanks go to my family, in particular my parents, Joan and Steve Zozula: You're wonderful, and I love you.

Courting the Community

Introduction

Culture and Punishment

The summer of 2002 was the summer of the ice-cream war in Green-ville. The ice-cream truck jingle, the siren call of summer, incited dis-cussions of quality of life, complaints about noise pollution, and the future of the city. Mr. Icy, a local chain of ice-cream trucks, received four noise violations over a period of two months. One resident videotaped the Mr. Icy trucks as they roamed the neighborhood, sending the videotapes to the police as "proof" that the noise levels were much too high. The fight extended to the local newspaper's letters to the editor. One resident wrote:

> Mister Icy does not have the simple chiming music we fondly re-member from Greenville's earlier days. It's music that is loud and jarring, often for 30 minutes at a time, as Mr. Icy parks on a neigh-borhood street. This is a citywide problem.

Other residents tied the noise violations to larger problems in the city. Residents argued that the music "lure[s] children out after 9:00 P.M.," caus-ing them to violate city curfew laws. Others linked noise violations to the city's exodus of residents to the suburbs. One resident wrote, "Quality-of-life issues such as persistent, excessive noise directly relate to the city's ability to attract and retain residents."

Of course, not everyone agreed that Mr. Icy's music was cause for con-cern. Some residents wrote positive letters about city noise. One letter claimed that "it takes all kinds of ears to hear the city." In addition to the

Mr. Icy truck, residents heard "the sound of basketballs thumping; soccer teams being cheered on; neighbors calling to one another with gardening tips[;] . . . the lilt and patter of many languages and dialects." A less poetically inclined letter writer told those concerned with Mr. Icy to "Get a life." Not to be outdone, the Mr. Icy detractors responded:

> This kind of noise would not be allowed in the suburb, where the letter-writer, a former Greenville resident, now resides. He didn't stay in Greenville. That is what happens when quiet residents get a chance: They move . . . to surrounding cities that protect residents. Some may argue, "We're not talking about drug dealers or prostitutes." But without taking care of quality-of-life concerns, those are the only people who will stay in Greenville.

The noise complaints landed the owner of the Mr. Icy fleet, Alberto Davis, in Greenville Community Court, which handled the city's low-level offenses. Judge Balick, the only judge at Greenville Community Court, arranged for Davis to bring one of his trucks to the court parking lot. Davis played the jingle for the audience of residents, media, and court personnel. Residents booed, insisting, "He's playing it soft for the judge!" The judge found the noise levels to be acceptable. After the show-and-tell, everyone gathered back in the courtroom. The judge ordered Davis to keep the songs at the volume he had heard in the parking lot, to refrain from playing music more than a half an hour after dark, and to move locations or stop the music after repeating the same song six times.

In recent years, American cities have come to view quality-of-life issues as integral to successful communal life. Small-scale incivilities, such as a loud ice-cream truck jingle or someone urinating on a street corner, have come to signal far more serious problems, such as urban fear, community disinvestment, and even homicide. This transformation of how we view low-level urban problems was partially fueled by the popularity of broken windows theory, a theory of crime that argues that small visible signs of disorder will lead to the apocalyptic decline of a neighborhood (Wilson and Kelling 1982). As political forces and new policing strategies focused on cleaning up the streets and enforcing order, quality-of-life issues shifted into criminal justice matters. Litter, loitering, public drunkenness, and vending without a license, once considered simple nuisances, were recategorized as "quality-of-life crimes." In Greenville, an ice-cream truck's loud jingle played the beginning bars of the song of urban flight and decay.

In many cities across the United States, the institution that handles quality-of-life issues is the community court. Community courts, such as the one presided over by Judge Balick, are a relatively new form of justice, specifically designed to handle quality-of-life issues. Community courts maintain that so-called victimless crimes (such as littering, graffiti, and public drunkenness) jeopardize the well-being of residents, businesses, and visitors of an area. Whereas traditional courts might dismiss such cases or administer a small fine, community courts aim to "meaningfully punish" quality-of-life offenders. For example, an offender who vandalized a building may be court-ordered to paint over his graffiti. Someone arrested for public drunkenness may have to attend Alcoholics Anonymous meetings and report back to the court. When an offender meets the court's requirements, whether through community service, treatment, or other sanctions, the court wipes the case from the offender's public criminal records.[1] Community courts also involve nonoffenders in the justice process. Some community courts arrange "impact panels," where offenders, residents, and business owners meet to discuss how quality-of-life crimes negatively affect the neighborhood. Community court representatives engage in strategic neighborhood outreach to inform residents of the court's practices, to update them on cases, and to ask about their concerns.

If scholars were asked to account for the relationship between the "ice-cream war" and community courts, they would relate them to broader criminal justice trends. Some scholars would describe the judicial resolution of the "ice-cream war" as a rare form of emotive punishment in a justice system primarily characterized by detachment, efficiency, and group management (Feeley and Simon 1992). The scene of a defendant, his accusers, and a judge, all looking to resolve an issue around an ice-cream truck jingle, seems like a quaint throwback to a simpler kind of justice, what Jonathan Simon calls a "willful nostalgia" (1995). In a reaction against a detached and calculated justice system, the United States created new justice forms that allow people to express emotions. The "ice-cream war," these scholars would argue, is an emotional outlier in a criminal justice system that is otherwise detached, bureaucratic, and wiped of emotion.

Other scholars would argue that the "ice-cream war" and community courts are clear examples of an overzealous criminal justice system in action. These scholars would assert that behaviors previously thought of as simple inconveniences are now subject to regulation by the criminal justice system. The very idea that judges should spend time deciding on the appropriate volume of an ice-cream truck jingle demonstrates the ubiquity of criminal justice control in the United States. This new concern with quality-of-life crimes indicates increasing control over behaviors and ways of being that were previously viewed as trivial nuisances or symptoms of larger structural problems. The United States has elected to "solve" structural problems, such as homelessness and addiction, through criminalization, using the quality-of-life paradigm as "a punitive approach to . . . urban social problems" (Vitale 2008: 2). The creation and growth of a community court system has only solidified this trend. Community courts formalize the criminal justice regulation of modern urban incivilities and, by doing so, demonstrate how excessive and punitive the United States has become.

Are community courts a reaction against current trends in the U.S. criminal justice system, or are they indicative of these same trends? Both explanations are too simplistic. In my study, the community court is both highly emotional and highly punitive. Community courts straddle the middle ground somewhere between the two explanations. Community courts do aim to make the justice system more emotional and less detached. They involve community members in the process by inviting them to court and by soliciting crime concerns from residents and business owners. I witnessed people who work at the court beam when an offender successfully transformed his or her life and wipe tears from their eyes when an offender made heartfelt pleas for leniency. In other ways, community courts clearly expand courts' capacity for criminal justice supervision and make the consequences for low-level crimes more demanding and severe. Community courts can and do send people to jail for relatively low-level crimes. They require defendants involved in very minor crimes to commit to lengthy stretches of court supervision. Community courts enact a unique, hybridized form of justice that is both emotional and punitive. Because these community courts are simultaneously punitive and a reaction against punitiveness, they warrant a more nuanced investigation to tell us what exactly they are doing and why they are doing it.

A nuanced investigation of community courts can lead us to a deeper understanding of the current state of the American court system. These trends—an increasingly punitive criminal justice system, the proliferation of community courts, and criminal justice control of quality-of-life crimes—warrant interesting empirical questions. What are the relationships between rehabilitation and punishment? What constitutes the community? What makes criminals, and how do we unmake them?

Goals of the Book

This book is an ethnography of one community court, which sits at the busy intersection of a downtown area of a city in the United States. I call this court Greenville Community Court, which is a pseudonym, along with the names of court staff, defendants, affiliated organizations, and other individuals who appear in this book—a requirement of the Institutional Review Board (IRB) that approved my research.[2] By telling the stories of Greenville Community Court, this study accomplishes three basic goals.

First, this book explains how quality-of-life discourses are translated into court practices. Other fantastic scholarship has illuminated our understanding of quality-of-life crimes from various vantage points. We understand how ideas about quality of life are connected to economic, social, and political structures (Chesluk 2007; Vitale 2008). We understand how quality-of-life crimes are managed through police tactics (Katz, Webb, and Schaefer 2001; Golub et al. 2003). We do not, however, account for how courts process quality-of-life crimes, an important gap in scholarship to date. In this book, I show how community courts formed in relation to quality-of-life discourses and how community courts translate those discourses into practice. This work aims to help form a more complete understanding of the processing of quality-of-life offenses and, by doing so, paints a more comprehensive theoretical picture of how quality-of-life crimes are understood, punished, and treated.

Second, this study illustrates the how criminal sanctioning in community courts produces particular identities for the offender and for the organization itself. By looking at how Greenville Community Court processes cases, this ethnography is ideally suited to show how the court creates, enacts, and interprets ideas about crime, culpability, and justice. Community courts' ideas about culpability vary—they do not assume the same level of culpability across similar cases. Clearly, individual circumstances, such as an offender's criminal history and current charges, influence how court actors make decisions about appropriate punishment. However, in community courts, an offender's "presentation of accountability," by which I mean how well a defendant conforms to community courts' legal and extralegal demands, significantly influences sanctioning decisions. Decisions about appropriate sanctions and whether to be strict or whether to afford leniency are based on Greenville Community Court's ideas about a defendant's willingness to conform to court orders rather than about his or her criminal propensity.

Sanctioning decisions for the community court are about producing not only particular kinds of defendants but also a particular kind of organizational identity. This form of case processing, which allows for treatment or leniency when offenders perform accountability and jail time when offenders do not demonstrate accountability, is ultimately useful for community courts' organizational identity. How community courts justify and practice punishment and their underlying justifications for how and why they punish aim to demonstrate particular qualities of the organization itself. Routine punishment at community courts demonstrates the courts' effectiveness and paints these courts as rational, reasonable, and correct in their orientations.

Third, looking at how community courts operate helps situate them in discussions about punitive versus rehabilitative strategies. The sociology of punishment often views punishment as a pendulum swinging between two opposite positions, retribution and rehabilitation. Retribution, or punitive punishment, aims to make the offender "pay" for his or her crimes through the imposition of negative consequences, such as criminal fines or jail time. Rehabilitative, or therapeutic, punishment aims to change the offender from a criminal into a noncriminal. This punishment may still mete out negative consequences, but the primary goal is to transform the offender's behavior. Viewing punishment as a pendulum that swings between punitive or therapeutic orientations has left scholarship with a bifurcated sense of punishment. This way of thinking imposes a contrived categorization system in which punishment practices must either be punitive or therapeutic. As discussed above, community courts do not fit neatly into this grand narrative; they focus on individualized justice and aim to rehabilitate offenders, yet they also send low-level offenders to jail.

Community courts are better viewed in light of a growing body of scholarship that focuses on the flexible and nuanced features of punishment (Hannah-Moffat 2005; Matthews 2005; O'Malley 1999; Pratt 2000; Robinson 2008; Stuart 2016). This scholarship documents how restorative justice practices, therapeutic jurisprudence, risk/needs assessment, and other popular contemporary practices show that rehabilitation is alive and well in penality. Even tactics that appear inherently punitive may be more flexible and imbued with meaning that suggests rehabilitative overtones. This scholarship foregrounds contradictions within criminal justice goals, values, and practices—contradictions that pose important challenges for the study of the current state of criminal justice. Through this lens, we can understand community courts as unique sites of control, practicing justice in a way that disrupts our understanding of punishment orientations as monolithic, either punitive or rehabilitative.

Community courts provide a useful case to examine existing scholarly debates about punishment and rehabilitation, and this study sheds an important light on the current understanding of the U.S. criminal justice system. The existence and possibilities of community courts within a criminal justice landscape that is primarily categorized as punitive, rational, and detached challenge certain widely held ideas about where punishment is going, even as these courts attempt to put other ideas into practice. Community courts are, in part, a reaction against overly punitive trends, as they seek to reduce high recidivism rates through rehabilitative and crime-reducing sanctions. They are also complicit in the punitive turn, as they ensnare low-level offenders (whose crimes may have previously gone unpunished) in a rigorous process of court supervision. This case study aims to show that punishment is not monolithic. Considering community courts as both separate from and as part of the punitive turn enables a more comprehensive view of the criminal justice landscape. Focusing on this unique form of justice invites a discussion of criminal justice trends that avoids overaggrandizing the logic of criminal justice tactics.

These three goals are united by an overarching concern with the relationship between culture and punishment. Punishment is an extraordinarily salient location from which to examine how culture "works." Much like how a small sample of blood provides doctors with an overview of a body's functions, punishment is an institution that provides social scientists with an extraordinary amount of information about how society structures its ideas. Foundational sociological theorists were concerned with issues of punishment: Émile Durkheim examined the relationship between social cohesion and crime. Karl Marx investigated how crime control was a mechanism of class control. Michel Foucault emphasized how penal institutions shifted alongside changes in power. Salient in these inquiries is the role of culture in defining crime and guiding rationales for dealing with it. Punishment is a site where cultural norms and values are elaborated, enacted, and contested. Punishment, then, is an integral part of sociological inquiry as we strive to understand the social world in general.

A community court provides an excellent venue to showcase how punishment creates meaning for groups of people. Because community courts are relatively new organizations, meanings surrounding their work are still dynamic. As community courts combine punitive and therapeutic logics, they provide a useful case in which to study seemingly opposing criminal justice goals. Since community courts directly involve their communities as punishment resources and benefactors of justice tactics, they provide an interesting case study to show relationships between justice systems and the communities they serve. The Mr. Icy vignette that opens this chapter illustrates how community members contest quality-of-life issues and how these debates about quality-of-life crimes map moral landscapes onto urban communities. Community courts are then a useful place to study existing scholarly debates around the enactment of punishment, retribution and rehabilitation, and the impact of justice tactics on local communities. These relatively new courts show how justice agencies draw on cultural resources to give meaning to punishment while attempting to create new and distinct penalities for the broader community.

Culture and Punishment

Much of the literature that we have on the role of culture in courtrooms is not well-suited to explaining how punishment organizes meaning in our social world.

One area that conceptualizes the relationship between culture and punishment is that of *legal formalism*. Legal formalism posits that cultural ideas do not and cannot influence punishment. Criminal justice agencies enforce the laws with rationality, objectivity, and fairness. John Roberts's opening statements during his Supreme Court nomination hearings provide an excellent example of legal formalism: he compared the role of a judge to that of an umpire in baseball, pledging, "I will remember that it's my job to call balls and strikes and not to pitch or bat."[3] While cultural changes may shape the creation or elimination of laws, the courts, according to legal formalism, serve only to act on the law as written. Courts are rendered a "black box" in which cases enter, are judged according to clear facts and guidelines, and exit with a correct application of the law. This perspective certainly appeals to our understanding that courts should be fair, just, and unbiased. It also protects against judicial activism, maintaining the separation between law making and legal decision making. Legal formalists view culture as an entity that should not and does not factor into courtroom decision making.

The next strand of literature that examines the intersection between culture and criminal justice agencies explores organizational culture. These "court communities" scholars (Eisenstein, Flemming, and Nardulli 1988; Flemming, Nardulli, and Eisenstein 1992; Ulmer 2005; Ulmer and Kramer 1996) argue that the courtroom is like any other workplace: people cooperate to make their work more efficient, to advance their own professional goals and careers, and to resolve conflicts within the group. Court communities are not limited to the courtroom itself; they also involve local political actors, local media, and local public opinions. Court actors handle cases in ways that are efficient, rational, and designed to help them advance their careers, and these considerations affect case processing. The organizational culture of courts can influence criminal charges, plea-bargaining decisions, and even the severity of a sentence. This scholarship helps us reevaluate the somewhat-idealized understanding of courtroom processing and shows how local patterns and cultures can influence case outcomes and trajectories. It also shows how micro- and mesolevel phenomena shape and organize case-processing outcomes.

The last group of scholarship on culture and punishment examines how the law expresses culture. Culture is conceptualized as an independent variable that affects the process, forms, content, and distribution of punishment. This body of literature argues that notions about certain crimes, criminals, genders, and racial groups influence enforcement and sentencing practices. For instance, feminist criminologists argue that ideas about girls and women translate into how we think about women who are perpetrators or victims of crimes (Chesney-Lind 1989; Howe 1994). Scholars of race and crime argue that stereotypes about racial minorities (in particular, black men) as aggressive, threatening, and criminal translate into more intensive criminal justice supervision (Collins 2004; Jones-Brown 2007; Russell-Brown 2009).

Aside from investigating how demographic groups are differentially punished, we can also look at how certain crimes and criminals come to be considered more or less dangerous over time, and therefore, more or less needing of punishment. For instance, the criminalization of certain types of drugs has been linked to xenophobia and racism (Musto 1997). This scholarship therefore argues that punishment embodies and reflects cultural meanings that exist in broader society.

All of these bodies of scholarship are useful for highlighting particular processes, goals, functions, and dysfunctions of the criminal justice system. However, these bodies of scholarship have some weaknesses that make each insufficient to examine punishment as productive of culture, necessitating the present study. The legal formalist approach views culture as though it is "turned off" in the criminal justice system. While it is certainly aspirational to say that justice is blind, fair, and uninfluenced by anything but "just the facts," in practice, that is not the case. People who work in courts vary in their understanding of how to interpret the cases before them, and litigants' resources (legal, economic, social, and cultural) influence legal goals and outcomes (Galanter 1974; Merry 1990). The court communities' perspective allows us to think about how meaning is constructed in a workgroup and in relation to other institutions outside the legal system, such as local politics and media. While this framework allows us to draw connections between the criminal justice system and other types of organizations, it does so at the cost of the substantive importance of the institution of criminal justice. The court communities' perspective is incredibly adept at highlighting differences between courts by interrogating differences in workgroup culture and local politics. However, it is less useful for studying how and why meanings of punishment matter beyond specifically local communities. The court communities' perspective is not equipped to deftly interrogate how local court practices are kinetically engaged with macrolevel cultural understandings of punishment and how those more macrolevel understandings shift and develop over time. The scholarship on how punishment and law embody cultural ideas allows us to connect macrolevel cultural values to microlevel case processing, but it also assumes that cultural ideals are readily adopted by the criminal justice institution. It does not allow us to think about how criminal justice organizations may interpret and, at times, resist preexisting ideas about crime and criminals. This scholarship does not show how the penal system actively creates culture and is not merely a recipient.

A more dynamic approach to the study of culture and punishment is presented by David Garland (1990), who views punishment as an important facet of social organization. He conceptualizes punishment as a "cultural agent," claiming that punishment, and institutions surrounding punishment, help shape broader patterns of meaning in society. Garland helps us see the relationship between culture and punishment as mutually constitutive rather than view culture as "causing" a particular penal outcome. He argues that

> punishment and penal institutions help shape the overarching culture and contribute to the generation and regeneration of its terms. . . . Like any major social institution, punishment is shaped by broad cultural patterns which have their own origins elsewhere, but it also generates its own local meanings, values, and sensibilities which contribute—in a small but significant way—to the bricolage of the dominant culture. (1990: 249)

This framework allows for punishment to be conceptualized as an independent variable, which can influence culture. It shows how culture can be created through punishment practices and how meanings surrounding punishment may be generated through penal actions.

Garland's work helps us think about community courts in relationship to and in dialogue with current penological trends. It allows for a discussion of community courts that does not take "the culture of punishment" as monolithic. Community court practices that do not fit into the macrolevel trend of punishment as wholly punitive may still be articulated and explained. Garland's framework permits an examination of dynamism and inconsistencies while still accounting for practices that are neither exactly punitive nor a vestigial form of justice administration that will soon be subsumed by the dominance of punitive policies. Second, this approach allows for an understanding of community courts as agentic institutions that can and do influence larger ideas about crime, justice, criminals, and the community. Finally, it takes the study of punishment as a worthy and unique endeavor rather than make punishment a subgenre of racial, class, and/or gendered inequalities or a particular articulation of state control.

This book focuses on discourses about and practices toward crime and criminals as a way to locate cultural understandings of crime and justice, criminals, and community. I studied one community court, Greenville Community Court. I observed court sessions at Greenville Community Court, attended meetings with court staff and other agencies, and took field notes on how workers, citizens, and the media understood, processed, and discussed community court cases.

Case-processing tactics at Greenville Community Court enact and create cultural meaning. Garland writes that

> implicit within every penal relation and every exercise of penal power there is a conception of social authority, of the (criminal) person, and of the nature of the community or social order that the punishment protects and tries to recreate. (1990: 265)

Greenville Community Court operates with an odd combination of meanings. Some offenders are able to be reformed in the eyes of the court. Others deserve punishment in the form of jail time. The court itself is both a cheerleader for offender success and a strict enforcer of proper behavior. The community, the local urban areas that the court serves, also have multiple meanings. The community is a place that encourages criminal activity (for instance, when offenders leave inpatient treatment, they often return to neighborhoods or social networks that promote criminal behavior). The community is also the place that heals criminality in that promoting positive communal ties is thought to be a rehabilitative force in offenders' lives. Finally, the community is something to be protected from crime, a precarious place where quality-of-life crimes are thought to constantly threaten orderliness and perhaps lead to larger crimes. The community gives the court legitimacy and authority but also acts as a strong critic of the court's ideas and practices. The multitude of meanings and the practices that inform, create, and challenge these meanings are interesting and worthy of investigation because community courts offer a "third space" that disrupts the essentialist, binary divide between punishment and rehabilitation that dominates academic and popular understandings of the U.S. criminal justice system, particularly the courts.

Flexible Times, Flexible Organizations

While this study of community courts contributes to understandings of punishment, it also comments on broader discussions around new organizational forms in contemporary life. Scholars use such terms as "postmodernity," "late capitalism," and "liquid modernity" to label the current historical moment. Real changes in the building blocks of society have radically altered how individuals and groups of people understand and organize their lives. Institutional building blocks with clear designs for living "no longer provide a long-term frame" (Sennett 2007: 4). As a result, this period of time is characterized by instability and uncertainty.

This "postmodern turn" coincides with the advent of new kinds of organizational forms.

These "liquid" or flexible organizations (Clegg and Baumeler 2010) curiously market themselves around their instability. They "demonstrat[e] signs of internal change and flexibility" and "reengineer, reinvent themselves continually" (Sennett 2007: 40–41). These organizations attempt to address the traditional institutions' failure to account for uncertainty by embracing and embodying the dynamic aspects of contemporary life. They do not attempt to replace traditional institutions in total; instead, they cater to specialized, niche areas of social life that were previously under the purview of more macrolevel institutions.

Community courts illustrate the rise of new flexible organizations in the criminal justice system. In the face of a failing criminal justice system, community courts forge a niche market around quality-of-life crimes. Serving a small subgroup of low-level offenders in hyperlocal geographic areas, community courts carve out a specialized space in the criminal justice field and brand themselves as innovative actors poised to solve pressing community-safety issues.

Legitimacy

For community courts to establish themselves as legitimate criminal justice organizations, they must draw from culturally resonant discourses to explain their existence. Organizational theorists tell us that new organizations must strike a delicate balance between appearing "innovative" while also "recognizable" (Ashforth and Gibbs 1990; Friedland and Alford 1991; Ruef and Scott 1998; Suchman 1995; Suddaby and Greenwood 2005). This book describes how community courts use different discursive tools to present themselves as legitimate, to distinguish themselves from other organizations in the criminal justice system, and to forge and maintain relationships with organizations outside this system.

Community courts are agentic institutions that coalesce seemingly dualistic and competing logics of retribution and rehabilitation. Greenville Community Court is harsh because it punishes low-level crimes more severely than traditional courts. Greenville Community Court is rehabilitative because it punishes low-level offenses with sanctions that aim to rehabilitate the offender, such as substance-abuse treatment or community service. Community courts, then, are simultaneously hard on crime and soft on crime. These competing logics illustrate the strengths of flexible organizations, demonstrating how community courts can market their adaptability and appeal to a wide audience. Heterogeneous, competing, or ambivalent institutional logics, like those of community courts, help institutions adapt to change, appeal to different stakeholders, and ultimately enable institutions to survive, as they are able to act opportunistically and reactively.

Greenville Community Court's competing logics help it appeal to different audiences, and they also help the court create new understandings of justice, punishment, and the community. This site is important to study because the courts themselves are involved in a project of socializing people into a new way of thinking. Community courts explicitly ask questions that are taken for granted in traditional courts and even in the criminal justice system as a whole: What are the goals of criminal justice? Where does crime come from? How should courts punish offenders? Because community courts actively and openly interrogate the meaning of punishment, their study can help illuminate how culture operates in traditional criminal justice organizations in which meaning making is far more routinized and subsumed under the logics of case processing.

Methods

When I started this project, I was enamored with the idea that businesses funded community courts and that community courts therefore functioned as a mechanism to rid cities of people and activities that hindered gentrification efforts. However, in the early stages of my fieldwork at Greenville Community Court, I did not see that assumption in practice. Instead, I observed judges, lawyers, and social-service providers working to get defendants into appropriate programs. I listened to frustrated residents express how they felt victimized by loiterers on street corners, litter in vacant lots, and disregard for the neighborhood. I heard social-service providers bemoan how few resources were available to accomplish the goals of their programs. I redirected this project's focus to reflect what I saw actually happening on the ground—choosing to study how the court interacted with and treated defendants and the community it aimed to serve. I briefly describe the strengths of my ethnographic approach, and I refer readers who desire a more detailed description to the Methodological Appendix at the end of the book.

Since I focus on discourses surrounding crime, justice, criminals, and the community in a problem-solving court, I adopted an ethnographic approach. This choice follows in a tradition of courtroom ethnographies that describe the relationship between larger cultural meanings and local practices of law (Barrett 2012; Emerson 1969; Feeley 1992; Kupchik 2006; Merry 1990). Through ethnographic observation, I trace how court actors' ideas about offenders develop and change over time and how those ideas are translated into action. For instance, I could trace how Greenville Community Court's ideas about a defendant change over time; cases that were initially seen through a "treatment lens" could shift over time to a punitive lens, depending on the number of times that a defendant had been to court, how that defendant behaved in court, and reports from sponsoring agencies about the defendant's conduct while under supervised treatment. Ethnographic research is uniquely capable of revealing how categories for understanding criminals are (1) mutable over time, (2) formed through interaction, and (3) not a priori. This final insight is particularly useful, given the macrolevel focus of the sociology of punishment.

The court itself has different audiences even outside the court: the residents concerned with quality-of-life crimes, law-enforcement agencies whose tactics can complement or undermine the organizational goals of the court, and other criminal justice agencies and social-service agencies that can aid or refuse the requests of the court. Ethnography illustrates organizational concerns for legitimacy by showing how court actors attempt to convert other people and organizations into their distinctive discursive framework. Ethnographic research highlights the communicative process to show how certain discursive tactics are successful or unsuccessful, given organizational goals. Ethnographic research was also incredibly useful for understanding how Greenville Community Court interacted with other agencies. It revealed how Greenville Community Court translated its flexible punishment logics to a variety of stakeholders. I witnessed how court officials highlighted or downplayed particular features of community courts to forge positive and beneficial relationships with residents' organizations, local homeless shelters, and social-service providers. These meetings revealed how community courts discursively deploy different aspects of their identities, depending on the audience at hand.

Overview

Chapter 1 provides an overview of community courts, detailing their philosophies and practices. Community courts draw specifically from legal and criminological theories and actively work to adopt those theories in their daily practices.

Chapter 2 situates community courts within historical criminal justice trends. Internal and external problems of the legitimacy of criminal justice institutions, the administrative and political appeal of community courts, and the problems associated with urban life contributed to the creation and popularity of community courts in the period when they emerged. The origin of community courts is not just a narrative of innovative people looking for solutions but part of the ongoing story of criminal justice's vacillation between rehabilitative and punitive extremes.

Chapters 3–5 focus on how Greenville Community Court creates meaning through routine case processing. Introducing the case-processing system at Greenville Community Court, Chapter 3 demonstrates how the court enacts criminological and philosophical principles on the ground. Chapter 4 describes how Greenville Community Court interacts with "good defendants," those people who arrive on time, attend all court dates, and act respectfully. Greenville Community Court structures its case processing to ensure that most defendants who enter the court will be good defendants, not only because doing so makes court actors' daily work easier but also because it reaffirms community courts' identity as benevolent, efficient, and effective. Greenville Community Court is often lenient with defendants, hoping that these defendants will ultimately prove themselves to be "good." Chapter 5 explains how Greenville Community Court decides which defendants deserve to go to jail. Retributive punishment has more to do with a defendant's failure to display appropriate accountability and deference than it does with actual criminal acts. I use the term "ambivalent justice" to describe the process by which the court sorts defendants into moral categories by virtue of how they respond to Greenville Community Court's orders. The court uses objective measures, such as failure to comply with court orders, and subjective measures, such as how a defendant communicates responsibility, to determine whether the defendant deserves jail time. The objective and subjective measures are problematic, in part because they assume that each defendant has an equal opportunity to comply with court orders and display accountability.

Chapter 6 takes readers outside the courtroom and into the world of people who interact with the court in other capacities. Greenville Community Court engages with resident groups, police officers, the media, and social-service providers. The community court's flexible mission, which allows it to be both therapeutic and punitive, serves the court well in its interactions with stakeholders. These competing goals are integrated in community courts in a complementary yet flexible way that enables them to draw on multiple sources of legitimacy to mobilize support and resources from distinct groups that make up "the community."

The Conclusion examines the lessons that community courts teach us about legitimacy of criminal justice organizations and contemporary social control. While community courts' impact on traditional criminal justice outcomes is inconclusive, it is clear that community courts excel at cultivating their own legitimacy as a criminal justice organization. Community courts' organizational legitimacy is best understood within a larger discussion of flexible organizations in the contemporary United States—namely, that specialized and flexible organizations have co-opted services and needs once filled by traditional institutions. I reflect on community courts' position in contemporary criminal justice in the United States, exploring the implications of filtering community efficacy, access to social services, and quality of life into criminal justice agencies.

Ultimately, I question the promise that community courts present a potential method to prevent crime.

1

Broken Windows, Broken People

t's 9:00 A.M., and Greenville Community Court is about a third full of defendants and their family members. Gary, the prosecutor, stands behind a small desk with a stack of manila folders on the left side of the courtroom.[1] He begins to call up defendants. A man received a violation for an excessively loud diesel truck. The defendant tells Gary that he believes the officer unfairly ticketed him, and he knows that other loud trucks drive through this neighborhood all the time. "He's not trying to be a dick to you," Gary says. "He gets calls from neighbors, and he has to just do his job. They can't chase everybody. Unfortunately, they got you." The defendant wants to pay a fine. Gary explains, "The judge doesn't give fines. You don't want to pay a fine, because then it's on your criminal record. You do this one day [of community service], and then it all disappears off of your record." Next, Gary calls up a young man for trespassing. The man shows Gary a piece of mail that verifies his address, and Gary tells him that the police report does not give him "any reason to pursue the matter further." They shake hands, and the young man leaves.

Gary calls other cases: a woman with a petty larceny charge. An older man charged with interfering with an officer who apologizes for missing his court date the day before. The exchanges between Gary and each defendant are one-on-one but not entirely confidential. People in the courtroom occupy themselves by quietly chatting or reading the newspaper. The morning reminds me a bit of being at the Department of Motor Vehicles, although it is more charged with nervous energy than intense boredom. While no one is acting out-of-hand, court marshals monitor people's behavior: "Sir, take your hat off"; as a woman dozes off, "Miss, you can't sleep here."

It is now 10:00 A.M., and Gary has finished with his pile of manila folders for the time being. Angel, a court marshal, announces that the court will take a fifteen-minute recess and that defendants may use the restrooms in the hallway or remain seated. Gary exits the courtroom via the door next to the jury box, which at Greenville Community Court is used for only the occasional outside visitors and me. There are no jury trials here.

Back in the staff hallway, Gary enters the office of Nick, the court manager. Gary teases Nick about his football team losing yesterday, and I tune out, unable to bring myself to care about sports. Gary then asks about Nick's morning so far. Nick, clearly miffed, has "yet again" received a call from a resident about a dog barking and has "for the third time" instructed her to call animal control. The conversation is interrupted by the judge, who summons Gary and Ralph, Greenville Community Court's public defender, into his office to look at the docket for today. In the judge's chambers, they review who might require court-supervised drug or alcohol treatment and discuss defendants who are already involved in some court-ordered treatment, deciding who is successful and who "needs jail time."

At 10:15 A.M., the marshals round up defendants who had left the courtroom. Twenty minutes later: "All rise for Judge Rodriguez." The judge enters the courtroom like a conductor about to orchestrate a symphony, robes billowing with his quick, sure strides. Everyone returns to their seats with straighter postures and serious, attentive faces. Judge Rodriguez opens court with a speech laying out ground rules and establishing the goals of the day:

Good morning and welcome to Greenville Community Court. [*He repeats the greeting in Spanish.*]

Please shut off all your cell phones. If one goes off during court, I will take it and donate it to charity on your behalf.

You have the right to plead not guilty and go to trial, where you will have the right to remain silent, confront the witnesses against you, and be proven guilty beyond a reasonable doubt.

If you choose to plead guilty in my court, you are giving up those rights in exchange for some type of community service, programming, or jail time. You successfully complete community service—we will wipe this charge off your record. It will be as if it never happened. If you do not successfully meet the conditions of your discharge—if you don't show up, if you don't do what you are supposed to do—I will sentence you to jail for up to the maximum the charges allow. Town-ordinance violation gets you twenty-five days in jail. Drug paraphernalia gets you ninety days. Criminal trespass one year. *Sigue?*

I do not impose fines. I do not give probation. Do community service, comply with treatment, or go to jail. It's just that simple.

No talking while court is in session. No giving the marshals a hard time. If you do, I may find you in contempt of court. If I find you in contempt, I will sentence you for up to six months in jail, starting immediately.

I will go over your individual rights as your case is called.

He then asks in Spanish whether anyone requires a translator, in which case the court interpreter reads some version of this speech from a piece of paper.

The first case of the day is a young black woman in her early twenties. Gary opens a folder as she walks up to go stand next to Ralph. Gary summarizes the report: she has a violation for breach of peace and trespassing. She claims she didn't do anything; instead, it was the girl she was hanging out with. The judge looks up from his computer screen from behind the bench and asks the defendant, "Why would you want to be friends with someone like that?" The young woman states that she doesn't know why, to which the judge responds, "Pick better friends, especially now. . . . [If y]ou show a lack of concern about cases pending here, I'll show a lack of concern for letting you stay in the community." Her case is continued for a month from now.

Gary calls the next case, a white man in his fifties charged with a larceny 6, which is a misdemeanor for stealing property valued under $250. His last court date was a month ago. Ralph announces that the man is currently enrolled in general equivalency diploma (GED) classes. Judge Rodriguez asks the man how he likes the program. He smiles sheepishly and tells the judge, "Instead of throwing their hands up, they're giving me a chance. Um, they have all the resources. . . . [I]it's unfortunate that I had to go through all this." The judge looks at the defendant and with a smile tells him, "That's what this court is about." Gary continues the case for next month, and the man exits the courtroom.

Next, an older woman is called before the court for prostitution charges, which are not announced, but I can tell from the markings on the docket.[2] She has previously been in this court three times for prostitution charges and drug charges. The judge seems fed up with her. He asks, "Is this what you want as your legacy? Is this what you want in your obituary? You have grandchildren—is this how you want them to remember you?" Then he speaks to her in Spanish, and she begins to softly cry. No one brings her a tissue. One of the court reporters, Barbara, says to the judge, "You're making me cry," as she starts to tear up. The judge announces that they are taking her into custody and continues her case for two weeks. Angel, the court marshal, walks over to the woman and escorts her through the door that leads to Greenville Community Court's lockup.

Gary announces that they are waiting on reports and lockups (people who have been arrested the night before as well as people who are currently incarcerated but still have pending cases). It's 11:10 A.M. and time for another recess.

This is a typical morning at Greenville Community Court. Readers who have served on a jury or had a court case themselves may recognize some features: periods of hustle and bustle punctuated by long court recesses, court marshals regulating proper courtroom behavior. Other aspects of Greenville Community Court's average day may strike some readers as odd, such as the time and energy spent on such low-level concerns as trespassing and petty larceny; the teamwork between the judge, the prosecutor, and the public defender; and the emotionally charged interactions in the courtroom.

Community courts do things quite differently from traditional courts. Community courts exclusively handle low-level offenses, such as prostitution, public drunkenness, trespassing, and fare beating. Community courts limit their cases to this group in the belief that courts can positively influence offenders and the community by intervening at the lower end of the spectrum of offenses. These courts aim to make positive changes by linking offenders to social services, by providing sanctions that reestablish ties to the community, and by deterring people from committing crimes in the future. Cases referred to community courts are typically punished with court-ordered treatment (substance-abuse counseling, anger-management classes, drug-treatment programs), community service, or jail. Community courts also believe that by intervening at the lowest level of offenses, they help deter more serious crimes, such as assault, robbery, and homicide.

The first community court opened in 1993 in midtown Manhattan. Described as a "public/private partnership," Midtown Community Court was funded by the New York State Unified Court System, the Fund for the City of New York, and the Center for Court Innovation (a nonprofit organization that was founded to establish Midtown Community Court). Midtown Community Court was first developed as a "demonstration project"; its founders conceptualized it as a criminal justice agency whose programming efforts could change and evolve to meet the needs of various offenders and community members. Midtown Community Court was also intended to develop tools and models that could be adapted to other cities to meet particular local needs.

Currently, thirty-seven community courts operating in the United States and four community courts outside the United States trace their lineage directly to Midtown Community Court (Center for Court Innovation n.d.; Lang 2011). The Center for Court Innovation has expanded its role from running Midtown Community Court to overseeing multiple specialized courts in the New York area and acting as the New York State Court system's independent research branch. Community courts have been endorsed by leaders at the White House Office of National Drug Control Policy and by Assistant Attorney General for the U.S. Department of Justice Office of Justice Programs Laurie O. Robinson (Center for Court Innovation 2012). In 2012, an annual conference for community courts drew three hundred attendees from seven different countries.

Decisions made in community courts are directly informed by criminological and jurisprudential theories. Court administrators and practitioners explicitly reference these theoretical orientations in their literature, origin stories, and conversations about their work. For instance, in my time working at Greenville Community Court, Judge Rodriguez asked that some in-

TABLE 1.1. THEORETICAL PRINCIPLES OF COMMUNITY COURTS		
Theory	Description	Implementation at community courts
Broken windows theory	Visible signs of disorder lead to increases in crime.	Focus on quality-of-life crimes Meaningful punishment Sanctions aimed at restoring neighborhood order
Therapeutic jurisprudence	Encounters with legal actors present offenders with opportunities for rehabilitative change.	Nonadversarial roles Personal interaction with defendants Judicial surveillance of defendants outside the criminal justice system
Restorative justice	Justice practices should ameliorate wrongdoings and reintegrate offenders into the community.	Community-service sanctions Victim-impact panels

terns and I compile articles about community courts to help outsiders understand the ideas behind them. This chapter first discusses community courts' guiding principles and how they are translated into action (Table 1.1 provides a shorthand guide). It then discusses how and why these guiding principles make community courts an appealing model for cities dealing with quality-of-life offenses. Finally, it critiques these philosophical models to orient readers to themes that emerge in later chapters.

Broken Windows Theory

Community courts' focus on low-level, quality-of-life crimes is rooted in broken windows theory. First postulated by James Q. Wilson and George Kelling (1982), it argues that visible signs of disorder in a neighborhood lead to increases in the rates and severity of crime in that neighborhood.

A simple thought exercise helps explain broken windows theory.[3] Imagine that your friend invites you over to dinner. He prepares a nice meal, you both chat at the dinner table, and your friend excuses himself for a phone call, leaving you at the table with your dirty dishes. You go to the kitchen with an empty, dirty bowl and spoon. If the sink is pristine, freshly cleaned with no dishes in the sink, you would likely clean your bowl and spoon, neatly place them in the strainer, and give the sink a swipe to make sure it's clean. If the sink is overrun with dirty dishes, and you can barely make out the shape of a faucet, you would likely cram your empty bowl and spoon somewhere in the mess and walk away. You are the same person in both scenarios, with the same morals and values, yet your behavior is different.

Broken windows theory argues that people's behavior is linked to environmental conditions. A visibly ordered environment deters criminal behavior, while a visibly disordered environment promotes crime. In our analogy, a clean sink is kept clean, while a dirty sink invites more dirty dishes. In broken windows theory, visible disorder could be litter on the ground, graffiti on buildings, or people drinking in the street.[4] However, broken windows theory is about crime, not messiness. It argues that visible signs of disorder in a neighborhood communicate that "no one cares" about it and that crime is permissible here. When people perceive that no one cares and that crime is permissible in the area, they engage in ever-escalating levels and rates of criminal activity. According to broken windows theory, signs of visible disorder will lead to larger crimes in several ways. People who commit small crimes and are not punished will graduate to more severe criminal behavior. Additionally, criminals from nearby areas will flock to the disorderly neighborhoods to commit crimes. Informal social-control systems will be rendered ineffective, as lawful residents will move out of the disorderly neighborhood or will isolate themselves out of fear (Kelling and Coles 1997; Skogan 1990; Wilson and Kelling 1982). As a corrections tactic, broken windows theory argues that meaningful punishment of low-level offenses reduces crime rates for a variety of offenses, including violent crime. It also follows that increasing the orderliness of a neighborhood results in decreased crime rates (Kelling and Coles 1997). Neighborhoods may aim to "fix broken windows" by cleaning up areas that are disorderly and increasing the visibility of social controls (for example, adding police patrols and posting "Neighborhood Watch" signs).

Community courts embrace the etiological and preventive narratives of broken windows theory and put them into practice. They establish that quality-of-life crime is indeed an important issue to residents, business owners, and community members of a neighborhood. Community courts also follow broken windows theory's thesis that without meaningful punishment, small crimes escalate. As such, community courts rally community members and law enforcement around quality-of-life crimes. They work with police departments to engage in quality-of-life or zero-tolerance policing, which is a kind of enforcement strategy that targets low-level offenses. They take quality-of-life crimes seriously and process them swiftly. In traditional courts, someone arrested for public drunkenness might spend the night in lockup but be released the next morning with "time served." In community courts, someone arrested for public drunkenness would spend the night in lockup and the next day be sentenced to ten days of community service or be court-ordered to attend weekly Alcoholics Anonymous meetings for a two-month period. Community courts not only embrace broken windows theory's emphasis on the importance of punishing quality-of-life crimes; they also apply the theory's lessons about preventing crime. Community courts sanction many offenders to community service in an effort to restore orderliness to the neighborhood through cleaning up trash in vacant lots, painting over graffiti underneath an underpass, and so forth. Some community courts specifically arrange offenders' community service so that offenders must clean the exact neighborhood or street block on which they committed their crimes.

Therapeutic Jurisprudence

While community courts explicitly operate with the understanding that the physical environment either promotes or deters criminal offending, they also follow the idea that criminal behavior may stem from an individual's personality traits, character flaws, or health issues, which can be corrected by the court. Community courts do not just attempt to repair broken windows, so to speak; they also attempt to mend broken people. This focus on rehabilitating underlying characteristics that motivate criminal offending is traced to the legal philosophy of therapeutic jurisprudence. Therapeutic jurisprudence emerged in the late 1980s as a critique of mental-health law, advocating that legal actors should think carefully about how to interact with offenders with mental-health problems. Instead of criminalizing people with underlying mental-health conditions, the criminal justice system should seek therapeutic interventions for these offenders and strategically interpret the law to produce positive outcomes (Wexler 2000; Wexler and Winick 1996). As opposed to liberal legal philosophies, which argue that a court must be objective, distant, and impartial, therapeutic jurisprudence contends that "the law itself can be seen to function as a kind of therapist or therapeutic agent" (Winick 1997: 185).[5] Under this philosophy, legal actors practice "individualized justice" by seeking a holistic view of the offender and making sentencing decisions based on his or her particular needs.

At community courts, offenders who are believed to have mental-health and/or substance-abuse issues motivating or contributing to their criminal behavior are referred to a treatment program. Community courts make referrals to substance-abuse counselors, anger-management teams, and mental-health facilities, among others. Although treatment referrals are not exclusive to specialized courts (many traditional courts also mandate treatment), the ways in which referrals are made and how they are enforced are different matters. Courts may refer an offender to social services regardless of the offense; that is, someone does not need to be arrested for an alcohol-related charge to be referred to alcohol treatment. This referral to treatment is motivated by the philosophy of therapeutic jurisprudence: when someone violates the law, community courts use this opportunity to link the offender to services that can treat the root cause of the person's criminality.

Community courts not only practice therapeutic jurisprudence by linking offenders to social services; they also apply the theory in case processing and sanction decision making. They operate with nonadversarial roles among the judge, the prosecutor, and the defender. As shown in the vignette that opens this chapter, the prosecutor, the public defender, and the judge work cooperatively toward a sentence that will most benefit the defendant (a much different orientation from that of courtrooms in which the defense attorney and the prosecutor are at odds, working on behalf of their clients, with the judge acting as an impartial arbitrator). Typically, community courts have only one judge, one prosecutor, and one public defender, which fosters tight-knit working groups.[6] They all work together to sanction the offender according to therapeutic principles. At Greenville Community Court, the judge, the prosecutor, and the public defender meet each morning to discuss the docket and to review the cases in court-supervised treatment. Before the action begins in the courtroom, they work out a "game plan" for cases that require specialized attention.

Therapeutic jurisprudence is not only practiced behind the scenes; it is also enacted in courtroom interactions with defendants. Community courts collect a great deal of information about each defendant to understand his or her specific needs and to better practice "individualized justice." They know the details about a defendant's violation and past criminal record, and they also know where the defendant works, where he or she lives and with whom, and how the defendant spends his or her free time. Judges in community courts are not dispassionate arbitrators of the law; instead, they choose various dramaturgical stances depending on what they think might be therapeutic for each defendant. During my fieldwork, I saw Judges Rodriguez and Corbett act in a variety of roles: the stern principal, the fed-up family member, the proud mentor, the enthusiastic cheerleader, and the dismissive disciplinarian. Their commitment to each of these roles and the ease with which they switched from one to another would have impressed seasoned professional actors. Scholars in other specialized courts witnessed similarly dramaturgical courtroom scenes, describing them as "therapeutic theater" (Nolan 2001). This theatrical presentation of justice does not happen in all cases; it is strategically used to motivate the offender to comply with the court's orders.

Broken windows theory and therapeutic jurisprudence present two etiological views of crime: environmental conditions and individual character flaws. Returning to the dirty sink analogy, broken windows theory would say that the dirty dishes need to be cleaned and that anyone who leaves a dish in the sink needs to be punished swiftly. In contrast, therapeutic jurisprudence would ask why a particular person was leaving a dirty dish in the sink. It would identify the underlying issue and then figure out an individualized plan to change the person into a tidier guest. Does the person need to be yelled at? Does the person need gentle coaching to clean the dish? Does a passive-aggressive note reading, "Clean your dishes!" change the behavior?

In my study of Greenville Community Court, I point to various contradictory penal logics that are enacted in the practice of community justice. The distinct visions of crime in broken windows theory and in therapeutic jurisprudence are just one example of this tension. Tensions also exist between the court's mission to serve "the community" by practicing individualized justice and to punish low-level crimes while focusing on rehabilitating low-level offenders. These tensions are partially resolved under the final guiding principle of community courts: restorative justice.

Restorative Justice

Restorative justice is an academic and applied orientation that argues that punishment should be focused on restitution and preventing recidivism. While offenders are punished under restorative justice, that punishment is tempered by community-building activities and tactics that reaffirm the offender as "fixed." For example, John Braithwaite (1989) advocates for reintegrative punishment, in which the offender makes amends and is welcomed back into the community through a ritual that marks him or her as rehabilitated, as having repaid his or her debt, and as once again a full-fledged member of the community. This practice is touted as helping reduce recidivism; the reintegrative label applied after someone has "paid back the community" prevents the stigmatization and subsequent identification with the criminal label that often results in continued criminal activity.

Community courts enact restorative justice in the types of sanctions given and the conceptualization of the victim. They argue that so-called victimless crimes, such as prostitution, littering, and underage drinking, do indeed have a victim: the community as a whole. As such, community courts often sanction offenders to "pay back the community" by cleaning up the neighborhood (e.g., removing litter from vacant lots or painting over graffiti), volunteering for local agencies, spending time at Big Brothers Big Sisters, or helping people at a local farmers' market. Community courts aim to reintegrate offenders by "nolling" cases. If a person successfully completes his or her court sentence (whether that sanction is community service or participation in treatment), the judge dismisses the case and eliminates the record of that offense. Community courts want to keep nonviolent, low-level offenses off a person's criminal record so they cannot negatively affect that individual's employment options or requests for financial loans.

Perhaps the most unusual way that community courts practice restorative justice is through the involvement of nonlegal actors in the process.

Community-service crews might be directly connected to local organiza-tions, such as food banks and other charitable organizations. The aim of these partnerships is to be mutually beneficial: local organizations get much-needed "volunteers," and community courts provide steady and meaningful community-service projects. Community-service projects are aimed at not only making the offender "pay back the community" for the damage caused by the crime but also building and mending the offender's bond with the local community. People who live or work in community courts' jurisdictions may also be involved in the legal process of punish-ment, such as by participating in meetings with offenders to create dia-logue about mutual goals for the community. For example, Midtown Community Court regularly facilitates "community impact panels," in which residents and business owners meet with three to five defendants for a mediated discussion about quality-of-life crimes and their negative impact on the community. Community courts might invite interested par-ties to tour their facilities, watch the court in action, or speak directly to defendants during a special court session.

The Appeal of Community Courts

The promise of community courts stems from these philosophical orienta-tions. Community courts' abilities to sell their particular brand of justice are central to their legitimacy as an organization. Before illustrating how community courts cultivate their organizational legitimacy in practice (which I do in Chapters 4–6), it is necessary to unpack the appeal of bro-ken windows theory, therapeutic jurisprudence, and restorative justice on their own terms.

Broken windows theory is the criminological equivalent of diet recom-mendations splattered across magazine covers: replace one soda a day with a glass of water, and you will lose thirty pounds in a year; clean up the litter in the park regularly, and you will prevent three homicides per year. This theory is so appealing because the solution to crime and crimi-nal behavior it presents is clear and simple. It argues that if law enforce-ment and court systems focus on enforcing, punishing, and preventing small crimes, then they will effectively prevent more serious and violent crimes. Broken windows theory masks more structural explanations for why and how crime happens, and, as a corrective tactic, such a perspective does not offer solutions for these more structural issues, such as poverty and joblessness. Instead, it focuses only on visible, superficial markers of urban disorder.

This focus on the superficial means that zero-tolerance policing makes an immediately detectable impact on neighborhoods. Residents and business owners see more police officers on foot patrol and people being arrested or ticketed for quality-of-life crimes. They notice community-service crews in bright yellow vests painting over graffiti on an underpass. In theory, increased police presence, arrests, and beautification efforts restore law-abiding citizens' feelings of individual and collective agency.[7] It is a far more visible law-enforcement tactic than others, and in that sense, it is easy to sell.

Many scholars argue that zero-tolerance policies and broken-windows policing are particularly attractive to urban areas undergoing gentrification (Herbert and Brown 2006; Parenti 2000; Smith 2002). Some argue that the appeal of zero-tolerance policing is connected to urban-planning goals. Steve Herbert and Elizabeth Brown write, "As urban centers compete with one another for increasingly footloose capital, and as consumption becomes more central to the economic health of cities, the aesthetics of the street are increasingly regnant" (2006: 769). Since community courts solely handle quality-of-life issues and are located predominately in urban areas, they serve a criminal justice function that did not exist prior to the popularity of zero-tolerance policies and broken-windows policing for newly gentrified (or gentrifying) neighborhoods. Indeed, private agencies sometimes provide funding for community courts. Midtown Community Court, for example, is (and has been since its inception) partially funded by the Times Square Business Alliance.[8]

Community courts' embrace of broken windows theory and therapeutic jurisprudence allow them to appeal to both liberal and conservative values for criminal justice policy. Community courts campaign in part on cost-effectiveness: rehabilitative programming is far less costly for taxpayers than incarceration. They argue that the meaningful punishment of low-level crimes not only reduces recidivism but also prevents offenders from graduating from smaller crimes to more serious crimes. Specialized courts also "free up" other courts to handle more serious cases. By taking the administrative burden of processing misdemeanor cases off other courts in the area, community courts open up space, time, and effort for more serious crimes. Specialized courts appeal to general liberal sensibilities in their focus on rehabilitative programs, giving people second chances, and creating partnerships with community organizations.

The cultural salience of therapeutic sensibilities provides another legitimating framework for community courts, especially noticeable in their practice of therapeutic jurisprudence.[9] Scholars note that the United

States is particularly ripe for a "therapeutic ethos" (Nolan 1998). The United States staunchly insists on individualized attributions of success and failure, especially as it comes to hardships that sociologists would usually describe as resulting from social forces. Community courts trace criminal offending to a root cause that can be solved through the application of therapeutic jurisprudence: resocialize people with anger problems, teach people who litter that they harm the community, and get people with substance-abuse issues into treatment. This therapeutic narrative in justice aligns well with what others have called the "medicalization of society" (Conrad 2007) or the "pathologization of human behavior" (Nolan 1998). In contemporary life, we apply medical diagnostic categories to an array of conditions and behaviors that were previously attributed to sin, character flaws, and so forth. A diagnosis provides not only an account of the problem but also a course of action to remedy it. By aligning with the primacy of individualized explanations for behavior in American culture, therapeutic jurisprudence applies a diagnostic frame of reference for the problem *within* and *not outside* the individual. Therapeutic jurisprudence provides a solution for cultural contradictions in contemporary American life between a (historically) puritanical focus on temperance and morality and a consumptionist ethos (Reinarman 1994; Reinarman and Levine 1997). The notion that each defendant should have a unique and specialized encounter with judicial structures aligns with postmodern understandings of niche markets and a fragmented public (Bauman 2013). Therapeutic solutions to criminal offending, with their attendant moralistic framework, medicalized solutions, and individualized bootstrap-ism, *make sense* in this cultural moment.

Critiques of Community Courts

On the face of it, community courts seem like a commonsense approach to low-level crimes. They extend a promise of safer and cleaner neighborhoods by promoting community involvement in justice and taking quality-of-life crimes seriously. However, the underlying philosophies of community courts raise some very valid concerns about individuals' rights in the justice system.

To start, broken windows theory is not empirically supported; empirical studies do not unequivocally find a relationship between disorder and crime. Wesley Skogan's 1990 study is regarded as the gold standard of empirical studies used to validate broken windows theory. Skogan analyzes neighborhood data from six cities in the United States and finds a relationship between disorder and crime. However, Bernard Harcourt's 2001 tour de force, *Illusion of Order: The False Promise of Broken Windows Policing*, dedicates a chapter to critiquing this study. Harcourt retests Skogan's data and finds that the relationship between disorder and crime exists for only one crime (robbery) and that those results are primarily driven by one neighborhood in Skogan's dataset. Harcourt's analysis raises significant concerns for scholars claiming that Skogan's study supports the causal relationship between disorder and crime. Perhaps one of the best tests of broken windows theory is Robert Sampson and Stephen Raudenbush's 1999 study of different blocks of Chicago. They find that the relationship between disorder and predatory crime is largely spurious and that disorder and crime can be explained by collective efficacy.[10] John Eck and Edward Maguire (2000) compare crime rates in the 1990s across major U.S. cities and find that cities that adopted zero-tolerance policing did not experience a greater decline in crime than cities that did not adopt broken windows–style tactics. Given this evidence, we cannot conclusively state that any relationship exists between visible disorder and crime, nor can we state that enforcement of low-level crimes decreases violent crime.[11]

The application of broken windows theory to zero-tolerance enforcement policies helps the criminal justice system engage in net widening and unnecessarily involves low-level offenders in the criminal justice system.[12] Quality-of-life initiatives may increase arrest rates by creating new laws or by enforcing already-existing laws with renewed vigor. For example, New York and California passed ordinances against "aggressive panhandling" that regulate the manner in which one can panhandle and quite often prohibit one from panhandling within twenty-five or so feet from an automatic teller machine.[13] These ordinances are vague enough to allow a great degree of officer discretion.[14] At Greenville Community Court, one employee told me that the "year before the court opened, there were seven public drinking cases in Greenville. In the first year we were open, there were seven hundred. You know, because before [police officers thought], "Why would I do this?" In this sense, quality-of-life initiatives' push for the policing and enforcement of low-level offenses may bring more people into the criminal justice system.[15]

When we consider the kinds of people who are likely committing quality-of-life crimes, we can see how the application of broken windows theory to criminal justice initiatives exacerbates already existing inequalities. The areas targeted by quality-of-life initiatives, the application of officer discretion, and the kinds of people who may appear disorderly mean that, in practice, many people who are subject to violations and arrests are poor people of color (Fratello, Rengifo, and Trone 2013). In *Sidewalk* (1999), Mitchell Duneier describes how the criminalization of particular behaviors in Pennsylvania Station in New York City, such as sleeping on the subway, was intended to drive homeless people out of the train station. Neil Smith (2002) argues that zero-tolerance policies effectively criminalize poverty and operate as a tool to remove poor people from neighborhoods and to attract wealthier residents and the businesses that they frequent.

Community courts are complicit in this net widening, as they provide a bureaucratic processing structure equipped to handle these kinds of cases. Community courts may even be the catalyst for the adoption of new policing strategies. At Greenville Community Court, the prosecutor reported that in the early months of operation, the court's dockets were so thin that people could complete their community service on the date of their very first court appearance. Before the creation of Greenville Community Court, a police officer stated that he and his colleagues "had given up issuing tickets" for low-level offenses. The police officers knew that low-level cases would just be thrown out of superior court, so, he thought, "I'm not even going to waste my time anymore." Many police officers did not believe that community court would work. "Our own CSO [community-service officer] said, 'Ha. Ha. Never work. They'll go through the same revolving door.'" Thus initially, Greenville Community Court persuaded police officers to begin to enforce quality-of-life laws. It could be that community courts create an artificial need to fill dockets and that perhaps other "criminal justice agencies feel compelled to fill their caseloads by any means necessary" (Berman and Feinblatt 2005: 171).

The net widening around quality-of-life crimes raises questions about whether community court involvement produces criminogenic or prosocial outcomes for offenders. People who otherwise may have never been involved with the criminal justice system may end up in the community courts, and this introduction to the criminal justice system may set them up for undesirable outcomes. We know, for instance, that putting someone on probation instead of incarcerating him or her increases the person's likelihood of future incarceration because people on probation are more harshly scrutinized (Blomberg, Bales, and Reed 1993; Blomberg and Lucken 1994; Chan and Ericson 1981; Hylton 1981; Phelps 2013; Tonry and Lynch 1996).

By placing people under rigorous court supervision for days or even months, community courts may increase the likelihood that these individuals will end up in jail or prison. If the "town drunk" is put in the "drunk tank" once a week, he may continue to be a small-scale nuisance, but he will not face lengthy jail time for his addiction. If the town drunk is sent to community court, is sentenced to attend daily Alcoholics Anonymous meetings, and fails to do so, he will go to jail for a few months. The intense court supervision, whether that involves future and/or multiple court dates or no new arrests for a particular period of time, may be more intrusive and detrimental than the revealing door of "time served." As Issa Kohler-Hausmann writes in her study of misdemeanors at New York criminal court (not Midtown Community Court), "the threat of prison is another means of social control" (2013: 355).

While community courts justify court supervision over very low-level crimes in the name of therapeutic jurisprudence, many scholars question the assumption that therapeutic goals are correct, moral, or otherwise advisable. A variety of criminological theories argue that the root causes of crime are such that rehabilitative efforts do not work and that criminals cannot be unmade. The forms that rehabilitation takes may also be questionable. Some have argued that the process of rehabilitation is not about making a person a noncriminal but rather about socializing offenders into white-middle-class norms (see Elias [1939] 1978). James Nolan (2001) argues that because problem-solving courts heartily champion therapeutic discourses, individual defendants may not have the expert knowledge to assert their rights or desires. Problem-solving courts interpret offender opposition or resistance to therapeutic goals as *even more* reason to intervene with treatment, as the offenders are clearly in the throes of their disease. Indeed, the discourse of therapy and the therapeutic self is so encompassing and so endorsed by expert voices that, in practice, there is no viable alternative (Foucault 1979; Rosenhan 1973).

Therapeutic jurisprudence is also coercive and paternalistic. Net widening may not only ensnare more behaviors and people under criminal justice control but also extend the purview of criminal justice supervision. Therapeutic jurisprudence allows for an increased degree of state surveillance and control, as individualized justice may involve judicial interventions into one's family, work, and home life (Malkin 2003; Nolan 2009). Kelly Hannah-Moffat and Paula Maurutto argue that therapeutic jurisprudence "legitimizes the roles and relevance of new practices and kinds of knowledge as well as new modalities of penal power" (2012: 211). By attempting to reform the criminal, community courts collect data from offenders' private lives, and any failure in any walk of life may be interpreted and sanctioned as a criminal failure.

Defendants must enter a guilty plea to be eligible to have their cases tried at the community court. If they enter a guilty plea and successfully complete the sanction the community court gives them, their case is "nolled" and stripped from the record. In some ways, this practice binds offenders to community courts for an indefinite period of time. This practice of submitting a guilty plea may be particularly coercive; although defendants may *want* to pursue a trial and maintain their innocence, the prospect of the time, money, and effort involved in a criminal trial may deter them from exercising their right to due process. Indeed, some scholars describe the pre-adjudicative nature of cases at specialized courts as "coerced volunteerism" (Burns and Peyrot 2003; Nolan 2009). Finally, therapeutic jurisprudence as applied to defendants with substance-abuse issues raises ethical questions regarding the degree of consent and confidentiality that defendants are able to exercise (Seddon 2007).

Conclusion

Community courts base their mission and practice around the guiding principles of broken windows theory, therapeutic jurisprudence, and restorative justice. Community courts use these principles to guide their division of labor, sentencing practices, and conceptualization of their mission. Ultimately, community courts believe that "meaningful punishment," which aims to involve the community in the justice process, results in safer communities and a more efficient and humane justice process. To others, the potential costs of community courts greatly outweigh the benefits. Broken windows theory's focus on quality-of-life crimes allows for the criminalization of behaviors that are associated with marginalized groups. Under the banner of therapeutic jurisprudence, community courts expand criminal justice surveillance into a host of attitudes and behaviors of low-level offenders with medicalized behaviors and conditions. While beautification projects and "paying back the community" appear to be beneficial to all, in practice, community courts privilege a particular notion of community that is racialized and classed.

The coming chapters trace how Greenville Community Court's implementation of these theoretical bases affect offenders as well as the organization itself. I show that, ultimately, community courts' embrace of these multiple and sometimes conflicting logics allows them to make a case for themselves as unique, effective, and responsive organizations.

2

Ordering the Court

Community courts market themselves as a fully innovative form of justice. Branded as "novel," and "alternative," they capitalize on the idea that their approach is the most state-of-the-art option for dealing with criminal offenses. However, a brief glance across the recent history of punishment in the United States challenges this idea that community courts are a new innovation. Instead, they are the inheritors of long-standing disputes over the goals of criminal justice. They embody changes in the cultural meaning of crime and tensions surrounding modern urban life. They are products of growing criminal justice professionalization, technology, and expanded surveillance. They capitalize on a particular brand of community engagement that finds healthy soil in urban areas where community efficacy is frequently disputed.

Community courts were born out of a crisis of legitimacy surrounding the criminal justice system in the 1980s, which led to a host of new criminal justice goals and practices (Fagan and Malkin 2002; Garland 2001). This crisis was caused by shifts in penal policy, changes in the criminal population, and the criminal justice system's inadequate resources. These changes caused frustration for criminal justice practitioners and the public. The first part of this chapter discusses the broad shifts in the American criminal justice system as it transitioned from rehabilitative to punitive goals and the attendant problems that emerged. This historical perspective helps us understand how community courts surfaced as a solution to two key problems: (1) procedural issues of revolving-door justice and (2) public frustration with the criminal justice system. This brief historical overview illustrates the trajectory of judicial goals as moving away from and then back toward rehabilitative sanctions. Community courts merely caught the wave of restorative justice as the tide changed.

The second half of the chapter addresses why community courts focus on quality-of-life crimes. We find our first clue in the bustling Times Square neighborhood in New York City, where quality-of-life crimes became a lynchpin connecting concerns of criminal justice practitioners with policing tactics, political agendas, and business-development interests. Real-estate and business interests, in Times Square especially, supported targeting quality-of-life offenders, as they allegedly discouraged desirable residents, businesses, and consumers from investing in the area. Already-frustrated criminal justice experts, now overwhelmed by dockets crowded with low-level nonviolent offenders, saw an opportunity to create a new specialized court focused solely on these cases. In this new specialized court, criminal justice practitioners could use rehabilitative programs and strategies to address underlying issues of criminality for quality-of-life offenders. For our second clue, we zoom out of Times Square and examine broader cultural trends linking "the community" to criminal justice efforts. The chapter closes with a discussion of the political and administrative appeal of the community court model and how that appeal has allowed it to proliferate in the American justice system.

The Decline of the Rehabilitative Ideal

In an editorial in the American Criminology Society's main publication, Mary Almore declares that criminology's "espoused 'love affair' with rehabilitation . . . is over" (1977: 147). This "decline of the rehabilitative ideal" (Allen 1981) would prove to be an important turning point in criminal justice, as it ushered in the more punitive criminal justice policies of the 1980s and 1990s. In a rare instance of political confluence, political liberals and conservatives alike aimed critiques at the rehabilitative goals of the criminal justice system. These critiques were further strengthened by increases in the crime rates and the politicization of crime. Out of the ashes of the rehabilitative criminal justice system emerged a more standardized and punitive version, one that eventually led to the resurrection of rehabilitative sentencing in specialized courts.

Sentencing practices—in particular, indeterminate sentences—were one of the key issues that propelled the shift away from rehabilitative goals. From the 1930s to the 1970s, punishment was, for the most part, decided on a case-by-case basis. There was very little oversight to ensure fairness in sentencing practices; statutes provided the maximum terms of probation or incarceration but rarely set minimum terms (Morris and Tonry 1991). This widespread discretion was intended to serve the rehabilitative goals of punishment: prosecutors, judges, and parole boards could individualize sentences to tailor punishment to fit the particular needs of each offender. Prosecutors set charges and were able to plea-bargain indiscriminately. Judges decided how someone was punished (probation, jail, or prison) and set the minimum and/or maximum lengths of incarceration for each offender.

Once in jail or prison, an offender had no official release date. Instead, the individual would be released when the parole board determined that he or she was rehabilitated and therefore fit to reenter society. In effect, no guidelines ensured a standard application of sentencing options, and no system of checks and balances sufficiently ensured that differences in sentences were fair. This variability left "prosecutors, judges, and parole boards . . . accountable for their decisions . . . only to their political constituencies and their consciences" (Morris and Tonry 1991: 21). This discretion in sentencing meant that a person could remain incarcerated for a very long period of time while awaiting the parole board's determination regarding his or her rehabilitative status.

In the late 1960s and early 1970s, scholarship exposing sentencing patterns and prison conditions revealed the dark side of the rehabilitative goals of justice in practice. Such publications as the American Friends Service Committee's *Struggle for Justice* argued that courts either arbitrarily applied indeterminate sentences or, more insidiously, applied sentences in racist or classist ways, producing disparities in sentence lengths. Citing a report from the Prison Reform Committee of the Florida Bar Association, *Struggle for Justice* shows sentence-length disparities for robberies in Florida: a man who stole someone's cash, wallet, and watch (valued at less than $100) without using a weapon was sentenced to five years in prison, yet another man who robbed someone at knifepoint of $18.52 received a life sentence. He had no prior convictions (American Friends Service Committee 1971: 126–127). Sociologist Bruce Jackson's (1968) article "Our Prisons Are Criminal," published in the *New York Times Magazine*, describes horrendous prison conditions and expresses disgust at the legal system. In describing Bridgewater's Correctional Institution for the criminally insane in Massachusetts (the subject of the infamous documentary *The Titicut Follies* and "the worst place [Jackson] visited"), Jackson recounts that one inmate had been incarcerated for thirty-seven years for drunkenly painting a horse to look like a zebra. Another sixty-year-old inmate had been in Bridgewater since he was seven years old: "His offense: running away from home" (B. Jackson 1968). These publications and exposés showed the coercive side of rehabilitative practices and the abuses that could stem from indeterminate sentencing in the name of serving rehabilitative goals. They were integral to galvanizing support for sharp oversight in sentencing practices and the abandonment of rehabilitative goals.

Publicity surrounding prison riots and rebellions also exposed the American public to prison conditions.[1] The 1971 Attica Prison uprising was particularly effective in this regard, although political liberals and conservatives would interpret the uprising's lessons quite differently (Berger 2007; Cullen and Gilbert 1982; Thompson 2017). On the morning of September 9, a small group of inmates escaped correctional supervision and within a few hours managed to take control of Attica Prison, holding forty-two guards and employees hostage. The prisoners' demands included recruiting correctional officers of color, hiring prison doctors who spoke Spanish, offering better education, and serving healthier food (New York State Special Commission on Attica 1972). The corrections commissioner agreed to meet most of the demands, but then a guard who had been injured during the rebellion died during negotiations. This death propelled Governor Nelson A. Rockefeller to order state police to overtake the prison. On September 13, helicopters clouded the prison with tear gas, and state troopers burst in, shooting thousands of bullets in roughly ten minutes. Twenty-nine inmates and nine hostages were killed during the storming of Attica, making it the deadliest prison "riot" in America at that point. While the New York Times first reported that the hostages who died were killed by inmates, either via slashed throats or severe beatings (Ferretti 1971b), and that one hostage had been castrated (Ferretti 1971b), autopsy reports showed that the hostages who died were actually killed by state troopers during the chaos of the storming (Ferretti 1971a).

Following the uprising, "the word 'Attica' instantly became a parable of the failures of US incarceration" (Berger 2007: 224). The Attica Prison uprising was salient for political liberals' and conservatives' claims that the criminal justice system needed to be reformed. Political conservatives took the Attica Prison uprising as a sign that criminals were out of control and could never be rehabilitated. Liberals viewed the uprising as indicative of the excesses of criminal justice. They were also particularly uncomfortable with the racial disparities that the Attica Prison uprising exposed, in which an all-white staff confronted a prison population comprising primarily black and Latinx inmates from urban areas. Regardless, conservatives and liberals agreed that the judicial system needed clear sentencing guidelines for punitive goals and fairness, respectively (Allen 1981; Friedman 1994). People's worst fears about the criminal justice system were validated through the media coverage of the Attica Prison uprising, thus only further intensifying the push for more state supervision of the criminal justice system.

Academic criminology is also deeply implicated in the decline of the rehabilitative ideal. More left-leaning perspectives, including labeling theory and neo-Marxism (both popular in the 1960s and 1970s), considered rehabilitation efforts to be more coercive and punitive than simple incarceration.[2] Conservative criminologist James Q. Wilson published *Thinking about Crime*, which argues that "[retributive] punishment is not an unworthy objective of the criminal justice system" and that "rehabilitation has not yet been shown to be a promising method for dealing with serious offenders[,] . . . while evidence supports . . . the view that deterrence and incapacitation work" (1983: xxiii).[3] Additionally, numerous published empirical reports conclude that rehabilitative efforts are ineffective (Bailey 1966; Lipton, Martinson, and Wilks 1975; Logan 1972; Martinson 1974; Robison and Smith 1971). The most famous (or infamous) of these reports, Robert M. Martinson's *What Works? Questions and Answers about Prison Reform,* was published in 1974. The so-called Martinson Report reviews data on multiple rehabilitative programming efforts and concludes that "nothing works."[4] Rehabilitation and indeterminate sentencing, then, were perceived by political liberals as cruel and contributing to crime and recidivism and by conservatives as wasteful and ineffective.

The idea of rehabilitation was under attack from all sides of the political spectrum (Allen 1981; Cullen and Gilbert 1982; Friedman 1993; Zimring and Johnson 2006). "For one brief moment in history, prisoners and police chiefs were united by distrust of the existing system for governing punishments" (Zimring and Johnson 2006: 276). The public viewed rehabilitation as unnecessarily cruel and/or entirely ineffective. The academy either doubted or openly critiqued rehabilitation as a worthy goal of criminal justice. This shared shift in perspective would help transform the criminal justice system into a more punitive and standardized system. In turn, this standardization would introduce a new set of problems that led to the resurrection of rehabilitative goals by specialized courts in the 1990s. Not all the motivation for reform, however, was motivated by what was happening within criminal justice institutions.[5]

The violent-crime rate saw large and steady increases beginning in 1963 and had more than doubled by 1970.[6] While public perception often does not match up with actual trends in offending (Roberts 1992), in this instance, the two went hand in hand. For instance, in a 1966 Gallup poll, crime was ranked as the second-most-important domestic problem. Prior to 1966, not enough respondents had answered "crime" for it to even be included in the list of problems. Crime, in turn, became increasingly politicized, as also evidenced by the popularity of crime or "law and order" as a political platform in the 1968 presidential elections (Rankin 1979: 200).[7] C. Ray Jeffery, the editor of the flagship journal of the American Society of Criminology, writes:

> Never before had the professionals involved in law enforcement, correctional administration, and the administration of justice faced a more difficult challenge. The crime rate is of national concern and our number one domestic problem. The recent Presidential election in the United States was run on the issue of law, order and domestic tranquility—citizens are afraid to walk the streets because of fear and violence and mugging. . . . The Nixon Administration is proposing an all-out fight on crime. (1969: 2)

Crime had become an issue of national concern, and the criminal justice system swiftly rerouted its goals and practices away from the whirlpool of rehabilitation.

The newly charted course of criminal justice steered toward punishing people for their crimes, a course of action that was implemented alongside an increase in the state's oversight of the application of law. Punishment that had once aimed to rehabilitate the offender was replaced by punishment that would be rational, standardized, and focused on giving the offender his or her "just desserts." As Franklin Zimring and David Johnson point out, "The irony is that the power of the state [was] expanded by those who dislike[d] and distrust[ed] state power" (2006: 277). By 1973, forty-nine states had instituted minimum mandatory sentences for some crimes. Parole releases had been either abolished or placed under strict guidelines in at least thirty-three states by 1975 (Morris and Tonry 1991: 24–25). The Sentencing Reform Act of 1984 federalized what was already happening at the state level: it increased mandatory minimum sentences for violations of federal laws and codified strict limits on judicial discretion.

The judicial discretion that was once seen as so problematic was now no longer an issue. The rehabilitative aims of justice were mostly abandoned.

But the newly standardized and punishment-oriented justice system introduced a new set of dilemmas, especially for the courts.

Problems with Standardization

Over time, many criminal justice practitioners came to resent the lack of discretion that they had ceded in the push toward standardization. They believed that the tools they had at their disposal—primarily prison sentences—were inappropriate for some offenders. They also thought that the justice system should work to solve problems related to crime rather than simply execute sentences. The "punitive turn" did not alleviate crime; punishment for the sake of punishment did not decrease the crime rate, nor did it deter individuals from reoffending after they were released from prison. It is out of this frustration that specialized courts were born.

The case of mentally ill offenders is especially instructive of problems with standardized justice and punitive punishment. The deinstitutionalization of people who are mentally ill occurred alongside the redefinition of penal policies, and the criminal justice system became one of the primary institutions of state interaction with these individuals. Conditions in state-run mental hospitals were not much better than in prisons, and activists sought to move mental-health services from large state-run institutions to community-based mental-health providers, which would enable more people to live in the community. Between 1955 and 1985, state and county mental hospitals reduced their resident patient loads by an overwhelming 449,000 people. More than 75 percent of that reduction occurred between 1965 and 1980 (Mechanic and Rochefort 1990). The aims of deinstitutionalization were noble, but the outcomes were quite problematic. While the expansion of Medicare and disability insurance allowed for the possibility of community-based mental-health services, in reality the investment in community mental-health initiatives profoundly failed to meet the needs of the mentally ill population (Kupers 1999). After the closure of state-run facilities, many mentally ill citizens were left without proper access to medication and counseling. Because people who are mentally ill may sometimes do things that are dangerous to themselves or others, some then came into contact with the criminal justice system, which then became responsible for punishing people for crimes committed at least in part due to their mental illness. Mandatory sentencing laws left little room for judges to consider an offender's mental health as a precipitating factor in criminality or as a reason for leniency.

Offenders with mental-health issues raised a conundrum for some criminal justice practitioners: Why should the criminal justice system punish people for crimes that could be prevented with proper mental-health treatment? If people were not responsible for their own criminality because they were unable to make prosocial choices due to mental illness, then punishing them for crimes with incarceration was as an ineffective response to deter their offending. Some criminal justice actors also saw this criminality as preventable: if people were under proper mental-health supervision, with a drug regimen and counseling, they would stop offending. Mentally ill offenders also led people to question the goal of criminal justice: Is the goal to punish someone who did something wrong, or is it to make people safer and criminals less likely to reoffend?

At this time, courts also saw an increase in offenders with substance-abuse issues. Drug cases overwhelmed courts due to increasingly punitive drug policies. These strict antidrug policies in part came from a strong antidrug movement, despite the fact that overall drug use was declining (Musto 1997). The policies were also motivated by a drug scare involving crack cocaine. Crack cocaine was highly addictive, inexpensive, and associated with the black underclass; therefore, it was easily demonized to promote strict minimum sentences for drug violations. The Anti-Drug Abuse Act in 1986 galvanized minimum mandatory sentences for drug possession (Musto 1997: 274).

Some court administrators found the mandatory sentencing of nonviolent drug offenders problematic. Much like the mentally ill population, drug offenders were seen as having a treatable form of criminality, and mandatory jail terms did not treat the root cause of their law breaking. Indeed, mandatory jail sentences for nonviolent drug offenders exacerbated crime rates and contributed to prison overcrowding. According to a drug court official interviewed by Rebecca Tiger:

[The] number one [problem] is the incarceration of addicted and mentally ill people. That is the only response to drug- and alcohol-driven crime. . . . During the eighties the crack epidemic really drove eleven million people into jail and we surpassed the million incarcerated mark in the late eighties and today we're at 2.2 million and the vast majority of these people are there because of their substance abuse, their addiction. We just don't think that's right . . . and they're coming out in worse shape than they were when they went in. (2013: 64)

As this quotation explains, some criminal justice practitioners regarded punitive sentencing as inappropriate for certain kinds of offenders. Furthermore, some saw that sentencing particular populations exacerbated other problems in the criminal justice system.

The punitive turn of the 1970s and 1980s in part helped fuel a dramatic increase in the prison population. The prison population grew almost 350 percent between 1973 and 1993 (Snell 1996). Mandatory minimum sentences boomed the prison population, especially with drug offenders, and severely limited judicial discretion. The mass imprisonment of offenders was impressively ineffective in reducing crime, and violent-crime rates continued to rise until the early 1990s. In a nationally representative study of recidivism among prisoners released in 1983, 62 percent were re-arrested within three years, and slightly more than 40 percent were reincarcerated (Beck and Shipley 1989). This pattern also appeared in a similar study of prisoners released ten years later—nearly two-thirds were re-arrested within three years, and more than 50 percent were reincarcerated (Langan and Levin 2002). The term "revolving door of justice" was a constant refrain to pejoratively describe how offenders entered and exited prison in an endless loop of reoffending.

Indeed, "economic, political, and social changes led the courts onto the frontline of managing policy issues . . . in ways that the legal system has not previously experienced" (Fagan and Malkin 2002: 902). As policy changes directly and indirectly led to the criminalization of mentally ill and drug-addicted people, courts became the primary institution for handling mental-health and substance-abuse issues. Yet minimum mandatory sentences left scarce, if any, rehabilitative options for these populations. Court dockets were overrun with nonviolent offenders, and many people considered it wasteful and inefficient to use time and money to incarcerate such offenders. Those who worked in criminal justice (and, to some degree, the public) viewed the court system as a bureaucratic machine that did little but shuffle people in and out of jail. Reformers within the court system were frustrated: they wanted to provide solutions to crime-related problems, but they were unable to do so under strict sentencing guidelines and punitive justice orientations. The judicial discretion that had been seen as so problematic for the enactment of justice at the beginning of this period was now sorely missed. This frustration led to the creation of specialized courts to provide more judicial discretion and renewed efforts at rehabilitation.

The Crisis of Legitimacy and the Birth of Problem-Solving Courts

The birth of problem-solving courts is linked to this "crisis of legitimacy in legal institutions" (Berman and Feinblatt 2005; Fagan and Malkin 2002). Beginning with the drug court movement, specialized courts were established to address multiple problems with the criminal justice system. They renewed judicial discretion and individualized justice. They provided criminal justice practitioners with a narrative that they were working to solve the root problems of offending rather than cycling people in and out of the justice system like a bizarre carousel. They also promised to help alleviate prison overcrowding by diverting people from prison sentences. While the crisis of legitimacy accounts for the specialized court movement writ broad, it does not explain the specific purview of community courts. Why did courts that focus on low-level quality-of-life crimes emerge?

The answer to this question necessitates an examination of both structural and cultural factors. Scholars who research the emergence of new organizations have shown that new organizations require material and cultural resources to succeed (Ashforth and Gibbs 1990; Suchman 1995). The birth of community courts in the 1990s illustrates how structural and cultural resources aligned to create and foster courts that specifically focused on quality-of-life crimes. The next section discusses the creation of the first community court in Midtown Manhattan to show how political, economic, and professional concerns aligned to give birth to the current community court system.

New York City and the Birth of Midtown Community Court

Community courts were born from the alignment of new policing strategies, political interests, and business interests. New interests and strategies, combined with the crisis of legitimacy in legal institutions previously discussed, led to the creation of a specialized type of court that would solely process quality-of-life offenders who committed low-level, victimless, and visible crimes. The creation of Midtown Community Court in New York in 1993 illustrates how these new policing strategies, political interests, business interests, and the crisis of legitimacy in legal institutions converged. New York City adopted policing tactics based on broken windows theory, which argues that low-level, visible crimes can lead to more serious offenses if left unpunished. These policing strategies targeted quality-of-life offenders and increased police presence in areas that were regarded as criminal "hot spots." This style of policing was also well-matched to then-mayor Rudolph Giuliani's focus on law and order. The Giuliani administration and the police's focus on quality-of-life crimes dovetailed with economic development efforts. Business owners and developers in Times Square were also interested in targeting quality-of-life offenders, as such crimes arguably detracted from the interests of real-estate and business enterprises in the area. Finally, the public welcomed these tactics, as they addressed visible crimes that affected people's perceptions of safety, control, and quality of life.

Midtown Community Court provided a refuge for criminal justice practitioners who wanted to solve problems they encountered in their work and practice greater discretion in punishment. The court model was flexible enough to appeal to multiple stakeholders. Business owners and residents who wanted to rid their neighborhoods of "troublesome" people were pleased by Midtown Community Court's exclusive focus on quality-of-life offenses. Even those who considered zero-tolerance policing tactics to be draconian supported Midtown Community Court because it linked offenders to rehabilitative services.[8] The court's flexibility in appealing to a wide variety of stakeholders with varying interests and different—perhaps even divergent—ways of conceptualizing criminal justice made this approach to criminal justice particularly striking.

In discussing the creation of Midtown Community Court, I show how varying interests converged to create a need for community courts. In doing so, I also illustrate how this model would appeal to other cities in the United States and abroad facing similar issues: making communities safer, making cities attractive to businesses and wealthy residents, making politicians happy with the criminal justice system, and making justice visible.

The Structural Roots of Community Courts: Enforcing Order in New York City

Much like other large cities in the United States at the time, New York City in the late 1980s and early 1990s had a host of problems. The financial crisis of 1987 led to cutbacks in public services. The unemployment rate nearly tripled from 1987 to 1992, reaching more than 11 percent: the highest level in fifteen years (Lyons 1993). The homicide and violent-crime rates in New York City peaked in 1990, with 14.5 homicides and 1,180.9 violent crimes per 100,000 people (Federal Bureau of Investigation n.d.). New York had the reputation of being an incredibly dangerous city. And, as previously discussed, people lacked faith in the criminal justice system's ability to make the city safer.

Giuliani was elected as mayor of New York City in 1993, after running on a platform focused on restoring order to the city. Specifically, Giuliani promised to target low-level criminals who detracted from New Yorkers' quality of life and safety. He appointed William J. Bratton to the position of police commissioner to help restore order to the city. Bratton had previously worked as the head of the New York Transit Police under Mayor David Dinkins, earning acclaim by introducing strategies explicitly based on broken windows theory. Under Bratton's leadership, the Transit Police swiftly arrested and processed people who committed low-level crimes or misdemeanors in the subway. They focused much of their attention on arresting fare evaders (people who jumped over or ducked under turnstiles to avoid paying for their subway rides). Advocates of this strategy argued that targeting low-level offenses, such as fare evasion, helped deter minor infractions, which freed law enforcement to concentrate on more serious offenders. "Many of those caught committing these small crimes were also guilty of larger crimes. One out of seven fare evaders had prior warrants out for their arrest. One out of 21 was carrying a handgun" (Kaplan 1997). Police claimed that these broken windows theory tactics helped them apprehend dangerous offenders. The question of what to do with people who were charged with these small crimes but *did not* have warrants or handguns on them would be answered by the newly created Midtown Community Court.

Giuliani and Bratton extended this zero-tolerance policing out of the subway and on to the New York City streets, focusing on public drunkenness, loitering, vandalism, littering, public urination, panhandling, turnstile jumping, prostitution, and other minor offenses (Giuliani and Bratton 1994). However, the unofficial mascot (or, better put, scapegoat) of Giuliani's quality-of-life campaign were the "squeegees" in Times Square. The squeegees were mostly black men who, unsolicited, cleaned the windshields of cars stopped at red lights and then asked for money from the drivers. They became synonymous with the problems of New York City in general and with quality-of-life crimes specifically. Mayor Giuliani reflects on the implications of the squeegees in a *New York Times* interview:

> It was amazing to me that people thought the squeegee problem wasn't important or couldn't be solved. A civilized society can't let people go around the streets intimidating other people. But a weird philosophical thinking had emerged about these quality-of-life is-

sues. If somebody was urinating in the street, the reaction would be, oh, we can't do anything about that. And then the idea would start to develop that there must be some inherent human right to urinate on the street. So the police started ignoring all kinds of offenses. They'd even stand by when drug deals were going on. The police became highly skilled observers of crime. (Quoted in Tierney 1995)

Quality-of-life crimes, then, had broader implications: how social life should be ordered, notions of civic responsibility, and the duties of law enforcement. But while these quality-of-life discourses were deployed, they were also explicitly connected to the idea that policing low-level offenses would dramatically improve law-abiding citizens' lives. In Bratton's words, "As minute a problem that might seem in the overall scope of a city with 2,000 murders, squeegees are of great significance because like fare evasion and like disorder on the subways, it's that type of activity that is generating fear" (quoted in Myers 1993: 23).

As if the criminal justice system was not already overwhelmed with nonviolent offenders, in New York City, the court system now needed to process cases stemming from quality-of-life initiatives. Since most of these offenses were misdemeanors, they did not command a mandatory minimum sentence. Courts would typically punish quality-of-life offenders by issuing "time served," meaning the time that they had spent in a holding cell between being arrested and appearing before a judge was sufficient punishment. This method of punishment did little to unclog the revolving door of justice or to placate residents and business owners who perceived themselves as victims of quality-of-life offenders. If the mayoral administration and the police wanted to punish low-level offenders and stop the cycle of recidivism, there was clearly a mismatch between police strategy and court procedure.

The Hell's Kitchen (now called Clinton) neighborhood, which includes Times Square, was one of the areas in which these battles over quality of life were most pronounced. By the late 1980s and early 1990s, Times Square was well on its way to being "reinvented." The "thriving strip of cheap action and pornographic movie houses, restaurants, martial arts supply stores, clothing boutiques, souvenir stands, sex shops, and other small businesses" (Chesluk 2007: 61) was replaced with a Disney Store and offices for MTV and Condé Nast. According to Greg Berman and John Feinblatt:

> Pre-Disney, pre-Giuliani, pre-Internet boom, the central business district in New York City was not exactly the most hospitable place in town. In fact, the word most often used to describe this neighborhood was "seedy." Porn palaces outnumbered cafes by a wide margin. Just blocks from Times Square, you could find trashstrewn avenues lined with prostitutes—sometimes as many as 250 a night. (2005: 60)

Times Square was in a period of transition between the "seedy" blocks that invited crime and deviance and the squeaky-clean streets that welcomed families of tourists.

Two public-private partnerships enabled this transformation: the 42nd Street Development Corporation (now Building for the Arts) and the Times Square Business Improvement District (BID; now the Times Square Alliance). The 42nd Street Development Corporation was able to force out undesirable businesses by declaring the street blighted. Redevelopers found ways to remove the sex shops and adult-entertainment venues from the area by successfully arguing that "the 'blight' of Times Square and Forty-Second Street threatened social and economic values both for the surrounding area and for the city as a whole" (Chesluk 2007: 39). The Times Square BID rewrote commercial-zoning regulations to eliminate sex shops from the area.

After these developers had removed the undesirable businesses from the area, they were still left with people perceived as undesirable—homeless people, people with substance abuse issues, shoplifters, and street vendors. While the New York Police Department (NYPD) enforced quality-of-life laws and regulations, they were not doing it efficiently enough to please the Times Square BID. This organization hired its own private security force to patrol the area, keeping an eye on undesirables and calling the police when someone should be arrested. The concern with quality-of-life offenders throughout New York City was amplified in Times Square as developers vied to attract wealthy investors. These developers and investors also hoped to draw in tourist money, and to do that, they had to ensure that tourists would feel safe in the area.

Policing strategies, political plans, and business interests all aligned on the issue of "quality of life." Police wanted to get tough on low-level crimes because they could presumably reduce the number of more serious crimes through such tactics. The Giuliani administration wanted to sanction low-level crimes to fulfill its campaign promise of retaking the city from people who frightened law-abiding citizens. Business owners wanted to crack down on low-level crimes because they (and the type of people who tended to commit them) were bad for business.

But the criminal justice system was unable to address quality-of-life crimes in a way that matched the interests of police, politicians, and businesses. Already-overcrowded court dockets could not devote much time or energy to nonviolent offenders. Midtown Community Court married the demand to punish quality-of-life offenders with legal reformers' ideas that some people were able to be rehabilitated and that courts should have access to a range of possible punishment options to better meet the diverse needs of offenders.

One of Midtown Community Court's origin stories traces its birth to a discussion between Gerald Schoenfeld, the chair of the Shubert Organization, and Herbert Sturz, a real-estate executive and former deputy mayor for criminal justice under Ed Koch (Anderson 1996). Feinblatt, the founding director of Midtown Community Court, describes its creation as originating from within the legal system and outside it:

> The court was born out of frustration. There was frustration within the court system about quality-of-life crimes. Judges felt they didn't have the tools to do their job. . . . But there was also frustration within the community. The residential community of Clinton felt that their neighborhood had been inundated with street-corner drug sales and with prostitution, and there was certainly frustration a bit further east in the Times Square area, which was terribly frustrated by its inability to create the economic development boom it had hoped would occur. In Times Square, there was a deeply held sense that crime had just taken a very serious toll on economic development and economic activity. . . . My friend Herb said that maybe the thing to do was to try an experiment, which was to have a community-based court right in the middle of Times Square. And [Schoenfeld] didn't miss a beat and offered up [what was called] at the time the Longacre Theater, which had been dark for a couple of years. . . . So with real estate in hand, suddenly the words ["]community court["] had some currency.[9] (Quoted in Chesluk 2007: 82–83)

Midtown Community Court offered a solution to many groups' problems and frustrations. It intersected policing strategy with a legal approach that would filter nonviolent, low-level offenders through a process that hopefully deterred them from reoffending. Every month, the court distributed reports to police officers so they could see the outcomes of cases. "Sometimes, if there is a warrant, the guy who made the arrest knows where that person is and can go right out and pick her up" (police officer, quoted in Anderson 1996). Midtown Community Court partnered with the police to solve problems related to crime rather than usher people through the revolving door of justice.

Mobilizing Community Discourses

Community courts were created to address specific frustrations of judges, residents, business owners, and politicians, but many of their successes in implementation and longevity can be traced to more cultural roots. Community courts owe much of their legitimacy and staying power to how they discursively frame their missions. Organizational theorists tell us that new organizations cannot be successful without proper narratives. These justifications for being must highlight an organization's unique characteristics while simultaneously framing these "innovations" within established cultural frameworks. A new organization must offer "legitimating accounts" (Douglas Creed, Scully, and Austin 2002) that link its logic and practice to existing cultural views (Meyer and Rowan 1977). Community courts draw on the discursive framework of "the community" and "quality of life" as legitimating accounts. In the following paragraphs, I describe how "the community" is a legitimating account that stirs nostalgic sentiments of a sheltered neighborhood, like a blanket wrapped around a child for protection from the cold.

Discourses of community are extraordinarily mobilizing. In their 1971 publication, *Community Studies*, Colin Bell and Howard Newby declare community to be a "god word." More recent scholarship argues that ideas of community are especially salient in postmodernity, as individuals are confronted with feelings of insecurity, dislocation in time and space, and an increasingly diverse set of options around identity and belongingness. "Communitarianism is an all-too-expectable reaction to the accelerating 'liquefaction' of modern life, a reaction [to] . . . the deepening imbalance between individual freedom and security" (Bauman 2013: 170). Scholars identify the community as an incredibly mobilizing framework due to its "highly nebulous" (Macleod and Johnstone 2012) meaning. The word "community" is used to invoke a nostalgia for simpler times, to mobilize diverse individuals into political action, and to express or create a shared value system (Herbert 2009). As Zygmunt Bauman writes:

Words have meanings: some words, however, also have a "feel." The word "community" is one of them. It feels good: whatever the word ["]community["] may mean, it is good "to have a community," "to be in a community." . . . Community, we feel, is always a good thing. (2001: 1)

The flexibility of the legitimating account of community is crucial to the legitimacy of community courts. Community courts stir nostalgia for imagined times of safer neighborhoods, mobilizing individuals around issues of crime and galvanizing a sense of shared community values around "quality-of-life" discourses.[10]

Community courts are but one manifestation of how the criminal justice system has profoundly reoriented around issues of the community. Scholars point to the rise of neighborhood watches, public and private partnerships around crime, the privatization of security, and the now taken-for-grantedness of community policing as key illustrations of the shift in criminal justice. Adam Crawford's work traces the rise of community in Great Britain's criminal justice system, arguing that under neoliberal governance, the state is no longer responsible for providing the needs of a society; instead, there is "greater individual and group responsibility for the management of local risks and security" (1999: 6). In his study on community-police relations, Steve Herbert (2009) finds that residents often described community in terms of providing security, predictability, and reliability. Community courts are then another manifestation of the increasing emphasis on community responsibility against crime.

Community courts' mission of restorative justice and the direct involvement of community members in the justice process capitalize on discourses of community. The identification of low-level, quality-of life crimes as a primary concern reflects these postmodern concerns around insecurity and incivility. There is a "moral rearmament" (Rose 2000) of the community itself and of members within that community against low-level crimes. The direct participation of community members in the justice process through impact panels, partnerships with private organizations, and data-seeking missions of the community court illustrate the "responsibilization of citizens" around issues of crime. The community court model has galvanized this "nice-feeling" word—"community"—into a profound and culturally fitting practice to incorporate residents and business owners into justice proceedings.

And, of course, the mission of community courts and the active promotion of "the community" are wonderfully appealing in practice. In the eyes of residents and business owners whose concerns were not being met previously, the community court model gives them a stake in the justice system. Community courts' strategies of listening to people's concerns and emphasizing that the organizations truly exist for community building makes this discursive approach particularly appealing. Community courts provide a formal organizational framework for "the community" to present a united front against crime.

It is no surprise that the fragmented experiences of postmodern life provoke communitarianism, and the path toward communitarianism promoted by specialized courts takes the form of individualized solutions vis-à-vis therapeutic jurisprudence. As Émile Durkheim, Claude Lévi-Strauss, and Zygmunt Bauman theorize, communities "cope with otherness" in one of two ways. The first strategy is to construct strong boundaries around the community and excise people, behaviors, or identities that threaten it. The second strategy is to incorporate the threat—"'devouring' foreign bodies and spirits so that they may be made, through metabolism, identical with, and no longer distinguishable from, the 'ingesting' body" (Bauman 2013: 101). Community courts practice both strategies. They aid in formally designating very minor incivilities as criminally punishable. This process shores up community boundaries symbolically and practically, as community courts can and do remove people from the area with jail time. Additionally, they provide structured rehabilitative practices whereby individuals whose behaviors threaten a community's quality of life undergo treatments meant to transform them from "deviants" into "community members" (a point further explored in Chapters 4 and 5).

Community courts are not just a quick fix to institutional pressures. Instead, they are a reconfiguration of meaning from within and outside the criminal justice system. They see the community as something meaningful that needs to be brought back into the justice system.

Conclusion

The differences in criminal justice policy from the 1960s to the late 1970s arose due to a declining belief in the rehabilitative ideal. The legal system changed by adopting standardized sentencing practices and punishing offenders, with no goals or strategies to rehabilitate them. Yet these practices failed to produce clear positive results. Policy changes brought new populations under strict criminal justice supervision, and crime rates, recidivism rates, and public concerns about crime continued to increase. In the late 1980s, the criminal justice system underwent yet another crisis of legitimacy, again raising questions about how best to punish offenders and what the goals of criminal justice should be.

The adoption of punitive strategies in the 1980s could not accommodate changes in the criminal justice population and increases in crime. The criminal justice system and its various agents were supervising more people than ever before, including offenders with mental illness who had recently been deinstitutionalized. The invention of crack cocaine with its attendant addict populations and gun violence introduced another concern for criminal justice. The punitive strategies did little to deter offending or reoffending. As a drug court judge summarized, "I think anybody who works in the criminal justice system, in the traditional justice system, realizes how little effect we're having on things. . . . The legal system has to change. . . . Overcrowded dockets and high recidivism rates in the criminal justice system are evidence of problems" (Nolan 2001: 45). The criminal justice system's crisis of legitimacy necessitated the adoption of new strategies in policing and in the legal system. One of the responses to the crisis was the creation of community courts.

The community court movement began in 1993 as new policing strategies, political and business investments, and legal actors converged around the management of quality-of-life issues. In New York City, where Midtown Community Court pioneered the concept of a community court, the mayoral administration was particularly concerned with "tak[ing] back the city" from criminals. Police tactics focused on low-level crimes with the aim of deterring larger crimes and/or apprehending those who posed larger threats to society. Real-estate developers and business investors in the Times Square area were also particularly concerned with quality-of-life crimes and criminals, which they thought detracted from their ability to draw in business. The interest in quality-of-life crimes aligned with criminal justice practitioners' desire to divert nonviolent offenders from the prison system and to revive long-abandoned rehabilitative practices in the legal system. Practitioners adopted philosophies and practices from the drug court model and from academic discussions of individualized justice and therapeutic jurisprudence to guide community courts' mission to meaningfully punish quality-of-life crimes.

Community courts embody modern approaches to the justice system. They take contemporary philosophies that theorize offenders' relationships to crime and offending and use that information to bolster positive ties to the community. Community courts understand the law as a tool to produce positive change, not as an apparatus to enforce literally and immutably. Community courts supervise citizens who are perceived as salvageable and therefore choose to spare them from the "revolving door of justice." The flexibility of the community court model allows it to appeal to stakeholders with opposing views on punishment. For stakeholders invested in rehabilitation, community courts mandate supervised treatment with an added incentive to comply. For those who believe that punishment itself should be the goal, community courts punish people whose cases would have been thrown out or given "time served" in traditional hearings. In community courts, the penal practices and strict by-the-books legal strategies of the 1980s are discarded in favor of individualized punishments (which aim to keep offenders out of prison) and avoidance of the negative outcomes associated with having a criminal record. Yet community courts still continue to process the new category of "quality-of-life offenders" and therefore do not theoretically or politically question their increased criminal justice supervision of drug addicts, people who are mentally ill, and other marginalized citizens.

The creation of community courts points to the agentic assertion of criminal justice practitioners against federal and state control over sentencing practices. The community court phenomenon also bears witness to the syncretism of the criminal justice complex as it incorporates new knowledge and ideas through a penological lens. Community courts resurrect and reinterpret the notion of the united community: involved in the collective creation of justice and sharing the same values. Rehabilitation is also focused on reintegrating offenders into the community, as opposed to rehabilitation practices from the 1930s to the 1970s, which separated criminals from the community in an attempt to rehabilitate them. Community courts aim to hold offenders accountable for the ways in which they harm the community, in part by keeping them *in* the community; after righting their wrongs, they are able to rejoin the community, reformed and ready to be productive citizens.

However, this notion of community is not as inclusive as it appears. Midtown Community Court developed in part due to resources that real-estate and business developers provided, underlining how beholden the notion of community is to specific interest groups. Giuliani and Bratton's focus on policing low-level, quality-of-life offenders further marginalized groups of people who were already on the fringes of society: sex workers, people who were drunk in public, unlicensed vendors. Therefore, policing so-called quality-of-life crimes promotes racialized inequalities in criminal justice practices and outcomes, like the sentencing outcomes that were so problematic to political liberals in the 1970s. Redefining "criminals" to include quality-of-life offenders (and their enhanced judicial supervision) becomes justified in the name of reformation and rehabilitation. Community courts aim to integrate quality-of-life offenders back into the community through treatment, education, and community service, but they also further justify the demarcation between community members and people who do not belong by filtering this notion through a criminal justice lens: criminals who can reform and change are community members, while those who cannot are indeed just criminals.

While community courts largely avoid the unchecked discretion and lack of oversight that characterized penology from the 1930s to the 1970s, they echo some troubling aspects of this era of justice. Community courts have tremendous discretion in sentencing and in offender surveillance, and they capitalize on this unfettered agency to punish crimes that are, objectively speaking, very minor. This discretion, coupled with their focus on rehabilitation, allows community courts to keep people under supervision for indeterminate lengths of time. Since offenders must plead guilty to have their cases heard at community courts, if they do not fulfill the conditions of the court—for example, if they fail at treatment or do not appear for a court date—they may endure criminal justice supervision for long periods of time. (Since the ultimate goal is to rehabilitate offenders, community courts give people many "chances" to succeed at treatment, which may mean that offenders remain under criminal justice supervision for much longer than they would have otherwise.) To the extent that community courts represent a contemporary form of justice, they may be repeating patterns that social scientists and criminal justice practitioners have already determined are problematic and harmful to offenders, such as a great degree of judicial discretion, the paternalism of rehabilitation, and the criminalization of poverty.

3

The Process of Punishment

Greenville Community Court is a small nondescript building across the street from the more architecturally grand superior court. Established in the late 1990s, Greenville Community Court was modeled after the first community court in New York City, with the mission of addressing "quality-of-life crimes that contribute to the deterioration of local neighborhoods" as well as "offering a helping hand to address the social issues that may be contributing to their behavior" (Martinez 2010: 20) Initial funding for Greenville Community Court was provided by the federal Comprehensive Communities Program that aims to "integrate law enforcement with social programs—and public agencies with nongovernmental organizations and individuals—to control crime and improve the quality-of-life" (Kelling et al. 1998). That money was supplemented with a grant from the U.S. Department of Justice and other funding from state agencies.

Violations in this city are filtered to one of the following courts: the housing court, the family court, the superior court, and Greenville Community Court. All low-level crimes committed in the city are first handled by Greenville Community Court. Typical low-level crimes include larceny under $500, public drunkenness, trespassing, disturbance of the peace, prostitution, possession of marijuana, and interfering with an officer. Greenville Community Court handles offenses that occur in all seventeen neighborhoods of the city, and approximately 15 percent of the court's caseload comes from suburban jurisdictions.

Greenville's population is under 120,000. The city is racially diverse: about 40 percent of residents identify as black or African American, about 30 percent identify as white, and about 40 percent of residents identify as Hispanic or Latino (of any race). The city has been attempting to attract younger, higher-income people to live in its downtown area: developers have constructed high-rise luxury apartment buildings, a hip new water-front district, and a recently opened convention center. However, most of the wealthy families are concentrated in a town that directly borders Green-ville. This town hosts bars, restaurants, a Whole Foods, a Lululemon store, and other companies that appeal to an upper-middle-class sensibility. Greenville Community Court handles the town's quality-of-life offenses:

Breach of peace
Criminal impersonation
Criminal mischief
Curfew violations
Disorderly conduct
Excessive noise
Illegal alcohol purchase
Illegal alcohol sale
Illegal possession of fireworks
Interference with an officer/arrest
Larceny
Littering
Loitering
Minor possession of alcohol
Prostitution
Public drinking
Public indecency
Public nuisance
Simple possession of marijuana
Solicitation
Threatening
Vending violations[1]

For the years in which I completed fieldwork, 32.5 percent of the city's population lived below the poverty level. For those sixteen years or older, 37 percent of Greenville's population were not in the labor force, and 10 percent were unemployed. The median family income was around $29,000.

Planning for the court began in the late 1990s, emerging from community concerns around quality-of-life crimes. Nick, the court manager, explained:

> In the early nineties, I don't know if you recollect, in Greenville [there were] serious gang problems. I mean, it was like the Wild West. People were getting shot every day. It was brutal. Residents couldn't go outside. *It was the Wild West.* The feds came in. . . . They put away a lot of real bad people on the RICO [Racketeer Influenced and Corrupt Organizations] Act stuff and gang stuff. And they . . . got twelve to fifteen years, stuff like that. . . .
>
> Although you know, it never really went away, but it got a lot more peaceful. And I think community people looked around a lot of the community and said, "What's affecting us?" And they said, "Quality-of-life stuff."

A group of residents visited the superior court and watched how it processed quality-of-life crimes, learning that these cases were either dismissed or taken off the docket without any repercussions. In other words, quality-of-life criminals were not punished for their actions, aside from being arrested or having to show up for a court date. Nick continued:

> And a lot of the residents . . . found out about the first court, Midtown, in Manhattan, which opened in 1993. They [took a trip to Midtown Community Court]. A lot of the community groups liked what [they] saw. . . . [T]hey went to . . . [the] mayor at the time, God rest him, and said, "We want this in Greenville. This is what's affecting us." And you know, of course, it was [the] nineties, glory days of money, and he had somewhat close to a million bucks in weed and seed money, and he approached the judicial branch [and] sa[id], "Look I have this money; would you guys be willing to do a community court like Midtown?" And [the] judicial branch said, "Yeah, we'll do it."

Judge Balick joined the community court movement a few months later, and the organizers began to establish relationships with social-service providers that would be integral to the court's functioning. Judge Balick was the perfect candidate for this initial project building. As a Greenville resident and an older white judge who had years of experience in

Greenville's court system, the community saw him as "their judge," balancing professional knowledge, personal charisma, and useful social networks.

How Defendants Came to Court

Defendants entered the court in two ways: through the front door and the back door. People who came through the front door had committed an infraction, which is less serious than a misdemeanor. The police caught them in the act, and they were given a summons with a court appearance date. Since Greenville Community Court emphasized swift justice, the court date was typically no more than two business days after the offense. Defendants who received a summons entered Greenville Community Court from the front of the building, first passing through a metal detector and then checking in with the marshals. Cell phones with cameras were not allowed inside the building. The entryway of the court was wide and paneled with light wood walls. Wood benches lined either side of the entry way. If people sat on these benches in the entryway, they were instructed to enter the courtroom on the right side of the hallway.

Greenville Community Court sometimes featured local art in the entryway, which made the space seem more welcoming. The artwork was either made by people who lived in the area and depicted the city, or it was made by prisoners involved in art programs. While I was conducting fieldwork, the most positively discussed exhibit was that of a local college student who showcased the "vibrancy" of one neighborhood in the city in her photos of barber-shop patrons, local bodegas, and residents sitting outside their homes.

Several offices were on the left side of the entryway. Toward the front of the building were the bail commissioners' offices, and toward the rear of the building were the social-services and community-service offices. At a glass window, much like one would find in a bank or a doctor's office, community-service coordinators gave defendants paperwork to complete and answered their questions. Behind the glass window, community-service coordinators sat in cubicles, many of which were empty. Also on this side were restrooms. (The women's room was noticeably clean and well-kept. I do not know the condition of the men's room.)

Defendants who had been arrested entered the court through the back door. Misdemeanors, such as public drunkenness and prostitution, warranted immediate arrest. If the police arrested someone who would be processed in Greenville Community Court, they first took the offender to a holding cell "across the street" at the superior court for the night. The following morning, court marshals from the superior court drove those offenders to Greenville Community Court, where they entered through the back entrance. They then waited in holding cells in the back of the court for their cases to be called. People who worked at the court called these defendants "lockups." Lockups also included people who were already incarcerated but had a court date at Greenville Community Court. These lockups were readily distinguished from those who had been arrested the previous night by their bright prison jumpsuits. There were two holding cells at Greenville Community Court, one 8' x 10' and one 10' x 12'. When men and women lockups entered the court, the marshals segregated them by gender. Only one holding cell contained a toilet (in full view of the rest of the cell), and both cells had one large Plexiglas wall. Two marshals were usually stationed in a room adjacent to the holding cells to monitor the lockups through the Plexiglas and with video feed from cameras in the holding cells' ceilings.[2]

Holding cells were located in a space behind the judge's bench, away from view and access from all nonofficial court personnel. Lockups remained in the holding cells until the judge called each case, at which time a marshal escorted the defendant, ankles and wrists in shackles, into the courtroom. Defendants entered the courtroom from behind the judge, on the right side. After their cases, no matter what the resolution, they were escorted back into the holding cells while the required paperwork for the court's decisions was processed. It was not uncommon for lockups to disrupt the court session from behind the scenes by screaming, crying, moaning, or talking loudly while in the holding cells. The culprits behind such disruptions were typically drunk or high, had mental-health issues, and/or had been sentenced to prison and were very upset about it.

Court staff members (usually one of the bail commissioners) interviewed all types of defendants before their cases were called. The bail commissioners compiled such information as age, education, residence, employment history, medical problems, and prior criminal record. Criminal record information was then cross-checked with law-enforcement databases to determine whether the defendants had any outstanding warrants, pending cases, and so forth. The bail commissioners prepared this information for the judge, the prosecutor, and the public defender to peruse prior to the court's official opening of the docket.

Greenville Community Court had only one courtroom, which was brightly light, clean, and sparse. The furniture was light-colored wood. Two sections of seating held those awaiting their cases and the people accompanying them. A low wooden separator demarked the courtroom's seating area from its official space, where court personnel conducted business. The prosecutor had a podium and a desk he used to hold his paperwork (he preferred to stand behind the podium). The public defender stood behind an identical desk to the judge's left. A jury box also sat to the judge's left, against the wall. Since Greenville Community Court did not hold trials, the jury box was used as seating for observers with some official status, such as people who worked or interned at the court, visitors from local high schools, or bureaucrats from other countries. The judge's bench sat higher than the other furniture and was flanked by an American flag and a flag with the name of the court. In front of the judge sat the court stenographer and other record keepers. To the judge's right was a seat for witnesses, although that seat was never occupied, as the court did not hold trials.

Setting the Stage

Court officially started at 10:00 A.M., Monday through Friday. Defendants' tickets were issued with the appearance time of 8:45 A.M. so that processing could happen more efficiently. Defendants checked in with a marshal, who then relayed their presence to the prosecutor. To assess the situation before the court was officially "in session," the prosecutor called each case as early as he could. Each defendant approached the prosecutor to discuss his or her case in front of the court, but the conversations were informal and semiprivate. The prosecutor reviewed the police report and past criminal history and discussed with each defendant the sentence he planned to recommend to the judge. In many cases, the prosecutor told defendants, "If you plead guilty, you can do [however many] days of community service, and if you stay out of trouble, we can dismiss the case." When the information from the bail commissioner indicated a possible mental, psychological, or emotional problem, the prosecutor then used his time with the defendant to discuss treatment.[3]

While some people in the courtroom needed to discuss their initial summons with Gary, the courtroom audience was not entirely first-time defendants. Some people in attendance had continuing cases; they may have been undergoing treatment and were making an appearance to report on their progress, or the judge may have wanted them to appear for court dates to motivate them to stay out of trouble. Occasionally, but not regularly, defendants were accompanied by private lawyers or social workers. Family or friends accompanying loved ones or awaiting defendants in lockup also sat in the courtroom.

Court Employees

Community courts are nonadversarial courts in which the judge, the prosecutor, and the public defender work together to make sentencing decisions that they think are most appropriate for each defendant. Greenville Community Court employed only one judge, one prosecutor, and one public defender, so these three actors had quite a bit of power. They could make decisions about appropriate sanctions, and as long they did not exceed the maximum jail time allotted for the crimes, their decisions were not scrutinized. Since the judge, the prosecutor, and the public defender engaged in direct and informal communication with defendants, they also had a lot of power in terms of how they presented the criminal charges and sanctions. According to therapeutic jurisprudence, how the court acts toward an offender may be more influential than the sentence itself. Therefore, presentational style and content are as important as, if not more important than, the sentences in determining offenders' behavior.

Two judges presided over Greenville Community Court during the course of my study. One was a Latino man, Judge Rodriguez. He was tall and elegant, but he moved with the pace of someone who had consumed one too many cups of espresso. When I first observed the court, Judge Rodriguez had been there for four years. He transferred to family court during a gap in my fieldwork and was replaced by Judge Corbett, a black Dominican woman. Judge Corbett was short, wore her hair in intricate braids, and displayed an unamused poker face. She was far less jocular than Judge Rodriguez, although when I observed her, she had just started at the court and perhaps had not yet developed close ties with the court staff.

Other members of the team included Gary, the prosecutor, and Ralph, the public defender. Gary often cracked jokes in court with a mischievous smile, while Ralph was very mild-mannered. As the court was nonadversarial, the judge almost always agreed with Gary's sentencing recommendations, and Ralph only rarely raised an objection. All three worked with a cohesion in sentencing goals and sentencing guidelines that made the process of deciding appropriate sanctions quick and easy.

Punishment or Treatment?

As a specialized court with a focus on individualized justice, Greenville Community Court had a wide variety of sanctions at its disposal. Community-service projects might involve picking up litter in the neighborhoods where the offenders had committed crimes, working with a local farmers' market, or cleaning trails at the local organization that teaches at-risk youth horse-riding skills. Mediation was typically used when a misdemeanor resulted from a dispute between two individuals (for instance, when two women were charged with a breach of peace when they fought over who could use a treadmill at a local gym). Outside agencies provided substance-abuse treatment, which could be inpatient (meaning that the person lived at the facility) or outpatient (meaning that the person resided somewhere else). Juveniles could be placed under the supervision of the bail commissioner, given a curfew, referred to a program for at-risk youth, and/or fitted with an electronic monitoring device. The court could forbid people from going to particular places if they had made threats or trespassed on these properties. The court also imposed some creative sanctions. Judge Corbett often continued defendants' cases for two weeks, instructing them to return to court with completed job applications for a position at the hospital down the street. Students charged with underage drinking or disorderly conduct were sometimes sentenced to write essays about their misconduct or to apologize to the community.

Figure 3.1 shows the process that cases followed throughout their time at Greenville Community Court. Since part of Greenville Community Court's aim was to punish offenders without giving them criminal records for minor offenses, the preferred outcome of a case was to be nolled. If a defendant successfully completed community service, classes, and/or a treatment program, the court would nolle the case. By nolling a case, the court in effect dismissed it. The nolle removed the case from the defendant's record, although it was still listed in the internal records of the state's criminal justice system. The defendant did not have to be present for his or her case to be nolled. The case could be reopened within thirteen months if there were reason to, although I never heard of any actual cases in which that happened.

If a defendant did not comply with court orders—if he or she did not report to classes, community service, treatment, or the like—Greenville Community Court noted a "failure to appear" (FTA). When a defendant failed to appear, the court issued a warrant for his or her arrest. Sometimes, the prosecutor would wait a day or so before issuing a warrant, in case the defendant had mistaken the court date or had an emergency situation. The issuing of a warrant did not mean that police would show up at a defendant's home or place of work to arrest him or her. Rather, if a defendant were to be caught violating the law at some point in time, whether

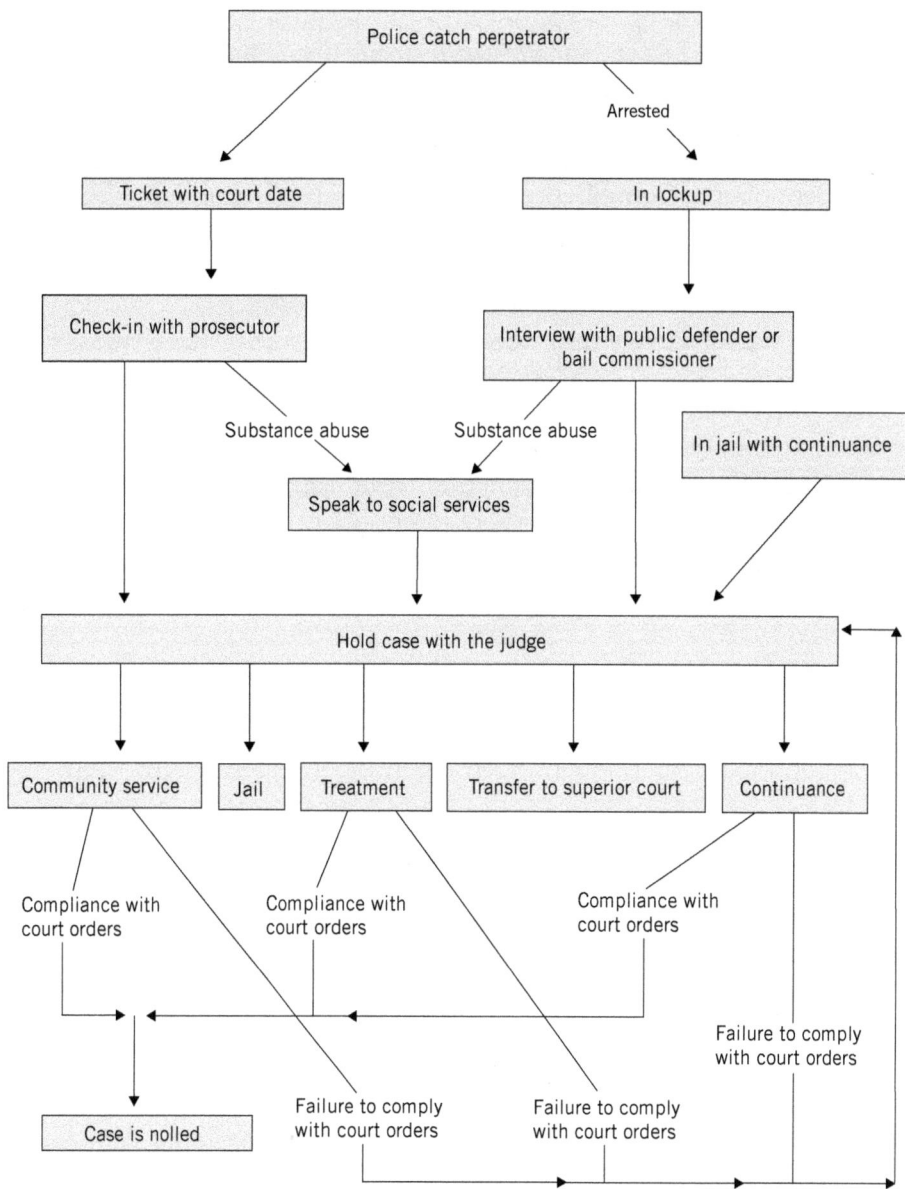

Figure 3.1. Case processing at Greenville Community Court.

that be a speeding violation or something less mundane, he or she would be arrested on the spot and appear in Greenville Community Court to answer for the FTA and the new charge, if the charge fell under that court's purview.

The court also had the ability to put people in jail. If Greenville Community Court considered a defendant to be beyond help or deserving of incarceration, the defendant would be put in lockup and then taken to jail or prison. The court also used lockup to assert its power to the people in the courtroom. For instance, if a defendant misbehaved in the courtroom (e.g., by speaking out of turn, swearing, or sleeping), the judge would put that person in lockup for a few hours or in jail for a night. The judge also regularly locked up minors or young adults who returned to the courtroom with poor reports from parents or treatment centers.

Sometimes the judge used jail more reluctantly. If a defendant was "waiting for a bed" (i.e., waiting for a spot to become available at an inpatient facility), he or she would be held in jail until a bed "opened up." Minors who were arrested could not be released from the court's custody without the presence of a legal guardian (e.g., parent, family member, or social-service agency). This stipulation sometimes meant that a minor would be in jail for days waiting for someone to either post bail or to get in touch with the court.

Like Judge Judy

Community courts' focus on individualized justice and therapeutic jurisprudence means that courtroom interaction is particularly important for understanding how punishment operates. In community court, the focus is on rehabilitating rather than on punishing, but, as we have seen, the court still has the ability to send quality-of-life offenders to jail. The contrast between treatment and jail time is made in explicit interactions with defendants while court is in session. The court deploys a dualistic framework, pitting rehabilitation and restoration against jail time, in an attempt to motivate offenders to comply with court orders. The court also strategically deploys emotion (or a lack of emotion) in its interactions with defendants to further encourage their compliance.

This tension between following the court orders, which aim to be restorative and/or rehabilitative, and disobeying them and receiving jail time is a stark illustration of community courts' ability to incorporate "seemingly disparate logics . . . into a coherent project" (Werth 2013: 237). Community courts are able to act rehabilitatively or punitively, depending on the situation at hand. Greenville Community Court acted in ways that aimed to motivate offenders to comply with rehabilitative goals, which could include using informal language, gathering and discussing information about an offender's life, threatening or imposing jail time, and praising offenders who were complying with court orders.

Days at the court had an emotional tempo that ranged from intensely boring to incredibly powerful. Despite community courts' position against merely shuffling people through the criminal justice system, they still have the drudgery of bureaucratic paperwork associated with legal work. Cases that had been nolled needed to be called while court was in session so that they could be officially recorded. Sometimes the judge could not sentence someone in court because he or she had not received a letter from a treatment agency testifying to the offender's progress. There was also the almost daily occurrence of the lockups arriving later than scheduled; the judge could not arraign offenders in absentia, so the people who were waiting for loved ones to be arraigned would have to wait longer than planned. During my fieldwork, a new law went into effect to protect the privacy of juvenile offenders. This law meant that the court needed to be cleared of "unofficial personnel" when it processed juvenile cases, even if Gary, the prosecutor, merely needed to make an official report on a juvenile matter (e.g., that someone was under supervision or that a juvenile's case was nolled). This requirement meant that everyone in the seating area of the court needed to leave the courtroom, the doors needed to be locked, and after the case had been handled, the courtroom had to be reopened so that everyone could reenter. The judge usually called for one or two recesses between 10:00 A.M. and lunch at noon: sometimes the judge needed to discuss cases with the prosecutor and the public defender, the bail commissioner needed to interview more people, or the court was waiting for lockups to arrive. Because of these logistical delays, some people who were waiting for their cases or the cases of loved ones to be heard would become bored and antsy. Marshals regulated the behavior of people in the courtroom, shushing them, insisting that they close any reading materials, and asking them to spit out the gum they were chewing.[4]

Other times, the courtroom proceedings were incredibly intriguing. Some people cried and screamed when the judge sentenced them to jail. Some people cried tears of happiness when the judge invited them to come up and shake hands for a "job well done." The judges often raised their voices when speaking to juvenile offenders, asking them whether they thought they were "tough guy[s]" or telling one, "Your aunt doesn't have enough money to get you out of jail. You just spent how many days in jail?

[Two days.] Just think of that in terms of months!" Whenever well-meaning folks asked me about my fieldwork, I responded, "It's like watching *Judge Judy* in person." This description allowed me to explain what my fieldwork was like to people who were unfamiliar with courtroom interactions and helped me capture how the judges interacted with some defendants. The description was also indicative of how the emotionally charged content of the court influenced my feelings during fieldwork. My heart swelled when someone graduated from the Women's Diversion Program. I felt intimidated when the judges yelled at defendants who continued to reoffend. When defendants gave particularly terrible excuses for their behavior, I chuckled to myself. These responses troubled me; sometimes I felt as though I were consuming the failures or successes surrounding someone's criminal behavior for pure entertainment. I was not the only observer who got caught up in the emotional roller coaster: the court reporters had a box of tissues on their shared desk, in case they cried during someone's case. However, my emotional reactions became less pronounced the longer I was in the field. Toward the end of my fieldwork, Judge Corbett had punished college students who had been caught underage drinking by having them write essays on their relationship to alcohol. When Judge Corbett hugged the students after they read their essays aloud, and the gathered audience clapped, I stole a glance around the room, wondering whether anyone else found this display to be even *a little* overindulgent.

The emotional discussions between court staff and defendants, then, were primarily about motivating offenders' behavior and giving meaning to the punishment process. This intent followed from the idea of therapeutic jurisprudence, which argues that punishment must be individualized to suit an offender's needs. Instead of merely giving out sentences that were meant to motivate behavior without context, Greenville Community Court situated and personalized the meaning for those sentences to better motivate offenders' behavior toward the court's goals of rehabilitation and personal transformation. The emotional exchanges may have affected more than just the defendants themselves, as all cases, except for those involving minors, were called before the full court.[5] People who were waiting for their cases to be called, those who accompanied them, and those who were waiting for offenders in lockup were instructed to sit quietly and watch the interactions between the judge, the prosecutor, the public defender, and the current defendant. This practice is theoretically interesting because it highlights the performative aspects for "court in session," not only for one's own case but also for cases that had not yet been called. That is, the court specifically organized the docket if specific cases would be advantageous in terms of presenting a particular image to a particular defendant or group of defendants. So these emotional exchanges may also have been used as to motivate the compliance of unrelated offenders who were watching. The court also used unemotional exchanges to regulate other offenders' behavior. This strategy was more obvious to an observer, as the judge and the court staff chose when to adopt a more formal, by-the-books presentational style.

Relationship to the Superior Court

Greenville Community Court occupied an uneasy relationship with the nearby superior court. According to Greenville Community Court personnel, superior court employees often referred to Greenville Community Court as the "the circus," and claimed that defendants performed a "song and dance" to garner lighter sanctions. They also called it the "revolving door," referring to a perceived high recidivism rate.[6]

Court staff were quite aware of these nicknames. Many of the marshals who had friends working in other courts and had themselves worked in other courts repeated these nicknames to me. These comments would be prompted by "a regular" returning to the court and/or when the marshal personally disagreed with how the court had handled a case (e.g., "That girl graduated the program and has been here four times. That's why they call us 'the revolving door'"). One marshal was particularly vocal about her dislike for the court's practices, calling it "a waste of taxpayers' money" and insisting that "if someone wants to become a better person and turn their life around, they can do it. They can find out where to go."

Other workers at the court (the court manager, bail commissioners, the prosecutor, the judge, and the public defender) perceived these nicknames as unfair and insulting to their work. It was often said that the superior court "[didn't] care about the people they process[ed]." One of the bail commissioners repeatedly told me that the lockup cells at the superior court were dirty, smelly, and disgusting. The public defender talked to me about the abysmal waiting time for defendants' cases to be called. Court personnel thought that the superior court purposely delayed transferring lockups to Greenville Community Court in an effort to delay their work. Public denunciations of superior court were also made while the community court was in session. For instance, a parent of a minor waited all day at the superior court, constantly asking marshals and clerks when her daughter's case would be called. No one told her that her child's case was not on the docket there but across the street at Greenville Community Court, so the daughter needlessly spent a night in jail.[7] This issue was discussed in detail the next day when the case was heard, during which the community court judge profusely apologized on behalf of the superior court.

Greenville Community Court staff also critiqued the superior court for its different jurisprudential orientations. There was a refrain that people at the superior court were careerists who wanted to pursue only high-profile felony cases. Community court employees often stated that the superior court had the personnel to practice rehabilitative justice but lacked the "attitude" and "willingness" to do so. Still, Greenville Community Court staffers believed that they were making a major contribution to the good of Greenville in general and to the superior court, specifically.

As one employee explained:

> [Employees of the superior court] call it "comedy court" . . . because it's low-level crimes. "It's not glamourous murders like we do and dangerous narcotics trials." . . . But you can also see their backlog of cases. For every case that we increase, their caseload [goes] down. . . . They used to have one of the hugest backloads in cases in the city. We process cases very efficiently. We're very fast, and we always have been, you know, while still maintaining the integrity of the court. . . . [T]here's always been a lack of respect [and] I think maybe even some resentment because . . . fundamentally we're here because the community said, "You're not doing your job and we're not happy. We want this."

Reproducing Inequality

Greenville Community Court as an institution conceptualized itself as practicing a "fair" form of justice that alleviated racial and economic inequalities in the criminal justice system because, as Nick, the court manager, explained:

> Greenville has heavy minority populations, populations that have been disenfranchised by law enforcement and courts, and you know, sometimes rightly and sometimes wrongly. But historically, you know there's skepticism. But . . . in this court, I'd say if you do what you're supposed to do, you're gonna get a dismissal. We're trying not to criminalize anybody, but, you know, your neighbors also want this enforced. They don't want you out there drinking a

beer on the sidewalk, smashing the bottle, you know, playing your tunes with your boys until 3:00 in the morning. . . .

And we aren't targeting anybody in particular. And we handle everybody the same: fairly. You know the fine policy here. We don't take fines . . . because, as I always say, why should a corporation vice president wearing a nice suit and tie [who] go[es] out on Main Street at 2:00 in the morning and [is] . . . howling at the moon . . . [be treated any differently from] somebody who is living on the street with a needle hanging out of his arm and schizophrenic and standing next to him and howling at the moon doing the same exact thing? And the street person has to come in here and do three days of community service. . . . And why should the vice president be able to come in here and pay a $100 fine, which is probably no skin off his teeth anyway? And the money just goes to a general fund; there's no payback to the community, and there's no accountability of that person to the community. It's a level playing field [here] in that sense.

As an ethnographer, I did observe the court staffers trying to treat people fairly. Greenville Community Court has a commitment to individualized justice, procedural fairness, and promoting defendant accountability. Despite this commitment to fairness, however, Greenville Community Court plays a part in exacerbating inequalities. Although Greenville Community Court is committed to promoting fair treatment, it is only one stop in the criminal justice process.

Two specialized dockets of Greenville Community Court may help readers begin to piece together how individualized justice and bureaucratic efficiency unintentionally reproduce inequality. On Thursdays, the court handled all cases that had been referred from the wealthier town that neighbored Greenville. The Thursday defendants were noticeably younger and whiter, and they were more commonly accompanied by private attorneys than other defendants. Court actors called Thursday "suburban day," but an intern at the court told me that a better name would be "scare the suburban kids day," as the judges and the prosecutor acted far more theatrically than with other defendants and presented a great deal of "tough love." Additionally, the Women's Diversion Program was specifically designed for women who were arrested on prostitution charges. It was a two-week outpatient program run by Greenville Community Court staff that combined mental-health counseling, substance-abuse treatment, and self-esteem-building activities (among other things). Participants in the Women's Diversion Program were afforded much more leniency than other offenders because they were viewed as less culpable for their actions than any other offender group; they were considered to be victims of male pimps and of drug and alcohol problems.

The practice of therapeutic jurisprudence allows for similar cases to be handled differently in an effort to best motivate the offender to desist. The pronounced sanction threats on suburban day and the specialized programming for women involved in sex work illustrate how Greenville Community Court processed cases according to the perceived unique needs of each offender group. So "fairness" of procedure was sometimes at odds with therapeutic jurisprudence, which directs court actors to tailor sanctions toward individualized needs.

Conclusion

Greenville Community Court processes all low-level offenses for the city. The court's main objective is to resolve as many cases as possible through sanctions and to have offenders leave with clean records. Greenville Community Court perceives itself as doing good work for the people of the city—by addressing quality-of-life problems that are at the least a nuisance and, according to broken windows theory, are contributing to the commission of more serious crimes and by providing a solution to recidivism. The court sees itself as complementing and contributing to the work of other agencies; it aids the superior court by handling low-level offenses that would take resources away from more serious offenses, and it aids treatment agencies by supplying them with people who have judicial motivation to succeed. Yet sometimes these agencies fuel bureaucratic delays.

The court's mundane work of processing some cases contrasts with the emotionally charged interactions of other cases. Sometimes the emotional cases are positive, such as when someone has successfully completed court-ordered treatment. Other emotional cases are sad or scary, such as when the judge tells people that their actions hurt them and their families, or when the judge bellows at defendants who continue to reoffend. These responses are quite different from those in other courtrooms, in which defendants have little if any direct communication with judges. These emotional discussions, the relationship between the community court actors, and the structure of case processing are designed to facilitate therapeutic jurisprudence: to help people reform and have positive interactions with the law.

These emotional cases also attempt to imbue the courtroom experience with meaning. Recall that community courts emerged in response to a system that was viewed as unable and unwilling to address real problems associated with crime. Community courts see themselves as addressing the quality-of-life issues that matter to people who live and work in the communities they serve. Greenville Community Court sees itself as providing these solutions by sentencing people who have committed victimless crimes to community service to repay their debts to the community and by placing people in treatment when it is deemed appropriate. Emotional performance is one of the tools at the court's disposal to help motivate offenders' behavior. The aim to provide solutions to problems related to crime in the community sometimes is in an odd relationship with the court's role as, primarily, a legal institution with the primary goal of punishment. This tension is particularly noticeable in cases when jail time is threatened as a motivational tool to get offenders to comply with treatment.

For all the treatment-based and community-restoring properties of Greenville Community Court, it is still very much that: a court. Its goal of "meaningfully punishing quality-of-life crimes" means that it has a great deal of discretion in handling cases. The processing at Greenville Community Court leaves a lot of room for variation in sentences: the crimes are either infractions or misdemeanors, yet the range of sentencing options at the fingertips of its staff are vast. Each defendant must plead guilty to hold his or her case at Greenville Community Court; this stipulation allows the court to send people to jail if they do not comply with court orders. The tension between the criminal justice system's legalistic functions and its therapeutic functions are well documented in drug courts (Murphy 2015; Nolan 2001; Paik 2011) and juvenile courts (Emerson 1969; Kupchik 2006), and they lay at the core of community courts.

Because specialized courts emerged as a result of the crisis of legitimacy, they do not have the staid legitimacy of more traditional courts. Even though many people in the American public and in the legal system believe that the criminal justice system is broken, not everyone agrees that specialized courts are the solution. They are relatively untested models, and they still have to prove their legitimacy to themselves, offenders, and stakeholders. Greenville Superior Court and those who work in it certainly perceive Greenville Community Court to be wasting time and resources. How, then, does a court that handles minor offenses—and does so with relatively informal procedures—create a legitimate identity?

4

Good Defendants and Good Courts

After Greenville Community Court had been open for a few years, an independent consulting agency conducted an evaluation of it. The study compiled data from court cases and included interviews and focus groups with defendants, court staff, community members, police officers, and other key stakeholders. The defendant interview data (which the report refers to as "client exit interviews") comprise about a third of the text of the full report. An additional fifteen pages is dedicated to descriptive tables of client characteristics and responses. Defendants were asked, "Do you think Community Court is a good idea?" (about 95 percent reported yes). "Was [your] sentence fair?" (about 75 percent responded that it was). "Did [the] judge treat you with respect?" (about one out of ten said that he did).

When I first began my research at Greenville Community Court, Nick handed me a copy of this evaluation, suggesting that it could help me with my "report." I read through the evaluation, searching for traditional measures of effectiveness, such as recidivism and treatment-compliance rates, but they were nowhere to be found. Instead, I read quotes and survey responses concerning what court actors, defendants, and community members thought about Greenville Community Court. I asked myself, "Why does this report, which aims to study the 'impact of Community Court,' devote so much time and space to what defendants think and how they feel about Community Court?"

Tom Tyler's classic book *Why People Obey the Law* offers some insight into this question. Tyler finds that the key to understanding rule-following behavior is legitimacy. Legitimacy is "a generalized perception or assumption that the actions of an entity are desirable, proper, or appropriate within some socially constructed system of norms, values, beliefs, and definitions" (Suchman 1995: 574). One might think that people obey the law because they believe in it (e.g., people will not steal things because they believe that stealing is morally wrong). In this sense, individuals have internalized the norms and values of a society and act accordingly. Tyler's work complicates this idea by showing that rule compliance is less about one's moral compass and more about one's perception of fairness in interactions with legal actors. In court settings, legitimacy is deeply connected to procedural justice—specifically, "judgements about 'how hard' the authorities try to be fair" (Tyler 1990: 151). People comply with court orders when they believe that they were "considered" by court actors, that they were treated politely, that court actors expressed concern for their rights, inter alia. While defendants desire that courts' decisions align with what they want to happen, their compliance with the law is not primarily motivated by self-interest. Instead, they are more likely to comply if they view the outcome and the process as "fair," which in turn lends legitimacy to the court.

I frame this chapter under Tyler's findings about legitimacy building to illustrate how daily case processing at Greenville Community Court was a display of organizational legitimacy. This chapter describes how Greenville Community Court practiced legitimacy-building strategies in interactions with defendants to promote compliance. Court actors listened to people's concerns and paid them individual attention. They deployed a "carrot-and-stick" technique in multiple ways to convey procedural justice and to maintain compliance. Court actors emphasized the fairness (and sometimes the leniency) of Greenville Community Court's sanctions, often contrasting them with the potential for harsher sentences and greater hassle if defendants took their cases to the superior court. They also emphasized the rewards and consequences of compliance with Greenville Community Court's orders: Do what we tell you, and the case will be removed from your record. Don't do what we tell you, and you will serve jail time.

This chapter begins with a look at how Greenville Community Court processed its simplest cases: those that warranted community service. While these cases were quite routine, they show the energy and attention that court actors invested in conveying procedural fairness and ensuring offender compliance. Next, I turn to cases that required court-supervised treatment, highlighting how interactions included threats and praise to motivate offenders to succeed in treatment. Through the cases presented here, I illustrate how Greenville Community Court practiced legitimacy-building techniques in daily court processing. The goal was not just offenders' compliance but a part of a larger responsibilization mission by which the court aims to resocialize offenders into productive citizens. I also argue that these presentational tactics may have been a rouse, as they undermined due-process rights and justified coercive tactics.

A Few Days or a Few Months: Community-Service Sanctions

Community service is the most widely used sanction at community courts, and it is also often the first step in the sentencing process; if defendants fail to complete community service, then they face more severe penalties. The court's goals for community-service cases are for people to agree to the sentences imposed, for them to perform the prescribed assignments, and for their cases to be dismissed. The court motivates defendants to complete their community service through bureaucratic and performative strategies that make community service seem relatively easy and the best option possible. Through these administrative tasks, the court also engages in legitimacy-building strategies by presenting itself as a "good court," one that is rational and reasonable and has the defendant's best interest at heart.

When defendants entered Greenville Community Court each morning, they were instructed to discuss their cases with Gary, the prosecutor, before the court docket officially opened. If the prosecutor decided to sanction a defendant with community service, he discussed this option with the individual in a way that emphasized its ease and highlighted the "carrot"—that the case would be dismissed after completion of the assignment.[1] He would often say, "If you do [however many] days of community service, then your case will be nolled, and it's as if it never happened."

Gary did whatever he could to make community-service times suitable for defendants. The prosecutor usually happily offered to work around the defendants' schedules before they even broached the issue; he scheduled community service on defendants' days off from work (if they were employed) and on school breaks for defendants who were full-time students. The notable exceptions to the prosecutor's niceties were the rare defendants who acted as though the whole court process was a terrible infringement on their time and energy. For example, one morning, a middle-aged white man in a stylish suit arrived at court, exuding a rushed and self-important air. His attitude couldn't have been more clearly demonstrated had he tapped his foot and audibly sighed while checking his watch. After going through the cases before court in a normal fashion, Gary called this defendant and reviewed his police record. Gary said, "Ehhhhhh . . . had a little too much to drink, I suppose. Disorderly conduct. Well, they're only charging you with disorderly conduct. [I'll do] one day of community service." The man curtly responded, "I work. Can we do it on a Saturday?" Gary told him, briskly and dismissively, "No weekends. Only days that the court is in session." Since the next two weeks of community service were full, Gary scheduled him for the following week.

Even though community service was scheduled with the prosecutor prior to the court docket's officially opening, defendants still needed to enter a guilty plea before the judge. Like the prosecutor, the judge also encouraged defendants' compliance with community-service sanctions. The judge reiterated the incentive of the case dismissal and emphasized the potential jail sanction that would be imposed should the defendant fail to appear. For most defendants entering guilty pleas in exchange for community service, the judge had a prepared dialogue:

Judge: How do you plead to the charge [number and name]?
Defendant: Guilty.
Judge: You just heard the facts of the case; is that what happened?
Defendant: Yes.
Judge: Is anyone forcing or threatening you to enter a guilty plea?
Defendant: No.
Judge: Are you under the influence of any drugs or alcohol as you
  stand before me here today?
Defendant: No.
Judge: Mr. State's Attorney, Mr. Public Defender, any reason why I
  should not accept this plea at this time?
Prosecutor: No, Your Honor.
Public Defender: No, Your Honor.
Judge: Let it show that the defendant pleads knowingly, willingly,
  and intelligently to the charges. You understand that you could,
  if you wanted to, go to trial on this matter, where you could
  plead not guilty, have the right to remain silent, confront the
  witnesses against you, and make the state prove its case beyond
  a reasonable doubt?
Defendant: Yes.
Judge: You are giving up those rights because you have come to an
  agreement with the state to complete [however many] days of
  community service.

Defendant: Yes.

Judge: You understand that if you do not complete community service, then I will order a re-arrest and sentence you to prison for up to [however many] days. And I can do that even if you're not here.

Defendant: Yes.

For each defendant entering a guilty plea, the judge gave some version of this statement.

Sometimes the judge abandoned the script or interjected commentary, particularly if it strengthened the presentation of the court as being generous toward defendants. An exchange between the judge, the prosecutor, and Ms. Joseph typified this interaction. Ms. Joseph, a black woman who appeared to be in her fifties, was appearing in court for larceny charges. Gary said, "The defendant was at [a local grocery store chain] and stole a pack of cigarettes. While she bought other items, she stole the cigarettes." The judge said, "Ms. Joseph, you could face up to ninety days in jail for larceny." Then the judge turned to Gary and asked, "What's the state's offer?" Gary replied, "Two days of community service." Taken aback, the judge responded, "Really?" Then he smiled and said to Ms. Joseph, "The state is being very fair. . . . Do you accept this offer?" Ms. Joseph smiled and replied, "Yes." The judge then began the exchange to enter a guilty plea into the record.

Community-service sentences are constructed to maximize offenders' compliance and emphasize community courts' legitimacy. Greenville Community Court attempted to maximize offenders' compliance by making community-service dates work for the defendants and by emphasizing the ease of completing community service over appearing at more court dates. The "carrot" of a nolled case was contrasted with the "stick" of potential jail sanctions and lengthy legal processes. Greenville Community Court played a one-sided game of "good cop/bad cop" with the superior court by contrasting its sanctions with the harsher sentences at the superior court. It emphasized that community service was a plum deal and far better than what defendants would get at the superior court.[2] Greenville Community Court also built organizational legitimacy in interactions with defendants relegated to community court. Court actors highlighted the leniency of proposed sanctions, as in the case of Ms. Joseph, when the judge incredulously described the state's offer as "very fair." The underlying message was that the court was reasonable and doing whatever it could to help Ms. Joseph and all other defendants get their cases resolved. These compliance and legitimacy-building activities were bolstered by the court's practice of individualized justice: personalized attention and discussion with court actors supported the court's presentation of looking out for each person's best interest.

The Problems with Guilty Pleas

Defendants must enter guilty pleas to have their cases processed at community courts. Because Greenville Community Court's raison d'être was to keep cases and resolve them, it sometimes accomplished this goal through a bit of manipulation. At times, defendants insisted that police reports were incorrect or maintained that they did not do anything wrong. In these cases, Greenville Community Court highlighted the choice between a *known* and *short* punishment there and an *unknown* but *potentially longer* punishment at the superior court, should the defendants pursue trials. Defendants' concerns were filtered through the official court process to make them conform to the script that Greenville Community Court offered the most reasonable, efficient resolution.

My data show that the right to plead not guilty at Greenville Community Court was illusory. While always offered as an option, the right to plead not guilty was an option only in theory and not in practice. Court actors presented a compelling argument: they had the expertise and insider knowledge to discuss likely alternative (and less favorable) outcomes, and they presented the court as being on the defendants' side. It was nearly impossible for a defendant to exert an opinion that clashed with Greenville Community Court's construction of reality.

Mr. Barge's case at the court illustrates the typical way that Greenville Community Court dissuaded defendants from exercising their due-process rights. Mr. Barge, a young black man, entered Greenville Community Court with a trespassing charge. According to the police report, he claimed to be waiting for a ride outside a multifamily building but could not name anyone who lived there. When he talked to Gary about the case, he insisted that he was not trespassing. After about four minutes of back and forth, Gary said to him, "You are entitled to plead not guilty on these charges and bring the records that [show] you have a right to be on that property to court across the street, and you may go to trial. We'd just give you one day of community service." Mr. Barge then asked, "Do you have Saturdays?" Gary said, "Nope. Community service [is only] on the days court is in session, Monday to Friday." The man said, "That's impossible. I work." Then Gary told him, "Then stay here, and the judge will assign you a trial date. But if you just want to get this over with, then it's only one day of community service. It's up to you." The defendant replied, "All right. I'll do the community service, but I work the third shift, so I'm not out of work until, like, 8:00 A.M." Gary and the defendant discussed and agreed on a date for community service. Since the man worked right down the street from the court, Gary told him, "Just get here right at 8:00 A.M. And that's OK [that you're coming straight from work]. Just make sure you get here right at 8:00 A.M."

So even though Mr. Barge insisted that he had not done anything wrong, he still ended up completing community service. Gary did tell him that he could plead not guilty and go to trial, but if he "just want[ed] to get this over with, then [it was] only one day of community service." The presentation of going to trial and amassing records that would show that the man had a right to be on that property was contrasted with the relative ease of completing one day of community service. Even though Mr. Barge was employed and insisted that his employment made it "impossible" to complete community service on a weekday, Gary helped him schedule a time that would work and guaranteed that as long as he arrived right at 8:00 A.M., he would be fine. Mr. Barge's initial statement that he had done nothing wrong was reframed into a conversation about the ease of completing community service over the hassle of going to trial. It is entirely possible that the defendant was just testing Gary to find out whether he could get him to dismiss the case outright, but Mr. Barge's case illustrates the typical exchange between court actors and defendants who claimed they wanted to plead not guilty. Greenville Community Court's narrative of the relative ease of sanctions contrasted with the unknown hassle of taking a case to trial at superior court always prevailed.

When cases like Mr. Barge's were called before the court, the judges altered their language to reflect the defendants' hesitancy regarding the charges. They would sometimes state, "You might not agree with all of the facts, but you agree with the *general core* of what happened," or "You may not agree with all of the facts of the case, but do you agree that this is *the gist* of what happened?" For example, when a man arrested for loitering had some reservations about the police report, the guilty plea acknowledged those reservations:

Gary: How do you plead to loitering?
Defendant: Guilty.
Gary: Your Honor, [the] defendant was standing outside of El Bar-

rio Supermarket for five minutes without going in. He was obstructing the entrance, and people had a hard time getting in and out. Two days of community service.

Judge: Is anyone forcing or threatening you to enter a guilty plea?

Defendant: No.

Judge: Are you on any probation?

Defendant: No

Judge: You may not agree with all of the facts of the case, but do you agree that this is what happened?

Defendant: Yes.

Judge: And you are going to take two days of community [service], because you understand that by taking this case across the street, you face up to twenty-five days in jail?

Defendant: Yes.

Judge: Any questions?

Defendant: Nope.

The court took concerns that defendants had about the credibility or content of information in police reports and filtered them through the court's logic of resolving the cases quickly and without much pain on the defendants' part. Court actors argued that defendants should accept that the police reports, while perhaps containing some inaccuracies, reflected "the gist" of what happened. This practice very much aligns with Tyler's discussion of "considering defendants"; the court modified its presentation to convey that the defendants did not completely accept the police reports. The court was able to get people to comply with community service by citing how much more time and energy would be expended should they choose to pursue trials. In the matter above, the ease of two days of community service was contrasted with the potential sanction of twenty-five days in jail if the defendant were to plead not guilty and be found guilty at trial. Even when people did not agree with all the facts of the cases against them, the threat of jail time persuaded many to enter guilty pleas.

In my entire eleven months observing cases at Greenville Community Court, I never watched a defendant plead not guilty and take the case to trial.[3] In fact, only two defendants during the course of my fieldwork argued with the judge against entering a guilty plea, both of whom were unsuccessful. To confirm my observations, I asked a marshal who had worked at Greenville Community Court for several years whether any defendant had successfully pled not guilty; he assured me that the court "would never let that happen" and that at most the judge would hold a pretrial hearing at Greenville Community Court.[4]

While many readers could correctly assume from my data that Greenville Community Court violated due process, a brief overview of plea bargaining at traditional courts affords some necessary context. In traditional courts, defendants are also dissuaded from entering not-guilty pleas and pursuing their cases at trial. Like community courts' carrot and stick, the "bargaining in the shadow of trial" thesis (Bibas 2004; Nagel and Neef 1979) states that defendants engage in heuristic reasoning to decide whether a plea bargain will be less costly than going to trial. Studies of legal actors show that courts prefer plea bargains to trials, as they increase workplace efficiency, reduce the number of trials, and minimize uncertainty (Dixon 1995; Eisenstein and Jacob 1977; Engen and Steen 2000). However, plea bargaining may be coercive or manipulative, as it preys on people's fears of punishment (Blumberg 1966), and many scholars argue that innocent defendants may be pressured to accept pleas (Kohler-Hausmann 2018; Schulhofer 1992; Scott and Stuntz 1992).

While circumventing due-process rights in not unique to specialized courts, the specific case of community courts holds interesting lessons about increased criminal justice control over very low-level offenders. Chapter 1 discusses concerns about net widening in problem-solving courts. Community courts' focus on quality-of-life crimes means that defendants are brought into the criminal justice system on very low-level charges. Then, due to institutional pressures to enter guilty pleas, these defendants have no recourse to effectively dispute their charges once they are brought to community courts. In traditional courts, these offenders would just be sentenced to time served. In fact, police officers may not even issue citations for quality-of-life crimes, knowing that the defendants would be sentenced to only time served. Because Greenville Community Court exclusively handled low-level offenses, and because it meted out harsher punishment for low-level offenses than traditional courts, the problems with a lack of due process in practice are more pronounced. Additionally, Eric Lane (2002) posits that community courts' commitment to their communities as stakeholders may further complicate due process in action; judges may not be independent and may act instead in the interests of the communities they represent rather than apply the law in a fair and unbiased manner.

My ethnography shows that at Greenville Community Court, concerns about organizational legitimacy had a greater impact on due process than did issues of judicial independence. Greenville Community Court actors heard and acknowledged defendants' concerns, yet they emphasized that their pressure to enter a guilty plea was in the defendants' best interests. They did not allow cases to go to trial because doing so would undermine the essence of the court's purpose. Community courts exist to punish quality-of-life crimes and to reform offenders. Greenville Community Court, in part, exists to help make the work at the superior court more streamlined and focused on serious offenses. If Greenville Community Court allowed defendants to plead not guilty and to have their cases transferred to the superior court, it would appear that the community court was not doing its job. Given the widespread practice of plea bargaining, pursuing trials for the relatively minor cases at Greenville Community Court would be perceived as frivolous and wasteful.

The Catch-22 of the Guilty Plea

Mr. Winston was one of the two defendants I witnessed discussing the option of pleading not guilty with the judge. Mr. Winston possessed clear knowledge of the court system's inner workings, presumably from his prior engagements for other offenses. Sally Engle Merry's (1990) study of two low-level criminal courts finds that people who have repeated interactions with legal discourses are socialized into how to frame their claims so that they can better exert their demands. These findings echo Marc Galanter's (1974) argument that the legal system privileges "repeat players" who have institutional knowledge.[5] Mr. Winston had amassed quite a bit of institutional knowledge, yet he was not able to game the system.

Mr. Winston, a handsome black man in his thirties, entered the court. Gary, the prosecutor, said, "Mr. Winston could be a persistent larceny offender. I'm not going to heap [on] twenty-four convictions, most of which are for larceny. I'll let you resolve everything with one year." This statement meant that Gary wanted to put him in prison for one year to resolve all of his pending larceny charges. Mr. Winston, who, with his twenty-four prior convictions, knew better than most defendants how the court worked, countered, "But if I plead guilty, then if I get out, other courts can use that [plea] against me." The judge brushed this concern aside: "Let other courts do what they want to do." Mr. Winston was in a conundrum: "But it's a catch-22. If I plead guilty here, then that's on my record, and if I don't, then I could get worse over there [at the superior court]." He paused, smiled charmingly, and asked, "How about six months?" The judge laughed and smiled, saying, "That's fine, we can joke about it. I think I'm giving you a major break here. If you go [to the other court to pursue a trial], and you get found guilty, by the time you're out, I'll be retired." Mr. Winston conceded this point and pled guilty in exchange for one year of jail time.

Mr. Winston pointed out the design flaw of the pre-adjudication sentencing policy at Greenville Community Court. If he pled guilty there, other courts could see that information and may use it against him in the future. Greenville Community Court's policy of keeping offenders' records "clean" did not apply to defendants with more serious cases in progress, those sentenced to jail time without conditions, or those who failed to comply with court orders and then served jail time. However, most, if not all, people who were sentenced to jail at Greenville Community Court without conditions had previous criminal records, as in the case of Mr. Winston, so the accumulation of one more guilty plea and one more charge was not of as great a consequence as it would have been for an offender with no prior criminal record.

The court still presented itself as a "good court" to Mr. Winston. First, the prosecutor said that he would not charge Mr. Winston to the extent that he could and would instead let Mr. Winston resolve the case with a one-year prison sentence. Gary maintained the presentation of procedural fairness, even when Mr. Winston presented his objections to pleading guilty at Greenville Community Court. The judge, who at first played the case as aloof, relaxed his attitude as Mr. Winston attempted to negotiate a shorter sentence, saying, "We can joke about it." After establishing that Mr. Winston was personable, the judge reemphasized that Greenville Community Court was on his side and offering to "giv[e] [him] a major break here"; he added that if Mr. Winston pled not guilty and was found guilty in the superior court, he would serve a very lengthy sentence. This performance of the "good court" was reinforced by the manner in which the prosecutor and the judge presented this information: they laughed, used informal language, and framed the decisions that they were making as if they were personal decisions made by people who knew Mr. Winston well (e.g., "I'll let you resolve everything with one year" and "I'm giving you a major break").

Greenville Community Court's case processing emphasized procedural fairness and leniency. Greenville Community Court's practice of circumventing due process was deeply rooted in the court's goals of producing compliant defendants and maintaining defendants' perception of organizational legitimacy. The court set up a discursive binary between pleading guilty at Greenville Community Court and pleading not guilty at the superior court: Greenville Community Court will give a reasonably short sentence that can quickly resolve the case, whereas the superior court will give an unknown but potentially longer sentence after a defendant goes through the hassle of a trial. The crime that landed someone in Greenville Community Court was not the focus; instead, it was the resolution of the criminal charge.

The Reformed Self

Greenville Community Court sanctioned about a third of its cases to complete court-ordered social programming, such as substance-abuse treatment, mental-health counseling, or anger management. Given that part of Greenville Community Court's mission was to address underlying problems that caused or contributed to people's criminality, defendants who suffered from something like substance-abuse or mental-health issues were placed in treatment. For instance, if someone were arrested for urinating in the street because he was frequently drunk, then Greenville Community Court would sentence him to substance-abuse counseling rather than letting him dry out in lockup overnight and issuing a "time-served" sentence the following morning (a common occurrence in traditional courts). Greenville Community Court believed that it addressed real issues of criminality rather than cycling defendants through a process of arrests, jail time, and re-arrests.

Greenville Community Court incentivized compliance with court-ordered treatment using the carrot-and-stick approach, as with community-service cases. However, Greenville Community Court's legitimacy-building strategies here were not just about procedural fairness but instead about effectively reforming low-level criminals. The interactional strategies centered on producing a sea change in offenders to transform them into responsible citizens. While still conveying procedural fairness, interactions with defendants in court-ordered programming additionally constructed legitimacy narratives: that criminals *can be reformed*, that court-ordered treatment is effective, and that community courts are effective at reforming criminals.

Greenville Community Court did not merely aim to produce defendants who successfully completed treatment; instead, it wanted offenders to be fundamentally transformed. Studies of drug courts show that rehabilitating an addict involves more than just ceasing his or her drug consumption; it involves creating productive citizens with habits, behaviors, and lifestyles that conform to mainstream expectations (Kaye 2013; Murphy 2015; Nolan 2001; Tiger 2013). James Nolan finds that drug court advocates sometimes describe their courts as "taxpayer factor[ies] . . . making these people responsible and more accountable" (2001: 64). Sociologist

Rebecca Tiger's informants describe drug courts as "a resocialization process" and as particularly invested in "personality changing" (2013: 103). They describe rehabilitating offenders in drug courts as not just making addicts into nonaddicts but also transforming them from drains on social resources to societal contributors and producers of resources. Treatment, then, is about the production of good citizens rather than people who refrain from committing crimes.

Like drug courts, Greenville Community Court aimed to radically resocialize offenders. However, Greenville Community Court's goals of transformation were oddly juxtaposed with its methods of achieving those goals. Court actors used threats of harsher sanctions to encourage compliance, much as they did in community-service sentences. This focus on punishment avoidance sometimes undermined the goal of transformation, as an offender's motivation for change may have been only to avoid serving time in jail.

Motivations to Comply

Getting an offender to successfully complete mental-health or substance-abuse counseling is not easy: when someone is sanctioned to treatment, to fulfill the conditions, he or she must show up for treatment dates and court dates and stay clean through the period of court supervision. While Greenville Community Court offered some in-house mediation services and the Women's Diversion Program, the majority of court-ordered social programming occurred at agencies outside the court. Therefore, much of the success that a person had in treatment was out of the court's hands. In fact, Greenville Community Court could do very little to "make treatment stick." Once someone was in treatment, the court's power was basically limited to compiling reports from treatment providers and encouraging, reprimanding, and/or punishing the offender on his or her periodic "check-in" court dates. Since these courtroom interactions were the only tool the court had to influence treatment outcomes, they were important to the court employees.

When defendants came into court with good treatment reports, Greenville Community Court encouraged their progress. The following short exchange illustrates a typical court date for someone successfully complying with court-ordered treatment. A short young white woman stood at the public defender's desk. The judge asked, "How are you feeling?" In a high-pitched, childlike voice, she replied, "Good." He said, "You look good!" She had been compliant with treatment, but, as the judge explained to her, "You have four files [separate but related charges] here. So, the state wants to see a little more." Her case was continued for a month. This kind of brief encouragement was common for people in treatment. Defendants at Greenville Community Court did not get lengthy pep talks from the judge, sobriety chips, or small incentives, which are common in drug courts. Instead, the motivation was just a short, pleasant interaction with the judge, sometimes little more than "Keep up the good work." The minimal positive investment in defendants who were doing well in treatment was due to the inevitability of failure for many defendants (a theme that the next chapter explores in detail).

Sometimes, people did not comply with their treatment. They showed up to court with bad reports from their treatment agencies: they missed appointments, talked back to counselors, or tested positive for drugs or alcohol. Failure at treatment did not immediately revoke their place at Greenville Community Court: defendants were typically allowed one bad report from a treatment agency before the court would sentence them to jail. When defendants did come in with bad reports, however, Greenville Community Court attempted to motivate them through shame, the threat of jail, or both.

In one case, a man wearing jeans and a preppy sweater returned to court on his continuance date. He had been in outpatient treatment for one month and had previously been arrested twenty or thirty times, according to the prosecutor. The judge said, "The letter says he was 'rude, uncooperative, and declined help.'" The defendant protested the report, saying that it was "not true." The judge, raising her voice, said, "I expect you to comply with my staff. My staff is not here to lie; they're here to give a helping hand, point you in the right direction . . . so you don't spend five years in and out of jail like you have!" The judge decided to "give [him] another chance" and continued the case for another two weeks. In this exchange, the judge reprimanded the defendant, but in doing so defined the court's goals and intentions. The judge argued that the court had the defendant's best interest in mind and wanted to help him avoid jail. She redefined the relationship between the defendant and the treatment staff as sharing mutual goals rather than as including a treatment staff tattling on a defendant.

Jail time was not the only "stick" the court had in its arsenal to promote treatment. The court also used knowledge of an offender's life to make a more compelling argument about a person's need to change. With people whom the court knew to be embedded in mainstream society, interaction might focus on career goals or offenders' familial obligations. With people who appeared to be disconnected from society, the motivation beyond threats of jail time was harder to instill. In the following example, the court attempted to motivate a man with mental health issues to change by shaming him and by using his relationship to the people at the court to illustrate his difference in behavior when he was unmedicated.

Mr. LaCombe, a black man in his late forties, was escorted from the holding cells. Ralph, the public defender, said that he was "well known to New Beginnings," the state-run, community-based mental-health program where Greenville Community Court referred many cases.

The judge added that Mr. LaCombe was "well known to us, too." Once the defendant stood next to Ralph, he began to talk very quickly, unprompted by any question from court staff. I could not understand what he was saying or talking about. After about thirty seconds of listening, the judge interrupted, "Do you want to go back on meds? We can talk when you're on meds." The defendant, still fidgeting and still speaking very quickly, replied, "We can always talk. We're talking right now." The judge responded, "You're a different guy when you're on meds." The defendant brushed this assertion aside, saying, "Some say that." The judge insisted, "Trust me; it's a *fact*." Then the prosecutor entered the discussion: "Last week, Mr. LaCombe couldn't even be presented in court because of the condition he was in." The judge asked, "Do you remember what condition you were in last week and why we couldn't let you into the courtroom?" The defendant answered, "No." Raising his voice, the judge loudly said, "You were covered in your own feces and urine!" Confronted with this information, the defendant looked a little bit shocked but then disagreed and continued to speak in a very quick cadence. I was unable to make out what he was saying, aside from general protests that he was not in the holding cell covered in his own waste. The judge firmly said, "Yes. You were. [We are] releasing you on a PTA [promise to appear]." The defendant asked, "What about my bond?" This question was odd because he was being released, not sent back to jail. The judge replied, "I'm releasing you on a PTA; do you want me to give you a bond?" The judge then had the marshal escort him back to the mental-health counselor, who would place Mr. LaCombe back in treatment at New Beginnings.

Notice here that no one discussed the crime, only how Mr. LaCombe behaved while unmedicated. The court aimed to get him back into mental-health treatment by telling him that it was "a fact" that he was "a different guy" when he was medicated and that "[they could] talk when [he was] on meds." The prosecutor and the judge also worked together to tell him and the entire courtroom that he was covered in his own feces and urine when he was last scheduled to appear. The primary goal was to motivate Mr. La-Combe to return to mental-health treatment and to get back on medication. The court accomplished this task by telling him the positive outcomes of staying on his medications (i.e., "We can talk" and "You're a different guy") and by contrasting the negative outcomes of going off his medications (the judge could not talk to him and the defendant had soiled himself and had no memory of it).

The Paradox of Judicial Motivation

Greenville Community Court motivated offenders to commit to treatment through threats and through appeals to reason, yet these tactics were at odds with the moral and emotional goals of personal transformation. The court instructed and incentivized defendants to undergo treatment as a way to avoid jail sentences. However, the court expected that through treatment, defendants would embark on a journey of personal transformation. The judges often said, "I like when people go into treatment, but not as a way to stay out of jail," or "A drug education program is not supposed to be a way to stay out of jail." Yet in the initial hearings, the prosecutor, the public defender, and the judge all explicitly presented treatment as a way to avoid a jail sentence. This pattern made for a nuanced understanding of the relationship between personal transformation and court-ordered treatment: personal transformation could be judicially motivated, but it was not achieved when a defendant just went through the motions of treatment. While the court explicitly used the threat of jail time to motivate offenders to comply with treatment, it did not want defendants to conceptualize treatment as a jail-avoidance strategy. The goals of personal transformation and the tools that the court had to motivate personal transformation did not always fit together.

The following short exchange between the prosecutor and the judge illustrates this tension between the coerced nature of court-ordered treatment and the goal of personal transformation that was supposed to take place. Gary, the prosecutor, called up the next defendant, who wasn't there. Gary said, "Illness in the family. Rescheduled for two weeks from today." The judge, looking at a report on the defendant, added, "It [appears] that he is doing very well in the program, though." Gary flashed the judge a smile and waved the defendant's folder meaningfully. The judge acknowledged this gesture: "I know he owes six years." Gary replied, "And Your Honor indicated that he'd give him six years if he didn't [do well in the program], so he has incentive." The judge did not particularly like this comment, saying, "Let's hope he is doing it for his own need for change," and then moved on to the next case.

People who study specialized courts often highlight this tension between punitive and rehabilitative goals: courts serve to punish people using the criminal justice system and to treat people for issues that fuel criminal behaviors. While Greenville Community Court used punitive tactics to motivate compliance, those tactics were at odds with the court's responsibilization goals. Good defendants who underwent treatment may have been initially motivated to avoid harsh sanctions. They may have also been motivated to comply with court orders, as they considered the court to have legitimacy: defendants believed that the court was fair. The threats of harsher sanctions and punitive actions were justified because the court considered them to be external motivators that would spark a need for personal transformation.

Presentations of Accountability

While getting people into treatment for drug use is a big part of a community court's caseload, treatment is also used for a variety of other "social issues," such as sexual victimization, alcohol abuse, mental-health issues, anger-management issues, and so forth. The punishment process at community courts, like at drug courts, is then "not so much about rehabilitation as *habilitation*" (Tiger 2013: 103; emphasis in original). Yet at community courts, the scope of criminal offenses under the purview of treatment and social programs is far broader. While drug treatment at drug courts is rooted in a medicalized model of addiction, the broad array of "social issues" that are deemed worthy of treatment at community courts is treated with a battery of programs that are not necessarily medically based.

While the community courts' goals of the reformed self are explicit for people who are in treatment, they also apply to people who are not in any court-ordered programs. Greenville Community Court aimed to socialize offenders into noncriminal behaviors through their encounters and interactions in the courtroom and by connecting them to resources outside the court.

Researchers have shown that drug courts aim to teach offenders accountability (Burns and Peyrot 2003; Paik 2011; Tiger 2013). Defendants can show that they are accountable by "taking ownership to fix their problems . . . and confessing when they fail in their attempt" (Paik 2011: 3). This means that offenders who relapse and readily admit to it are extended more leniency than offenders who lie about using, and that offenders who have sought employment since their cases opened are viewed more favorably than those who have not shown such initiative. Kerwin Kaye argues that drug courts and treatment institutions "foster particular types of agency that pertain to a 'productive citizenship' while disallowing other pertaining to a purported 'drugs lifestyle.'" (2013: 4). Treatment institutions and drug courts, then, are not solely about teaching offenders how to get and stay clean; instead, they include a program of taking responsibility, surrounding oneself with the "right" friends, participating in legal work, and so forth. Much like drug courts, community courts aim to teach people accountability. As drug courts link drug abuse to unproductive habits, poor friend networks, and low self-esteem, community courts link low-level crimes to these same undesirable behaviors and traits.

Therapeutic jurisprudence as practiced by community courts invokes a similar narrative to sobriety stories. Much like an addict must hit "rock bottom" to make real steps toward change, therapeutic jurisprudence looks at the defendant's encounter with the court as a kind of "bottoming-out" event. Greenville Community Court favored people who showed accountability, even if they were not addicts. The good defendants at Greenville Community Court understood and embodied the court's mission and showed that they were accountable. By taking positive steps to better their positions in life, they displayed their accountability and the changes that their encounters with Greenville Community Court had motivated.

Mr. Pierre's story illustrates how accountability was practiced. He missed his court date at Greenville Community Court, resulting in a failure to appear (FTA) citation and a violation of probation. Mr. Pierre entered the courtroom from lockup. His FTA indicated that he was not taking the community court process seriously, yet he turned himself in to the police when told he had violated probation. Ralph, the public defender, explained, "Mr. Pierre is already in a full-time educational program, five days a week, from 9:00 to 2:30." The judge looked unimpressed and didn't say anything. The defendant raised his hand and added, "I have a paper, if I may show you. It's a letter stating that I am in this program. They know about my interest in real estate, you feel me? This school would help me get half of the money to go to real-estate school. I don't have $500, but they'll pay $250. Feel me?" The judge said, "Every time, I give you a chance." Mr. Pierre insisted, "I wasn't even doing anything. The cops just knew me from around. Feel me? I didn't even know I had a violation of probation. I turned myself in as soon as possible. I completely forgot. I came prepared." The defendant began rifling through his pockets and started pulling out various pieces of paperwork. I found Mr. Pierre's demeanor quite endearing: he was trying so hard to avoid getting placed in jail for his violation of probation. The judge relented without even glancing at the impressive amount of paperwork now amassed in a mess on Ralph's desk. "OK, we'll release you on a promise to appear." The defendant thanked him, stuffed all the papers back into his pockets, and returned to lockup. When he had left the room, the judge started laughing and said, "Feel me?" mimicking the phrase the defendant had used for emphasis. The prosecutor and a few of the court reporters giggled.

In this exchange, Mr. Pierre displayed his accountability. He turned himself in when the cops told him that he had violated his probation. He made sure that he had paperwork to back up his claims that he was enrolled in an educational program and was thinking about pursuing a career in real estate. The court extended him leniency because he showed that he was taking responsibility for his actions and himself. He was released without punishment for the FTA and was given another chance to make his next court date.

Accountability, then, is partly about taking responsibility for one's actions. But it is also partly about making changes that will help one live a productive life. Under therapeutic jurisprudence, one of the guiding principles of community courts, the law is regarded as a force for positive change in terms of how the court and court members act toward defendants, not only formally through sentencing but also informally through their demeanor, speech, and procedures. Cases like Mr. Pierre's embody the ideals of therapeutic jurisprudence. Mr. Pierre was involved in an educational program—which was not court-ordered—was enthusiastic about his participation, and successfully indicated to the court that he was actively working toward self-reform.

Accountability may be problematically applied in courts that operate with a significant amount of judicial discretion, such as drug courts, juvenile courts, and community courts. A defendant's display of or failure to display accountability may affect the court's sanction length, type, and severity (Nolan 2001; Paik 2011; Tiger 2013). In community courts, the resocialization of defendants takes on a wider scope than in drug courts or juvenile courts. In drug courts, notions of accountability and resocialization are supported by medicalized understandings of the nature of addiction (however flawed those notions may be; see Tiger 2013). In juvenile courts, understandings of young adults or children as less culpable and more mutable than adults support the logic of teaching and emphasizing accountability (Barrett 2012; Emerson 1969; Kupchik 2006; Paik 2011).

Again, these understandings are rooted in particular cultural notions of childhood, responsibility, and criminality. Community courts target a wide array of offenders for resocialization: juveniles, sex workers, people who are mentally ill, addicts, and people with anger problems. As we saw in the example of Mr. Pierre, even those without any diagnosable issues are co-opted under the logic that offenders should display accountability. In community courts, almost everybody needs to be resocialized and made more accountable.

This attitude is problematic in deeming more people unsuitable for participation in society and in need of therapeutic criminal justice intervention to become productive citizens. The kind of accountability that community courts aim to instill in offenders is laden with particularly classed notions of responsibility. Anthropologist Benjamin Chesluk (2007) writes about the racialized and classed lessons at a job-training program at Midtown Community Court in his book on the redevelopment of Times Square. Participants in the job-training program, Times Square Ink, were all low-level offenders referred through Midtown Community Court. They were mostly black and Latinx people. All were poor. In his participation with the program, Chesluk finds that the jobs skills participants were taught (how to respond to interview questions, how to dress, and appropriate workplace conversation topics) were aimed at deemphasizing racial and class markers. He writes that participants learned a particular style of self-presentation that would aid them in acculturating to the neoliberal economics of Times Square. As with Chesluk's work, we can look at how accountability in community courts operates as a marker of productive citizenship.

Success Stories

Despite these problematic implications of accountability, community courts do want people to succeed at treatment. When a defendant completed treatment, and the case was ready to be nolled, the Greenville Community Court narrative reflected and enacted the goals of personal transformation. The judge often noted how good the defendant looked, perhaps asked him or her to share with the court what lessons had been learned, or commented about something personal, such as the defendant's parent or child. These "spectacles of sincerity" (Bauman 2013: 88) publicly narrate an authentic selfhood and tidy up loose ends and inconsistencies with performative ritual. The official process of nolling a case, which is an instrumental goal of the court, is then imbued with symbolic meaning. The defendant has transformed from an offender—sometimes an addicted offender—to someone who can now be a productive member of society. The symbolic meaning here is useful not only for the offender but also in the enactment of the type of justice that community courts favor.

The following exchange involved a man with a prior substance-abuse problem having his case nolled before the court. Mr. Montas, a young Latinx man in his mid-twenties, was called up. He wore a kind of uniform: a shiny blue jacket with a prominent insignia, a blue shirt, and a blue tie. Earlier that day, I had sneezed in court; he and the man who accompanied him (dressed in the same uniform) had said, "God bless you." Gary, the prosecutor, said, "Mr. Montas has been in Hogar Crea [for more than five months]. I'm going to enter a nolle on this one." Hogar Crea, I would find out, was a drug-treatment program developed in Puerto Rico that did not receive state funding or oversight and had very strict rules.[6] The judge said, "I want to commend you on a job well done. It's a difficult program, not easy at all. . . . [I]t doesn't give you, um, a lot of latitude. You're a completely different person. And I hope that you . . . take advantage of that." The judge asked Mr. Montas to approach the bench, and they shook hands. The judge said something to him in Spanish. Becca, an intern who was observing with me that day, whispered, "When I see cases like this, it makes me want to clap."

In this exchange, the judge acknowledged and highlighted Mr. Montas's successes in the program. He praised the defendant for a "job well done" in a difficult treatment program that required a lot of commitment and afforded little leniency. Mr. Montas was now deemed "a completely different person." The judge also spoke to Mr. Montas's future, noting that he "hope[d Mr. Montas would] take advantage" of his reform. And finally, the judge called him up to shake his hand and speak to him in Spanish, thereby enacting Greenville Community Court's commitment to personalizing justice.

Ceremonies like these have long been observed in drug courts and in addiction settings, such as Alcoholics Anonymous. They have been described as "reintegrative shaming" (Braithwaite 1989), "status return ceremonies" (Trice and Roman 1970), and "status elevation ceremonies" (Rouse 1996). The ceremonies aim to delabel offenders so that they will be less likely to recidivate. They "constitute legitimized public pronouncements that the offending deviance has ceased and the actor is eligible for reentry into the community" (Trice and Roman 1970: 539). The self becomes reconstituted through ceremonies and stories whereby one forms a new positive identity (Denzin 1987).

But these ceremonies do not only hold meaning for the person on whom the new status is conferred; they also communicate deeper aspects of the identity of the organization or group that confers the status. For Greenville Community Court, the performance of these status-elevation ceremonies also confirmed the court's rehabilitative goals. By claiming that a defendant had been rehabilitated, Greenville Community Court made organizational claims that court-ordered treatment works and that the court helps people make positive changes in their lives. These ceremonies produced emotion in those who witnessed them, either as courtroom observers or as Greenville Community Court staff. Notice how during the exchange, the intern, Becca, said that she always wanted to clap when she "s[aw] cases like th[ese]." I commonly observed court staff smiling or tearing up as a defendant was brought before the judge as a success. The acknowledgment that someone had overcome significant hurdles produced a good feeling in people who were watching the courtroom proceedings and who worked there.

Praising ceremonies were a joint construction between the defendant, the judge, and the audience. The actions that were performed for the benefit of the offender were also performed for the benefit of the institution. The following series of praising ceremonies took place on the same day. Notice how they included personalized comments and interactions, but all maintained a script of transformation and an acknowledgment of the work the court had done for each person.

The judge called from the docket a graduate of the Women's Diversion Program, which readers may recall from Chapter 2 is an outpatient program run by Greenville Community Court staff specifically for sex workers. She was a Latinx woman, around forty years old, dressed in jeans and a black shirt. The judge asked, "What, if anything, have you learned in the women's program?" The defendant responded, "I learned to stay out of trouble. . . . [It's a] good program. . . . [I learned] some things I can't say here." The judge said, "You look good! When I see these types of charges [prostitution], I see disrespect." He instructed her to approach the bench, where he shook her hand, said something to her in Spanish, and kissed her cheek. Her case was nolled, and she left the courtroom, smiling.

After calling four other cases unassociated with the Women's Diversion Program, the prosecutor called another graduate, a defendant in her mid-thirties. The judge said, "Wow. This is a great report. Best you've done in a long time, huh?" The defendant responded, "Yes, Your Honor." The prosecutor said, "I'm going to enter a nolle on this one. She's had a lot of supervised treatment." The judge explained, "Because of the quality of your compliance, we are going to enter a nolle on this case. I need you to stay in touch with your case managers. When you think about doing something, think about my face and what it's gonna look like when you come back. Come up to the bench." She approached. The judge stepped down from the bench to come around shake her hand. He quietly whispered in her ear, "Respect yourself," which I could hear only because of my close proximity. The defendant teared up a bit, smiled, and left. In between cases, the judge said, smiling, "Today is just one of those days." The prosecutor, smiling back, responded, "Our conviction rate is going down."

The next defendant, a woman in her late forties, had successfully completed about seven months of a drug-treatment program. The judge said, "You've done a magnificent job! I'm proud of you, too! I hope you now have tools for a better way to live your life." The judge asked her to approach the bench and shook her hand; the defendant smiled and left.

These praising ceremonies further illustrate how the processing of nolles for people who underwent social programming was constructed with particular meanings for the defendants and for Greenville Community Court itself. The defendants were now reformed and in possession of "the tools" for better lives. The defendants received acknowledgment for their hard work and success. They were recognized as "completely different [people]," having transformed from criminals/addicts to productive citizens. For the court, praising ceremonies reinforced the benefits and necessity of judicially coerced treatment. Gary, the prosecutor, joked that the court's "conviction rate [wa]s going down," an ironic comment given the court's explicit aim to nolle cases rather than to enter convictions. These ceremonies may have been strategically performed to showcase rehabilitated defendants to other defendants in the audience. Court actors also used these ceremonies as proof of the court's success, thereby appropriating the defendants' success. Through praising ceremonies, case dismissals were not the cause for celebration. Instead, the interactions' focus was the successful rehabilitation of the defendants.

Specialized courts use success stories to reaffirm individuals' commitment to their missions. Nolan (2001) finds that drug courts tell clients' success stories to the press and to one another. Using Gary Fine's (1995) typology of stories in social movements, Nolan argues that success stories reaffirm the drug court movement's participation and investment. These "happy endings . . . provide a morale boost and directly reinforce movement involvement" (Fine 1995: 136). In the status-elevation ceremonies at Greenville Community Court, happy-ending ceremonies were performed before a courtroom audience. The ceremonies that delineate the beginning of a new life and a new self provide a legitimizing narrative for community courts. They also help ease the tension between coerced court-ordered treatment and the desire for personal transformation. Successful cases justified judicial coercion and provided legitimacy by illustrating Greenville Community Court's status as the impetus for positive change in the lives of individual offenders, who were then personally transformed.

Greenville Community Court wanted people who were sentenced to treatment to succeed and create new and better lives for themselves. Part of the construction of success at Greenville Community Court was an individual's personal transformation from an offender to a productive member of society. The production of "good defendants" who succeeded in treatment involved a ceremony through which each defendant was labeled as "transformed." Everyone who successfully completed treatment—regardless of whether they had truly changed—was marked as such. The defendants were displayed as examples of personal transformation, and their success was attributed to the court's intervention. The status-elevation ceremony was meant to produce instrumental goals through symbolic means. By symbolically and ritually recategorizing defendants as transformed and rehabilitated, Greenville Community Court aimed to lessen the chance that they would recidivate, using the official conferral of a new positive status as a way to build ties to the community and to prevent relapses.

Undermining the Ceremony

But does this reintegrative shaming actually work? This question, while quite important, is more difficult to answer than one might expect. Very few statistical studies evaluate defendants' trajectories after they complete treatment and leave community courts' supervision. The Greenville Community Court evaluation report does not include recidivism rates, arguing that while reducing recidivism is "an important goal," people must be "realistic" in the understanding that the court's population will recidivate. Therefore, readers should not consider "recidivism as a critical measure" of Greenville Community Court's impact. However, the report does include data on prostitution recidivism: only 31 percent of those who had completed the pilot treatment program for sex workers returned to the court, a figure that is substantially below the national average. And still, low recidivism rates do not necessarily mean that defendants have ceased offending (perpetrators may just not be getting caught) or that they have become "productive members of society" with mainstream employment, familial ties, and responsible behavior. Therefore, it is an empirical question of whether these ceremonies produce desired instrumental outcomes. The lack of data on recidivism rates in community courts and the privileging of success stories lead me to believe that these courts' symbolic goals override traditional criminal justice goals.

Studies of other community courts may offer additional insight, though they present a variety of methodological and ethical challenges. Empirical assessments of community courts are often done by people hired by the Center for Court Innovation or by community court staff themselves (Lee et al. 2013; Sviridoff et al. 2002; Westat 2012). While I am confident in these researchers' methodological skills, it is still worth noting that there may be an unconscious bias to report in favor of community courts' effectiveness. Arranging proper control groups is yet another issue. Community court defendants who successfully complete court orders may be less likely to reoffend because of their experiences at court, or they may be less likely to reoffend regardless. Offenders who violate court orders are likely punished with jail time at community courts. This group presents a conceptual challenge: should these offenders be included in the "experimental group" of community court defendants, should they compose a subset of community court offenders, or should they be excluded altogether? Additionally, community courts have particular geographic jurisdictions (e.g., if someone is arrested in Greenville for public drunkenness, the case is referred to Greenville Community Court). If someone is arrested for public drunkenness in a geographically close area that is technically outside a community court's jurisdiction, that person will not be referred to a community court. Following social-disorganization theories, it is possible that people who commit crimes in community court jurisdictional areas have differential likelihoods to reoffend than those who commit similar crimes in other areas, net other factors.

Beau Kilmer and Jesse Sussell's (2014) study on recidivism rates in San Francisco sidesteps many of these design issues. They examine changes in recidivism rates over time within a San Francisco community court's jurisdiction and compare them to changes over time in neighboring areas that are not within the court's jurisdiction. They estimate that those who were arrested within the community court's jurisdiction experienced an 8.9 to 10.3 percent decrease in the probability of re-arrest after one year. However, some problems remain. Police officers working in a community court's catchment area may be more likely to arrest someone for low-level offend-

ing than police officers in other neighborhoods. It is also possible that police officers in a community court's catchment area are more likely to cite
people who a priori have very little likelihood of reoffending. Therefore,
this reduction in recidivism may be driven by arresting more people, a
greater portion of whom are less likely to reoffend. While Kilmer and Sussell's models control for criminal history and still find a jurisdictional effect, they note that their analyses do not explain *what* drives this reduction
in recidivism. While it could be the access to treatment and social services,
it could also be the swiftness of punishment at community courts, as the
average time between citation and court appearance is only five days (as
compared to an average of forty-five days in the control jurisdictions).

While these quantitative studies are necessary to show the impact of
community courts on treatment compliance and recidivism, recall that
Greenville Community Court primarily cared about narrative and defendants' experiences. While courtroom ceremonies marked as reformed defendants who had successfully undergone treatment, behind the scenes,
these ceremonies were readily acknowledged as presentations. The judges
aimed to show people respect and kindness; however, they also understood that some defendants would relapse and return to Greenville Community Court. For instance, a group of students from a local high school
visited court on a day that happened to have a lot of cases dispensed with
praising ceremonies (much like the court day described in the previous
section). During a recess, Judge Rodriguez had the group of students in
his chambers and explained what they had just seen:

[You have to show the defendants] some human respect, some
human kindness. Shake their hands and tell them they did good.
You understand that they've had to go through a lot. Right now, a
lot of them are on medication, and then after a while they feel so
good that they don't think they need the medication, so they go off
of it. But they really do need that medication, and by the time they
realize, in a couple of weeks, that if [only] they had kept taking the
medication, they're already back on the streets and back into
drugs. About four out of ten of them will be back.

The judge's description of what was likely to happen with the defendants who underwent treatment through Greenville Community Court
strongly contrasts with the presentation of reformed defendants in status-
elevation ceremonies before the court. This contrast highlights the court's
goals and functions as distinct from the understandings of individual ac-

tors who worked there. The presentation of the reformed self was understood as a ceremony that enacted particular ideas and meanings around the defendants at Greenville Community Court that were meant to produce particular attitudes and actions.

Conclusion

In the formal evaluation of Greenville Community Court, one of the biggest findings is that defendants, much like stakeholders and community members, were "overwhelmingly positive" regarding their experiences: "While the clients of the community court . . . might well have been expected to have a different, and perhaps more critical, view of the nature, process, and operation of the court than other community members and court staff, the themes voiced in this study . . . were remarkably similar among [clients, stakeholders, and court staff]." The "most important theme of [defendant] interviews," the report states, "was the humanity of the Community Court and the way the court responded to clients as individuals."[7]

Greenville Community Court aimed to make people into good defendants who get their cases resolved. Through the institutional processes and narratives, it set up its defendants for success. It scheduled court dates and community-service times around the defendants' schedules, and it encouraged and threatened defendants to motivate them to comply with treatment. This strategy is particularly evidenced with defendants who successfully completed treatment. The status-elevation ceremony was meant to instrumentally influence defendants to avoid the behaviors, actions, and tendencies that initially led them to Greenville Community Court. By positively relabeling people as "completely different," status-elevation ceremonies aimed to reduce the likelihood of recidivism. The process of punishment at Greenville Community Court not only was oriented toward instrumental outcomes; it also aimed to create particular meanings and attitudes in defendants.

One integral part of the punishment process was to make defendants responsible—responsible for coming to community service on time, for committing to treatment, for turning themselves in if they failed. Through the symbolic goals of personal transformation and offender accountability, Greenville Community Court aimed to make the punishment process connect people to mainstream values, goals, and orientations. Ultimately, the production of good defendants was seen as crucial to the production of good people.

The organizational and symbolic goals of Greenville Community Court sometimes led to problematic issues. The pre-adjudication model, whereby defendants must enter guilty pleas to have their cases handled by Greenville Community Court, might result in a lack of due process. The goals of personal transformation and accountability "justified" increased court supervision and monitoring of defendants' behavior under the banner of "transformative" rehabilitation. And the focus on making offenders believe that Greenville Community Court was working with their best interests in mind might limit the perceived options that defendants had for resolving their cases.

The measures of success in specialized courts may indeed be viewed as more holistic or symbolic than traditional criminal justice outcomes (Nolan 2001). Nick once told me a story about what he considered to be one of the court's greatest successes. During my fieldwork, a Federal Bureau of Investigation (FBI) case led to the ultimate conviction of two men for human trafficking, fraud, and coercion. The woman who provided the impetus for the FBI's investigation was in the Women's Diversion Program at Greenville Community Court. She had confided to the program's leader that she was forced into sex work: her aunt had set her up with a man who wined and dined her. What at first seemed like seduction soon became grooming for sex work. The man coerced her into sex work and used her to recruit other women to engage in sex work from which he would profit. Nick said that it was incredible that she had "felt comfortable enough and trusted us enough to come forward with this information." Nick viewed this woman's example as a success story because of the role of the Greenville Community Court program and its staff in making the defendant feel comfortable coming forward with difficult information that led to the apprehension of some serious criminals. This perspective aligns with the court's organizational narrative that targeting small crimes was important and could help prevent more serious crimes as well as its focus on the importance of defendants' perception of Greenville Community Court as being on their side.

Greenville Community Court's case processing was oriented to producing positive attitudes toward the court itself. It presented itself as a "good court." Through informal language, unsolicited advice, and personalized interactions with offenders, Greenville Community Court aimed to make defendants believe that they were being helped rather than punished. Greenville Community Court created an identity as a court that was on the side of the offender and was doing whatever it could to set up someone for success. The case processing at Greenville Community Court was intended to make offenders feel positive toward the justice process. Punishment produces an identity for not only the defendant but also the court, the state, and the community. As Jennifer Murphy writes about therapeutic punishment in drug courts, "An *individual's* transformation was enough evidence for the court staff that a drug court program was the best way to handle *society's* drug problems" (2015: 59; emphasis in original). In community courts, because the judicial process is so invested in making meaning and garnering support for this particular justice model, the pressure to stake an identity claim is far more pronounced.

Community courts' case processing, then, is set up to create good defendants and a good court. Successfully resolving cases through community service or treatment is integral to the production of these identities. But the reality is that not all defendants *can* be good defendants. People fail at treatment, do not show up for community service, or get re-arrested for the same crimes. How, then, does the court whose primary goal is to resolve cases allow for and explain defendants who do not succeed?

5

Ambivalent Justice

As a college professor, I have the necessary but unpleasant responsibility of calculating grades at the end of each semester to determine which students pass and which students fail. The students who fail my classes deserve to fail: they don't do the assignments, or they don't know the material well enough to pass exams or to construct satisfactory papers. I began offering extra credit in my courses as a way to deal with the guilt I felt about failing students. Now, when a failing student sends me a panicked email before the final exam or an outraged message after the final grades are posted, I can respond that I offered extra-credit opportunities that the student did not complete. The student had an opportunity to improve his or her grade but did not pursue it. But this tactic is somewhat devious, and it is built on working assumptions that I have about students that have proven true over the years. No student who fails the class has ever completed extra-credit assignments. This is not because students who are failing have managed to bump their scores into passing grades through a few extra-credit points. Instead, it is because students who fail classes are not the kinds of students who complete extra credit (and students who complete extra credit are not the kinds of students who fail classes). The extra-credit ruse in my courses allows me to further justify why a student fails the course, even though that student would have failed even if I had not offered extra credit.

My experiences in offering extra credit are similar to Greenville Community Court's offers of treatment, compliance, and nolles. The court offered these opportunities, but not every defendant took advantage of them. Some defendants failed to report for community service, acted up in court, entered drug-treatment programs only to fail drug tests, or disobeyed the rules. When offenders did not do what the court asked of them, Greenville Community Court sentenced them to jail time. When it became clear that defendants would not comply with court orders (perhaps after going to jail for a short period of time or being reprimanded in court), the court revoked its offers of treatment and sentenced them to jail. In these cases, the individuals "deserved" to go to jail because they had failed to take their responsibilities to the court and to themselves seriously. While some people "want and need help," others "want to serve a life sentence three months at a time." Jail time punished offenders who proved to be unamenable to the court's reformative tactics.

When Greenville Community Court sent someone to jail for failing to comply with orders for treatment, the courtroom interactions with that defendant reconceptualized the person. When defendants first entered community court, they were not considered wholly culpable for their actions; they were thought to have an "underlying social issue" that fueled their offending. However, after defendants entered court supervision, they were expected to be accountable and responsible for their criminal behavior. By virtue of being offered treatment, defendants were now conceptualized as being in control of the issue that had driven them to commit their quality-of-life crime(s). When defendants failed to comply with court orders and did not demonstrate accountability for their actions, the court recast its understanding of them as culpable for their actions. Greenville Community Court claimed that defendants who failed in treatment made rational (albeit poor) choices that led them to continue to act criminally. Jail time was imposed as a punishment for defendants' moral failing to display accountability and responsibility, not for the crimes they had committed.

As Chapter 2 illustrates, punitive and rehabilitative strategies are grounded in opposing origin stories about the root of criminal offending. Punitive strategies are based in classical theories of criminal behavior: people seek to maximize pleasure and minimize pain, so if we want people to avoid offending, we should make committing crimes painful through severe penalties. Rehabilitative strategies are based in positivist notions that criminal offending is caused by some underlying mechanism. According to positivists, if we isolate and address the underlying mechanism of offending, then crime rates will decrease. Each defendant arrived at Greenville Community Court under the rubric of positivism: the court believed that defendants had an underlying social issue that motivated their offending. Yet when offenders failed to comply with court orders, they were recast as agentic and amoral criminals who willfully chose to disobey.

I use the term "ambivalent justice" to describe the process by which the court sorted defendants into moral categories by virtue of how they responded to Greenville Community Court's sanctions. Given its embrace of therapeutic jurisprudence and its concerted effort to produce "good defendants," describing case processing at Greenville Community Court as ambivalent justice may seem contradictory. However, a practical reality of case processing at community courts is that not all defendants succeed. The flexibility of the community court model allowed Greenville Community Court to make sense of offender noncompliance that, in a more rigid organization, may have threatened central contentions of the court's success. Scholars identify ambivalence and ambiguity as important themes in therapeutic settings, especially around the treatment of drug users. Jennifer Murphy (2015) describes "the institutionalization of ambiguity" as a central organizing feature of how we manage drug users in drug courts and treatment centers. This ambiguity, she explains, results in moral constructions of "deserving" and "undeserving" clients. I similarly find that in community courts, an ambivalent stance toward defendants enables a moral sorting mechanism.

Ambivalent justice assumes that all defendants have equal opportunity to comply with court orders and/or to succeed at treatment. By using objective measures, such as completion of court-ordered sanctions, and more subjective measures, such as whether a defendant is making steps toward a noncriminal life, Greenville Community Court determined who deserved jail time and who deserved leniency. The court did not acknowledge how a defendant's social structural location may influence his or her ability to succeed at treatment or practice accountability. In this refusal to acknowledge differential opportunities, Greenville Community Court reproduced structural inequalities. Defendants who had more free time to devote to treatment, economic access to better treatment, more training in how to act in front of judges and lawyers, and more skilled ways of showing accountability fared better than those defendants with such resources. Just as my offer of extra credit serves only to further justify my failing a student, the court's offers of treatment and nolles ended up bolstering its claim that defendants needed to take responsibility for their actions and were punished for not doing so.

Making Community Service into Jail Time

The previous chapter describes how Greenville Community Court attempted to facilitate the completion of community service to motivate offender compliance. And yet some defendants still ended up in jail when initially all they had to do was show up on time to pick up trash for a few hours. When defendants ordered to complete more than a few days of community service did not report for duty, they were sentenced to jail. When calling these cases, the judge and the prosecutor often performed a discursive routine that indicated how reasonable and rational the court had been in giving community service and, by proxy, how irrational the offender was for not completing it. The following was one such example.

Mr. James had been in court a week earlier following a new larceny arrest. He went into a grocery store on Oak Avenue and "attempted to leave [the store] with detergent that he had not paid for." Gary, the prosecutor, had arranged for Mr. James to complete ten days of community service in exchange for not being treated as a persistent larceny offender, even though he had multiple larceny convictions. Gary and Mr. James had agreed on a schedule of community service for four weeks every Tuesday and Thursday, because those were the days Mr. James was off from work. He was scheduled for his first day today, and he had not appeared.

Gary called his case, saying, "I agreed not to treat Mr. James as a persistent larceny offender in exchange for ten days of community service. He was supposed to be here today, and he's not." Because Mr. James was in violation of the terms of release, he could now be treated as a persistent larceny offender and faced up to one year in prison. The judge announced that he was checking the computer for any new arrests, which could explain why Mr. James had missed his community-service date. The judge stated that there were no new arrests and then asked the public defender, "Has he contacted your office, Ralph?" (He had not.) The judge then spoke theatrically: "As is my custom, I advised him that I could put him in jail if he did not fulfill his community-service requirements. Given the fact that he could have been treated as a persistent larceny offender, I probably warned him that I'd give him ninety days. He was fully aware of the underlying charges and of the conditions of his discharge." The judge then ordered a re-arrest and imposed a twenty-four-hour hold in jail before Mr. James would be taken to court regarding the failure to appear (FTA) charges. He was later re-arrested and sentenced to ninety days.

The narrative in the courtroom placed blame on Mr. James while executing orders for his re-arrest. Mr. James was described as willfully choosing to be sentenced to jail. He was aware of the requirement to report for community service. He was aware that failure to complete community service would result in jail time. He did not call the public defender's office to explain his absence or to reschedule his community service. Mr. James was ultimately viewed as culpable for his jail sentence, as "he was fully aware of the underlying charges and of the conditions of his discharge." Notice how much discussion surrounded Mr. James' re-arrest orders: the judge dictated his actions and explained how Mr. James had not complied with court orders. The judge explained all the benefits that Greenville Community Court had extended to Mr. James. Mr. James was then discursively painted as responsible for his own re-arrest.

Greenville Community Court typically ordered arrests for defendants, such as Mr. James, who failed to appear after agreeing to somewhat-lengthy sentences of five to ten days of community service. People with fewer required days of community service were usually given more of a break if they did not report to court. It was unwritten protocol that if someone ordered to perform only one or two days of community service failed to report, the prosecutor's office would wait to file the FTA charge. Gary usually noted this delay in court, saying that the office would wait to see whether the person called with an excuse or an explanation. Sometimes, court staff even called these defendants before court adjourned for the evening, insisting that they report for community service the next day. This leniency was sometimes extended to people who appeared to be committed to completing their community service. For instance, Mr. DeSoto, another defendant, had been sentenced to five days of community service. The prosecutor said, "He did four days; today is his last day, and he didn't come in." The judge advised the public defender to call him and have him come in tomorrow. The prosecutor added, "Otherwise he's looking at a two-year sentence." Mr. DeSoto was given the benefit of the doubt because he had completed four days of his five-day sentence.

The decisions surrounding who was re-arrested for failing to complete community service and who was afforded some leniency were based on ideas of accountability, culpability, and rational decision making. Defendants with fewer days of community service faced shorter jail sentences. They may have reasonably forgotten about their community service or failed to call if they needed to reschedule because they were not facing very severe consequences if they missed a shift. If someone faced a longer jail sentence, the court assumed that the person would and should be extraordinarily cognizant of complying with court orders to avoid punishment. The court also thought that defendants who missed community-service dates did not respect the court and its orders. The court imposed jail time as punishment for failing to adhere to its orders and failing to show accountability rather than as punishment for the crime the person had committed.

Another example of the court punishing defendants' behaviors rather than crimes occurred early in my fieldwork. One morning, community service was suspended due to a conflict that broke out while the crew was raking leaves and cleaning up litter not far from the court. Edwardo, one of the community-service site supervisors, spoke to the prosecutor because two of the men on his community-service crew, Mr. Burton and Mr. Fine, had a "dispute." According to Edwardo, Mr. Burton had called Mr. Fine a drunk and a liar and had made a disparaging remark about the number of children he had fathered. The prosecutor called Edwardo, Mr. Burton, and Mr. Fine to appear before the judge. As Edwardo explained the verbal altercation to the judge, Mr. Burton interrupted repeatedly. The judge yelled at Mr. Burton, "Keep quiet and wait your turn!" Mr. Burton continued to interrupt the conversation between Edwardo and the judge but began to raise his hand like a grammar school student while he talked, as though the gesture granted him permission to interrupt. Despite the interruptions, Edwardo was able to tell the judge that Mr. Burton had "instigated the situation" and that Mr. Fine had approached Edwardo, saying, "I need to see the judge because Burton is making threats." At this assertion, Mr. Burton again interrupted, hand raised, asking whether he may bring a witness. The judge denied this request and imposed nine months of a one-year sentence on Mr. Burton. Two marshals essentially dragged Mr. Burton into lockup, legs trailing behind him, as he protested the sentence.

Taking Treatment Seriously

Greenville Community Court punished people with jail time for their lack of accountability, not for their crimes. With missed community service, it was easy to construe that a defendant had willfully and rationally defied court orders. However, with defendants who were in treatment for alcohol or substance abuse, ideas of culpability were more complicated. Because these defendants were medicalized, they were framed as less culpable. Defendants who complied with court orders were demonstrating accountability for their actions. But ideas of accountability vary. While accountability is in part about compliance, it is also about taking ownership of one's failures (Paik 2011), adhering to institutionalized narratives about criminality (Waldram 2012), and displaying traits and characteristics associated with a healthy, noncriminal lifestyle (Kaye 2013; Murphy 2015). When defendants failed to show accountability, through noncompliance, lying, or other defiant acts, Greenville Community Court punished them with jail time. The following example showed how defendants' accountability and where they were in the course of their cases influenced the court's decisions to impose jail sentences or to extend leniency. It also showed how the court's classifications of accountability were tenuous, mutable, and subjective when defendants had substance-abuse issues.

One morning, after calling two cases of people in drug treatment (one who had fulfilled the court's conditions and whose case was nolled for "a job well done," and one who had a good report but whose case was continued pending another month of treatment), Judge Rodriguez called Ms. Peterson to the stand. Ms. Peterson, a white woman in her mid-twenties, with long dark hair, was dressed in a crisp white blazer. The judge silently read the reports from her outpatient drug-treatment program as she stood before the courtroom. His eyebrows went up approvingly as he said, "Hmm!" The judge then congratulated her: "You look pretty good. Actually, you know what you look like? You look like someone who's ready to graduate from college. Good report. Keep up the good work." The defendant was quiet but smiling, and Greenville Community Court continued her case for one month, meaning that she would have to maintain her participation in the program and earn another good report from her treatment agency.

About fifteen seconds after she had left the courtroom, the judge looked at his computer, glanced up, and asked a court marshal to "get Ms. Peterson back in here real quick." She returned, looking nervous and fidgeting a bit. The judge asked, "Ms. Peterson, why didn't you tell us about your new case? I was just looking at the computer, and it just popped up. What are you charged with?" Ms. Peterson answered, "Driving with a suspended license." Raising his voice like a stern principal, the judge added, "And possession of narcotics!" The defendant maintained, "There were prescription drugs in the car, [and they came] out of a bottle," but the pills weren't hers. "Somebody left [the pill bottle] in my car," she claimed. "I know it sounds not true, but it is—" The judge interrupted her: "Are you on methadone? Do they have you on methadone?" She was not. Next, the judge asked, "If I have you drop a urine [sample], it will come out clean? It's a five-minute urine [test]; I'll know in *five minutes* if you're clean or dirty." Ms. Peterson, now defiant, offered a bit too readily, "It might show. I was on methadone a while ago." The judge threateningly assured her that it shouldn't show, as methadone leaves the system in "twenty-four to forty-eight hours. So it will be out."

The judge then briskly asked the court marshal who had fetched Ms. Peterson to escort her to the bail commissioner so that she could "drop a urine." The judge was very frazzled by what had just happened. I exchanged glances with Becca, an intern, both of us fairly shocked and curious about the outcome of the drug test.

The next defendant was Mr. Martinez, a black Dominican man. He was a persistent larceny offender with five other cases pending in three different jurisdictions in the state, but this was his first appearance in community court. The defendant stood before Judge Rodriguez and stated, "I need to get an attorney." The judge, a bit dismissive of that statement, said, "I like when people go into treatment, but not as a way to stay out of jail." Mr. Martinez seemed scared and began speaking very rapidly, ending his commentary with "I've been clean for a week now." The judge interrupted this train of thought with a somewhat rhetorical question: "Who gave you non-surety bonds?" This type of bond meant that he was in jail, but he was allowed to sign a document that promised he would pay the bond amount should he fail to appear in court. This situation was atypical for defendants in Greenville Community Court, who usually had bonds that required them to offer cash or property as collateral in exchange for their release. Since the judge often used short stints of jail time to get people to comply with court orders, he frowned upon people being bailed out. Mr. Martinez explained that he wasn't working at the time, so he could not pay for a surety bond, an answer that missed the meaning behind the judge's question (i.e., whoever gave him a nonsurety bond was foolish) and was incongruous with his earlier request to secure an attorney. The judge picked up on this inconsistency and said, "I think it's wise to appoint [Ralph] as your attorney. He's a good attorney. He listens." Mr. Martinez seemed confused that this appointment was an option—that the man who had been sitting near him through the entire process and who had been representing all the previous cases was also available to him. He replied, "That's fine. I'll talk to him." The judge asked the defendant to have a seat and passed the case for now so that he and his public defender could meet.

Next on the docket was the case of Mr. Sheppard, an older black man. Gary, the prosecutor, announced his presence by saying, "He came in this morning, and I detected an odor of alcohol. I think he may have had a little too much breakfast." The prosecutor mimed tipping a bottle to his lips, in case anyone missed his joke. Judge Rodriguez asked, "Have you been drinking today, Sir?" The defendant did seem drunk; his eyes were glazed, and his speech was a bit delayed. Mr. Sheppard replied, "Oh, that's from yesterday. I went into a shelter yesterday." The prosecutor interjected, "I didn't think he was out of control, just under the influence." The judge said, "I really don't like it when someone comes to my court when they've been drinking. That means they can't understand what is happening to them. You should be taken into custody." But then, with apparent change of heart: "Come in tomorrow. If I think you've been drinking, then I *will* take you into custody." Mr. Sheppard remained standing next to Ralph, appearing confused and drunk. Finally, he processed what the judge had said and responded, "That's it?" The judge reiterated, "Come in tomorrow." The defendant chuckled nervously and agreed before leaving the courtroom.

At this point, there was a lull in the action. The lockups had not yet arrived, so the defendants who had been arrested the previous night were still across the street at the superior court. A woman sat in the courtroom, clearly waiting for someone she knew, and Gary assured her that when the lockups arrived, he would call the case of her loved one first. Some other cases needed to be called, but the defendants had not yet arrived at court. So to kill some time, Gary began to file nolles for all the cases whose defendants had completed their community service. This process was basic paperwork, but it needed to be called out in front of the court so that the court reporters could stamp and file the proper forms.

During this lull, a woman in stylish jeans and a Latinx man in his early forties entered the courtroom. After the community-service nolles had been called, Gary called the woman's case. Like Ms. Peterson, she was also in a treatment program, yet her discussion with the court was very short. She was compliant with treatment and meetings, and so her case was continued for a month. Her interaction with the judge was noticeably brief and lacked any kind of emotional impact.

Next, Mr. Castillo, a balding man wearing a parka, was called up. He power walked toward the prosecutor, but one of the younger marshals intercepted him, slowing his momentum and directing him to stand next to the public defender. Judge Rodriguez read the report from Mr. Castillo's treatment agency: "It says here that when you went to the evaluation, you were drunk." Mr. Castillo paused for a moment, looking shocked and confused, and then said, "No-no-no-no-no. I was late." The judge replied, "You know, I expect you to be there in [sic] an ability to understand what is going on." Then Mr. Castillo protested, "No-no-no. I wasn't drunk." The judge tilted his face down to glare and said, "Well, I believe them. Take him into custody. Continuance for tomorrow." The defendant began to scream and cry: "Your Highness, I swear to God, I swear to my mom, I wasn't drunk." He begged, "God-God-God-God." Mr. Castillo seemed on the verge of hyperventilating, taking dramatic gasps of air. The younger marshal, Jay, escorted him into lockup as he continued to scream. Even from lockup, his pleas could be heard in the courtroom: "Your Highness! Your Highness!" Since someone *had* to say *something* to break the tension and to acknowledge the noise, Gary noted, "Someone called Your Honor 'Your Highness' yesterday, too."

Becca turned to me and whispered, "I'm going to start crying; I feel so bad." I responded, "Yeah, but it's only for one day; I don't think *I* would even flip out *that much* for one day in jail, you know?"

Since the lockups had not yet arrived, and all the cases the court could handle at this point had been dealt with, the judge called for a recess. Everyone relaxed in the courtroom for a bit. While we were in recess and no one was watching, the mood was more jovial. Jay, one of the marshals, emerged from the lockup area, smiling and laughing to himself. He walked in front of the judge's bench and said to everyone, "[Mr. Castillo] thinks Ralph's being mean to him." Ralph, the public defender, shrugged his shoulders to convey innocence and befuddlement, and everyone laughed. I laughed, too, because I didn't understand how Mr. Castillo could think Ralph was being mean to him.

I left the courtroom to see what Nick, the court manager, was up to; Becca came with me. Pam, one of the court reporters, was leaning into the doorway to Nick's office, talking about Mr. Sheppard. "You know," she said, "[the judge] should have thrown that other guy in jail, too. He was clearly drunk. He just gets a slap on the wrist and gets to come back tomorrow." Jay walked up behind Pam and confirmed, "Yeah, that guy was drunk." Becca and I agreed, and Becca changed the subject to say that she felt bad for Mr. Castillo for being put in jail. Nick assured her, "It's just a show sometimes. Then once they get into lockup, they calm down and just stop it." He was right: sometimes defendants who were upset when they were put into lockup did calm down. At other times, they would continue to cry and scream for quite a while. Mr. Castillo was in the latter category. I told Nick, "No, you could hear that guy [in the courtroom]." Becca commented that he had been screaming. I added that I was surprised that Nick had not heard him, saying, "You can probably *still* hear him."

Nick, Becca, and I chatted for about fifteen minutes about whether the lockups had arrived, or whether they even would arrive, and about defendants we knew and defendants we hadn't seen before. Jay poked his head into the office to share that "[Ms.] Peterson took off." Intrigued, Becca and I begged for more details. Jay explained, "She was in the room, and I'm giving her water and stuff, and Stacy [the bail commissioner] leaves the room and came back, and she was just gone. If she entered guilty pleas, she is just stupid. I'd rather stay here and face the consequences than just leave."

Shortly thereafter, court was called back into session, as the lockups had arrived. Gary, the prosecutor, called the Peterson case again, looked theatrically around the room as if trying to locate the defendant, and then said, "Oops. She ran away." Apparently, no one had informed the judge of this development during the court recess. He appeared shocked and angry: "What!? Before or after [leaving a urine sample]?" Stacy, the bail commissioner, stepped forward to say that she had "got[ten] a small amount of urine, but not enough to test. We gave her some water, and I left the room for a minute, [and then] she was gone." No one had seen her slip out. Ms. Peterson had indeed entered guilty pleas and posted bond. One of the court reporters called the bond (which involved a fancy speech that even included a "hear hear"), and it was officially forfeited. The judge ordered a re-arrest, and a new bond was set at $5,000 cash. Later, Ms. Peterson's case was transferred to a different jurisdiction, so I do not know her ultimate sentence.

The cases of Mr. Sheppard, Mr. Castillo, and Ms. Peterson represented three ways in which the court handled treatment noncompliance. Mr. Sheppard was given a continuance, Mr. Castillo was put into custody for the night, and Ms. Peterson was ordered to submit to an immediate drug test and then later re-arrested. While they were all offenders with substance-abuse issues who were not sober, their cases had very different outcomes.

Let us first consider Mr. Sheppard and Mr. Castillo, as their cases were very similar. Mr. Sheppard came to court drunk, and Mr. Castillo went to his evaluation drunk. Neither case was called before a particularly full audience; the only woman in the courtroom for both cases was waiting for her family member to arrive in lockup. Mr. Castillo and Mr. Sheppard likely lied to the judge about being drunk. Mr. Sheppard claimed he had been drunk the night before; Mr. Castillo claimed that he had been late, not drunk, at the evaluation.

The court gave these men different sentences because each was in a different stage of case processing and displayed a different degree of accountability. Mr. Sheppard was appearing in court for the first time for this offense. He had not entered a plea for this crime and had not received a prior sanction. The court insisted that people pled to crimes "knowingly, willingly, and intelligently" and not while under the influence of any drugs or alcohol. As discussed earlier, the court often used jail to regulate defendants' behavior in the courtroom. When people acted inappropriately, the judge could and did either put defendants in the holding cells or in jail. However, despite Mr. Sheppard's "breakfast," the judge did not sentence him to jail. This leniency occurred for two reasons: the rehabilitative goals of the court and the input of Gary, the prosecutor. The judge wanted to put Mr. Sheppard into treatment. He allowed Mr. Sheppard to leave with the promise to return the next day rather than put him in jail for the night to sober up because he wanted the defendant to go into treatment. Mr. Sheppard also showed some accountability. He had gone to a shelter the previous day, one presumes, in an effort to make it to court on time, which he did. Finally, Gary insisted that his behavior was not out of line, pointing out that Mr. Sheppard was "not out of control." The court extended Mr. Sheppard leniency because of the early stage of his case and because of its interpretation of his actions as displaying responsibility. The court wanted to sentence him to substance-abuse treatment; because he seemed accountable for his actions, letting him leave court was a show of goodwill. Even though Mr. Sheppard may have lied about not drinking before his appearance in court, Gary spoke on his behalf. In contrast, Mr. Castillo had already entered treatment and had failed to act with accountability. Even with a guilty plea entered and the threat of jail time hanging over his head, Mr. Castillo had failed to act appropriately regarding treatment by reporting to his evaluation while drunk. He also had not arrived to court on time, coming in mid-morning. A night in jail was a tool to motivate Mr. Castillo to comply with treatment orders; if he didn't comply after this incident, he would not get another chance.

The Greenville Community Court judges based their decisions to sentence defendants to jail on notions of accountability, but the expectations for accountability varied by case duration. As the severity of threatened punishment increased, so, too, did the expectations for accountability. Therefore, defendants facing longer jail sentences and defendants currently participating in court-ordered treatment were expected to act in ways that minimized their risk of being sent to jail. The court presumed that someone undergoing treatment should be acting responsibly.

Ms. Peterson's case also illustrates how Greenville Community Court punished people who failed at treatment and did not display appropriate accountability. Ms. Peterson failed to disclose her new arrest, and when she was called back to account for it, she omitted the narcotics charge. She then insisted that the drugs found in her car were not hers. When the judge asked about her methadone use, she claimed that she was not on methadone; then, after being informed that she would be tested for drugs, she revised her statement. (She may have claimed she was on methadone so that if she tested positive for opiates, she could claim it was methadone and not OxyContin.) Yet even after lying to the judge, Ms. Peterson was not sent directly to jail: she got the benefit of submitting to a drug test. After she ran away, and her re-arrest was ordered, Ms. Peterson's jail sentence was not deployed as a motivational tool; instead, it was used as a punishment for noncompliance with the court. Ms. Peterson lied to the court and ran away. It no longer mattered whether she tested clean or dirty; in the court's eyes, her behavior made her deserving of punishment.

In deciding which defendants to put in jail and which defendants to give a chance (or even a second chance) for leniency, the court assigned blame. People who acted in ways that communicated that they did not feel accountable, in ways that did not show that they were taking responsibility for their issues, were conceptualized as being *more* culpable for their actions. This contrast also had to do with the defendant's current stage in the punishment process. If the defendant had not been threatened with jail time and had not yet been sentenced to treatment, poor behavior was viewed as resocializable. But once someone started court supervision, any misstep could be read as an indicator that the defendant was no longer deserving of help and instead was deserving of jail time.

Constructing the Undeserving Offender

Community courts, like other problem-solving courts that aim to rehabilitate offenders, deploy particular notions of culpability and selfhood. The idea that offenders can be rehabilitated is rooted in positivist criminological theories, which argue that criminals are *made* through environmental, social, and economic factors. People engage in crime for reasons that are largely beyond their individual control: poor socialization, drug problems, poverty, and disadvantaged lives can shape people into criminals. If these criminals are made, then they can be *unmade*: they can be taught new skills that will address the issues that caused their criminality, and they can be guided to more positive behaviors, attitudes, and values that coincide with law-abiding behavior. Community courts argue that a large portion of offenders commit crimes due to some underlying social issue: drug addicts commit crimes because they need drugs, people who are mentally ill commit crimes because they are psychologically impaired, and juveniles commit crimes because they don't know any better. Community courts argue that offenders can be resocialized into nonoffenders through rehabilitative sanctions.

Yet this view of the offender as treatable is still squarely rooted in the idea of accountability—specifically, that the offender must take ownership of his or her life and must commit to making positive life changes. While the root causes of criminality may be traced to forces beyond the individual's control, the solution to criminality is rooted in the individual. The offender's encounter with a community court is a fork in the road where the defendant must make a choice: change his or her behavior or continue to offend. Some defendants do not comply with court orders after being threatened with jail or even spending a few nights in jail. When this happens, the court sentences the person to jail and withdraws any offer of treatment. At this juncture, the court must reconceptualize the defendant's criminality to withdraw treatment and issue a jail sentence. Whereas previously, a defendant was thought of as deserving help, needing treatment, and not completely responsible for his or her actions, when someone fails at treatment, the person must be reconceptualized. A defendant cannot be punished through retributive forms of punishment, such as jail time, if the person is not thought to be responsible for his or her actions. This is especially the case at community courts, as quality-of-life crimes generally do not pose any real danger to the community.[1] Courtroom narratives at Greenville Community Court painted defendants who were sent to jail as criminal, undeserving of leniency, and unwilling to change. These narratives rhetorically justified the withdrawal of treatment options and the imposition of jail terms. Defendants who failed at treatment more than once and subsequently were incarcerated were narratively transformed from offenders whose criminality stemmed from societal or personal issues to criminals who needed punishment rather than treatment and did not take responsibility for their actions. In this sense, a jail sentence was not punishment for a crime but punishment for a defendant's moral failures.

Greenville Community Court accomplished this reconceptualization of culpability through courtroom narratives about its defendants. Jaber Gubrium and James Holstein (1997, 2001) write about how institutions transcribe the self through professional expert schemas. They define "institutional selves" as "cultural and institutional images [that] set the 'conditions of possibility' [Foucault 1979] for who and what we might be. . . . These identities establish the general parameters for how the troubled self might recognizably and accountably be constructed" (2001: 9–10). Institutional talk and knowledge do indeed have the power to reconceptualize the person to justify an institutional action: schools define students as gifted or slow, psychologists define patients as mentally ill or of sound mind, and doctors define people as sick or healthy. Through amassing information on the defendant's criminal record, behavior in court, and character from other related agencies, the court creates an understanding of the person as deserving of treatment or deserving of punishment. When a defendant at Greenville Community Court failed to comply with court orders and display accountability, the institution reconfigured the defendant from someone deserving of treatment to someone who should be put in jail.

Ms. Irwin's case illustrates how the court narratively constructed accountability. Ms. Irwin, a white woman with bad skin who appeared to be in her forties, appeared in court on a larceny 6 charge, which meant that she had stolen items that were valued at less than $250. Gary, the prosecutor, called her case as she was escorted from lockup: "Ms. Irwin met with probation officer *yesterday* and got arrested yesterday night at 7:00 P.M." He explained that Ms. Irwin had been on probation since May of the previous year for narcotics use and had multiple FTA charges on her record. A few months previously, she had been charged with a new narcotics violation and was currently under five years of state supervision. Lino, a bail commissioner, also summarized Ms. Irwin's "extensive criminal history." The judge asked Lino and Gary whether they had a record of what time she had met with her probation officer and then answered his own question: "No, [the computer] doesn't [say], but I'd assume some time in the morning." Then he turned to Ms. Irwin and said, "So, you're given five years of probation because some judge feels bad for you"; then his voice raised as he turned to Ralph, the public defender: "[And Ralph], then a few hours later, she goes and steals $240 worth of stuff?!" The defendant offered, "I was supposed to go into detox last night." The judge snapped at her, yelling, "OH, YOU'RE GONNA BE DETOXED!" Gary commented that she had "sufficient convictions for a persistent larceny offender," meaning that the judge could sentence her to up to one year in prison. Yet the judge decided to hold off on imposing a sentence. Instead, he reverted to his "detached administrator" persona and said, looking at his paperwork, "Continuance [in one month]. Medical attention for withdrawal noted." One of the marshals escorted Ms. Irwin into lockup. Once she was out of the room, the judge looked at Lino and Ralph, smiling in disbelief: "See how many FTAs she has?"

The court constructed Ms. Irwin as brazenly committing crimes and ignoring opportunities to avoid jail. Gary and Lino gave details and a summary, respectively, of her offending pattern. She also had multiple FTAs on her record, which meant that releasing her on a promise to appear would likely result in more charges, as she would not show up for her court dates. Ms. Irwin stated her desire to be detoxed, which for people with less serious criminal records may have effectively demonstrated accountability and desire for change. However, Ms. Irwin's admission that she needed to be detoxed was not counted in her favor. In fact, the court narratively stripped this agency from her, as the judge told her that she was "gonna be detoxed," making it no longer her decision or dependent on her consent; it was the judge's decision, in sending her to jail, that she would be detoxed. This interaction also painted Ms. Irwin as being manipulative or lucky in her interactions with the criminal justice system, in that she received probation rather than jail time "because some judge fe[lt] bad for [her]."

When Greenville Community Court sentenced defendants to jail for a period of time, it did so by narratively conceptualizing them as culpable for their own actions. Initially, most offenders were offered the chance of treatment before being sentenced to jail. To be sentenced to jail, offenders had to be reconceptualized from people who deserved leniency to people who rationally chose to be criminals. The culpability underlying rehabilitative strategies, such as judicial supervision and court-ordered treatment, was compromised in that the defendants were viewed as not wholly responsible for their bad actions. But once they accepted rehabilitative sanctions, the offenders were recategorized as people who should be doing everything in their capacity to avoid jail. Judicial expectations of accountability and compliance increased in conjunction with the severity of potential sanctions and time under court supervision. When offenders displayed a lack of accountability and/or failed to comply with court orders after having accepted the court's conditions, their desire to change and deservingness of opportunities for rehabilitation came into question.

Prostitution Cases

Prostitution cases served as interesting examples of how Greenville Community Court constructed culpability. At Greenville Community Court, sex workers were viewed as victims of crime rather than as perpetrators. This view conforms with the paternalism hypothesis (Belknap 2001; Chesney-Lind 1989), which argues that female offenders are perceived as less agentic and in need of protection rather than punishment. A marshal at Greenville Community Court told me that prostitutes in holding cells "[sometimes] put on a show; it's sad." He described how prostitutes pulled up their shirts when the marshals walked by or when male defendants were brought into lockup. He continued, "That's the way they are, like they are so far removed from reality . . . so many problems in their life." Prostitutes at Greenville Community Court were women or girls with one exception. Early in my fieldwork, I asked Nick, the court manager, whether any male or transgender prostitutes were arrested. He said, "We've only ever had one male prostitute in court. . . . But you could tell he liked it," and then he described a male "cross[-]dress[ing]" prostitute who came to court dates in jeans, high heels, and lipstick. This statement further confirms the uniquely gendered understanding of culpability with regard to sex workers at Greenville Community Court.

During my fieldwork, Greenville Community Court housed an internal program for sex workers called the Women's Diversion Program. (It was previously called the Prostitution Program, but the name was changed to avoid further labeling and stigmatizing defendants.) The Women's Diversion Program combined mental-health counseling, substance-abuse treatment, sexual-health education, and self-esteem programming. It ran for three weeks every three months. It was an outpatient treatment program, which meant that sessions took place from Monday to Friday, and defendants lived at home, with friends or family, or at shelters during their participation. Sex workers received far more chances after failing to comply with treatment than other groups; on average, other defendants were allowed one or two chances at failing, whereas sex workers were allotted three or four because they were viewed as less culpable for their actions. They were seen as victims of criminal men and addiction rather than as agentic criminals and addicts.

Because sex workers were viewed as less culpable, if they were sentenced to jail for failure to comply, the circumstances were far more dramatic than those of defendants with substance-abuse problems. Typically, if women with prostitution charges failed to comply, the judge continued their cases each month until the Women's Diversion Program opened up and they were eligible to participate in the program again. When people in this program repeatedly failed to report for classes, tested positive for drugs, and/or were re-arrested after successfully completing the Women's Diversion Program, the court had to assert that they were not victims but responsible for their own actions.

Ms. Torres, a short Latinx woman in her late forties who looked far older, was called from lockup. Gary, the prosecutor, said that she was "facing nine months [plus] nine months consecutive because they are the same charges involving an officer." This description was Greenville Community Court's code for prostitution: an undercover police officer had offered her money in exchange for sex acts.[2] She had already participated in the Women's Diversion Program four times. The judge responded to the proposed year-and-a-half jail sentence by claiming it was "a bit . . . strong" and, in Spanish, asked Ms. Torres whether she would prefer to speak in

Spanish. She said she would, so the interpreter came forward. Speaking through the interpreter, crying and distraught, Ms. Torres said, "I was doing good in the program, going to meetings every day; I just relapsed once. . . . [G]ive me that next opportunity, [and] I swear to my mother, I swear to God." The judge responded sternly, "The time for crying and asking for more favors is over. I've given you every chance I could. I've given you every opportunity, and you throw them away." The scene was quite frenetic, not only because of the emotional charge of everyone's speech but also because the interpreter was working to translate the judge's statements while the defendant was still pleading in Spanish. She begged, "I promise." The judge responded angrily, "You always promise, and you break your word. If you want to, you can go across the street [to plead not guilty and have your case transferred to the superior court], but I'm not giving you any more breaks. . . . I gave you help, and you turned your back on it." He then paused and said, "I won't give you nine months, though."[3] He did not say what sentence he was imposing. She screamed and cried as the marshals escorted her into lockup. She pled, "No" as she clasped and raised her hands in a begging gesture and called out to the judge as she was being walked past his bench.

In this interaction, the judge punished Ms. Torres not for her crimes, which were vague to an outside observer, but for throwing opportunities away. She was narratively constructed as an amoral person who broke her word when she made promises and disregarded opportunities for help. She was narratively redefined from someone who had previously deserved help to someone who, in light of her failure to take help when offered, deserved jail time. She was beyond redemption because every time she got help, she didn't change.

When rehabilitative measures failed—when defendants failed to show up for community service, when they were re-arrested for similar or more serious crimes while under court supervision, and when they failed at treatment more than once—ideas about the origin of their criminality were reconceptualized. Those defendants who failed to complete community service were reconceptualized as unreasonable; they were given chances to get their cases dismissed without serving any time in jail, and they chose not to take advantage of those options. Those defendants who failed in substance-abuse or mental-health treatment were reconceptualized as not taking responsibility and acting irrationally. However, those defendants who failed in treatment were also reconceptualized from people whose criminality was treatable to criminals who were amoral and untreatable. They were reconceptualized as people who chose to be criminals, thus negating any use of social services or restorative-justice tactics. Bad defendants were then created through the institutional filtering process of Greenville Community Court. They did not enter the court as bad defendants, but through the process of failing at court orders and failing to follow through on their accountability and desire to change, their whole personhood was reconstructed in court as having never really deserved that chance after all.

Ambivalent Justice

The court's discourses surrounding people who were sentenced to jail masked structural inequalities that may make some defendants more likely to fail at compliance than others. While the court may have done everything in its power to provide the basis for success (by scheduling community service on days that worked for the defendant, by motivating the offender through the threat of a larger sanction, and by connecting the defendant to professional staff who had expertise in dealing with a criminal justice population), these presentational and organizational strategies were the only options the court had for motivating offenders. The court's presentation of equal opportunity for success ignored the resources, skills, and experiences that offenders brought with them to the courtroom. I use the term "ambivalent justice" to describe the idea that success in court compliance is widely and equally available to all defendants and that their failure to comply is due to their moral and individual failings. The court gives offenders tools and resources to motivate compliance and to succeed at treatment but steps back to see whether they will comply. The offenders' success or failure at complying with court orders is then read as an interpretation of their responsibility, morality and commitment to resolving their cases. Success or failure is read as an individual assessment of perseverance, dedication, and worth rather than as a manifestation of structural inequalities. The defendants who succeed in treatment or in presenting accountability likely have better resources and better connections and are better able to adapt to the framework of community courts. In Greenville Community Court's presentation of justice, opportunities for treatment were conceptualized as being endlessly open to all defendants. Success in treatment was presented as a matter of only an individual's dedication to the pursuit of treatment.

Accountability, which matters greatly in how community courts perceive offenders as deserving of leniency or harshness, is a classed and racialized cultural resource (Van Cleve 2016). Defendants' knowledge, abilities, and even desire to advocate for themselves in Greenville Community Court were forms of cultural capital. By "cultural capital," I mean skills, resources, manners, and ways of being that can be demonstrated, used, and expressed to demonstrate one's competency in a given situation (Bourdieu 1977; Lareau 2003). A defendant's knowledge and ability to engage in conversation with the judge, to provide favorable documentation and evidence, and to exhibit "proper" demeanor in court were influenced by that person's classed and racialized experiences.

The case of Mr. Wolfe demonstrates how more privileged people used tools and resources at Greenville Community Court to avoid jail sentences. Mr. Wolfe was a young white man, sixteen or seventeen years old, dressed in baggy white clothes that contrasted heavily with the suits and khakis of the other young men assembled for their court cases. He was accompanied by a private attorney and by his father, a police officer in the suburban jurisdiction where Mr. Wolfe was arrested. About an hour earlier, the judge and Gary, the prosecutor, had discussed Mr. Wolfe's case, and the judge had decided that he would put Mr. Wolfe in jail for one week. Mr. Wolfe was in court on this day to answer to a new charge, possession of alcohol by a minor. Upon reviewing this information, the judge said, "While in and of itself, it's bad, this [new charge] is while your case of marijuana possession is still pending." He asked the marshal to retrieve the file from the defendant's marijuana possession. The judge then elegantly and dismissively flung his hands outside the bench, leaned back in his chair, and tilted his chin upward in a stance that dared Mr. Wolfe and his attorney to convince him that the case was not as bad as it appeared.

The private attorney spoke on Mr. Wolfe's behalf, saying that is the defendant was receiving anger-management counseling from a Catholic charity organization. He produced a letter from Mr. Wolfe's mother, "who in many ways is the boy's toughest critic," which summarized her son's progress. He handed the letter to the judge and summarized its contents for the larger audience: Mr. Wolfe's mother stated that she saw progress and hope, especially since the defendant was connecting with his anger-management counselor.

The private attorney continued, "[Mr. Wolfe is] working full time, got a raise, is due for another raise in April. Everyone feels good. He feels proud. His parents feel good and are banking most of his money for him." The attorney added that "his parents are deeply concerned and involved." The problem, the attorney explained, was that when Mr. Wolfe got out of work, he had "nowhere to go and nothing to do. If nothing else, he comes to court every time."

The judge, holding his cards close to his vest, did not speak. The attorney continued, suggesting that "conditions racket up [more sanctions be imposed], rather than incarceration, if only to save his job." The judge finally broke his silence to ask Mr. Wolfe's father whether he had anything to say. He responded that his son was "fantastic at his job . . . giving us money every week"; he just "makes a few stupid choices." He also described how his son "really connects" with the counselor at the Catholic charity and how after talking to her, "he comes home like a new person."

The judge asked the lawyer whether his client would like to say anything. Mr. Wolfe was mute and blankly stared for a few seconds. The attorney interjected, "He's just nervous." The attorney had teed up the ball, and now the judge was ready to smack it out of the park. The judge replied, "He's not nervous when he's asking UPS guys to buy him alcohol. He's not nervous about hanging out in front of a liquor store and bringing his younger brother into this. He's only nervous when he's under the gun. . . . [He's only nervous] when he walks into my courtroom." The judge further explained that these charges represented only the times when Mr. Wolfe had been caught in the act: "Other times, he's doing it. He's just not being caught. Am I right, young Mr. Wolfe?" The defendant nodded.

The young man's father said, "I tell him, if he goes out with his friends and there is pot or alcohol involved when he gets in the car, he should just leave. He can tell them that he can't hang out. [He should explain that he is in] a compromised situation. If he could work sixteen-hour days, he'd be fine." The judge responded, "He should know that he should not spend his free time like that." The judge paused, sighed, and said, "Let me be honest: it was my full intention to take him into custody today." He contemplated his decision while audibly sighing. Finally, he said, "Increase bond to $25,000 [and] put him in lockup. I want to speak to the bail commissioner."

The young man's father and attorney were obviously displeased with the bond increase, but they quietly left the room. Later that day, the judge called them back and summoned Mr. Wolfe from lockup. Lino, the bail commissioner, stated, "The bail commissioner's office wants to see how the defendant can make amends with the town of [name of jurisdiction]. We will have Mr. Wolfe call a number at 9:00 P.M., five days a week, from his home phone. Then, someone will call him back to make sure that he's at home. He will submit to weekly urines. He will also look into working in the library or somewhere at night."[4] The judge replied, "This is his last chance. Next time, he'll go to jail. Any violation will be zero tolerance. One missed call, one new arrest, one noncompliance, you'll be arrested and go to jail."

The court wanted to send Mr. Wolfe to jail for not complying with court orders. However, the intense and well-orchestrated demonstration of accountability made an effective argument for why he should *not* go to jail. Mr. Wolfe was employed, and he was not causing problems at home aside from those related to his crimes. He was undergoing counseling. He also admitted to the judge that he was smoking pot and drinking at other times but had just been caught twice. Mr. Wolfe's parents, the private attorney, and, to a small degree, Mr. Wolfe himself convincingly presented that he was on the path to change his behavior. It could be that Mr. Wolfe was given leniency because he was a minor. It may also be true that Mr. Wolfe got off easy because his father was a police officer or because he had a private attorney. However, the judge had been aware of these factors prior to the courtroom interaction and had already determined that he wanted to take Mr. Wolfe into custody. The court instead afforded Mr. Wolfe leniency because of a well-executed presentation of accountability.

This case highlights the ability of a suburban, white, well-off family with working knowledge of the legal system to effectively and convincingly present information that showed their son was somewhat accountable and able to improve. Certainly, other people who did not come from privileged backgrounds could and did display accountability (for instance, the previous chapter's Mr. Pierre, who proved his participation in an educational program by pulling crumpled paperwork from his pockets). But Mr. Wolfe's case highlighted how accountability was easily accessed and presented by people with more economic and cultural resources.

The term "legal consciousness" refers to how people understand and use the law (Ewick and Silbey 1998; Merry 1990). Legal consciousness is developed through interactions with the law and abstract understandings of the law, rights, and citizenship. While one's legal consciousness is dynamic, it is also subject to social structural forces, as "law is understood experientially, in ways shaped by class, education, geography, and occupational position" (Cooper 1995: 510). While Greenville Community Court did its best to make defendants believe that it was there to help people dismiss their cases, it is possible that not all defendants interpreted the court's actions or intentions in that manner. People who understood the court system as being rational, the law as on their side, the police as protecting society, and counselors and treatment providers as aiming to help may have had very different responses to Greenville Community Court than people who viewed the court system as overly procedural, disinterested in their concerns, and preoccupied with punishment. In this sense, people's racial, class, and occupational backgrounds (among other things) likely shaped their legal consciousness. Sally Engle Merry (1990) finds that working-class people often enter civil courts with positive associations with the law, but as they struggle to get their cases heard and their grievances acknowledged, their perceptions become strongly negative. She shows how social-structural location and individual experiences with the courts combine to produce particular kinds of legal consciousness in people who attempt to use the courts to solve problems that they cannot solve themselves. While there is certainly room for individual agency and interpretation of the law, we should acknowledge how structural positions often shape people's understandings of courts, court processes, and legal rights.

Ambivalent justice is justified by community courts' aim to resocialize offenders into accountable and productive members of society. The resocialization process, particularly for those in court-ordered treatment, occurs beyond these courts' control. Drug-treatment programs, for instance, are typically housed at agencies independent of these courts; Greenville Community Court had little input into how people received treatment and merely received reports from these agencies regarding defendants' successes or failures. However, succeeding at treatment meant that people not only successfully abstained from drug use but also behaved appropriately while in drug treatment. Kerwin Kaye's (2013) ethnography of a treatment community shows that clients must abstain from any behavior that is associated with a "drugs lifestyle." Clients' compliance with mundane tasks, such as washing dishes, avoiding romantic relationships, tattling on other community members, and enduring the disciplinary actions of treatment community staff, are read as indicative of their commitment to treatment. Indeed, the ability to graciously execute mundane tasks and deal with the abuses in a treatment facility at times supersedes the need to stay clean. Leslie Paik's (2011) study of juvenile drug courts shows that the meanings of objective drug-treatment results become subjective as court staff interpret those results through their understandings of the offenders' patterns and types of drug use, the offenders' behavior surrounding the drug tests, and their perceptions of the testing facility's competency. So, interpretations of "failing" at treatment and treatment reports from agencies may be colored by outside agencies' definitions of success.

Ambivalent justice is firmly rooted in the idea that all offenders have equal access to success in treatment and compliance with court orders. It obscures structural inequalities by painting access to and success in treatment as equally available to everyone. Structural advantages or disadvantages may shape how people view the court system, how they respond to treatment, and how they express their attitudes, behaviors, and values. Accountability, a mitigating factor in the court's decision process, is a cultural resource that may be more easily displayed by people of privilege. Defendants with a particular kind of cultural capital may feel more entitled to opportunities and have a greater ability to access them. They may understand how to provide documentation or may have access to people with professional knowledge of the judicial system. The display of accountability—a respectful demeanor, a concerted effort to show responsibility, and an expressed desire to change—may be more easily performed by people with structural advantages. This idea is particularly important when considering Greenville Community Court's aim to resocialize defendants into noncriminal behaviors, attitudes, and values. The court provided all defendants with access to rehabilitative sanctions and punished those who did not conform to its orders to succeed at rehabilitation. By masking or ignoring structural disadvantages that limited people's ability to succeed in treatment, the court covertly reproduced inequalities under the guise of personal responsibility and accountability.

Greenville Community Court punished offenders with jail time in a way that preserved and affirmed its legitimacy. The court effectively sequestered defendants for whom treatment did not work by pushing them out of the community court system and into jail. This process maintained the court's rehabilitative emphasis. When treatment did not work, it was framed as an individual failure due to personal choices and moral shortcomings rather than as an organizational failure. When the judge sentenced someone to jail as punishment for noncompliance, the courtroom interactions emphasized the lack of reason and irresponsibility of the individual offender. The court was able to paint itself as offering a helping hand and as doing everything in its power to keep the person out of jail. By narratively constructing defendants who did not comply with court orders as irrational, irresponsible, and ungrateful, the court recast their criminality and personhood, turning them from individuals who needed help and were not wholly to blame for their actions into individuals for whom treatment and reason would never work.

Organizational Discourses versus Individual Feelings

One could certainly make the argument that imposing a jail term is not a function of the court itself but a function of the people who work at the court. This argument would suggest that people who work at the court become frustrated with the offenders who don't succeed and sentence them to jail in much the way a parent would make a defiant child go to bed without supper. But my data reveal that personal frustrations were not being aired out in Greenville Community Court. Instead, they show that the legalistic framework of the court limited and constrained the punitive and rehabilitative actions of the people who worked there. Even though the court practiced individualized justice and exercised a great degree of discretion in deciding case-processing tactics, particular institutional boundaries and logics had to be maintained for the court to function.

The people who worked in the court in non-decision-making capacities may have disagreed with the sentences that the court gave. For instance, in Pam's discussion with Nick about the different sanctions for Mr. Sheppard and Mr. Castillo, she opined that both men should have received jail time, especially given that Mr. Sheppard was obviously drunk when he arrived at court. These types of discussions also happened with regard to people who had received sentences that were thought to be too harsh.

Another example of court actors' openly questioning a sentence occurred during a meeting about expanding the Women's Diversion Program. In attendance were Anne (white, early thirties) and Denise (black, early forties), who ran the program, and Nick, the court manager. Denise had been hired within the year and as such was fairly new to the position.

The meeting began with a discussion about expanding the scope and eligible population for the Women's Diversion Program. Anne wanted to include programming for "everything these women need to get out of the life," but Nick cautioned that expanded programming cost money and that she needed to consider "who h[eld] the purse strings" for funding this program.[5] The discussion quickly turned to a defendant who had recently been put in jail for "one dirty urine." Denise commented, "Tanisha was doing so good."

Nick said, "I think it bothered [the judge] personally to have to [put her in jail], but he had no choice."

Anne asked, "Is there some way we could put a gray area in there? I don't want to say. . . . I don't want to say that I want them to pull the wool over our eyes."

Denise advocated for their client: "Tanisha's urines were clean, but then she went home, and there was nothing in place for her. That's not a good place for her to be. And I know why she used; she just has a hard time being at that place. She came in on Monday with attitude, so I knew something was wrong, because she wasn't herself. She was doing so good. But you know, she 'fessed up to it." Nick offered the somewhat-dubious proposal to give a continuance for a few days to see whether her drug levels would decrease (indicating that she had discontinued use). This offer was a bit impractical but doable within the framework of the court, but Anne then insisted, "The real problem is housing." Denise agreed: "She was in a place that was just no good for her."

Nick brought up his contacts who worked at homeless shelters: "You may want to develop some relationships with [the shelter directors]. I know there are a lot of male shelters, and [one director] said that if we ever really need a bed, to give him a call." They discussed a new hire for the Women's Diversion Program who, during the interview process, had shared information "about some transitional housing programs . . . things that we don't know about, and we've been here how long!?"

Nick said, "There's just so much bureaucracy to work through. Like, I know a lot of shelters and programs like that can only admit certain people, and they get scared to take our clients because their funding might be cut. Or, if they make an exception for some, then they'll have to start letting all offenders in, and I know they don't want to do that."

They discussed the merits and pitfalls of imposing sentences on a case-by-case basis. Anne noted, "We might want to be zero tolerance, though, because otherwise we're sending a mixed message out on the street. [But], I mean, sometimes, people are here for seven weeks, and then they slip and they're put in jail."

Nick said, "There's a second chance written into it [each sentence]." This answer did not satisfy Denise, who asked, "But what about some unforeseen drama that manages to happen all of the time? That if they pick up [use drugs] on the weekend, it doesn't mean she's back out?" Anne turned the conversation back toward what she considered to be the real issue: separating women from criminogenic networks. She said that "really basic needs are the thing" and that housing was needed away from the places that pushed women to use drugs. Nick said that he had talked to a developer and suggested that he build houses on vacant lots in the area, "because we could fill them. [But] he's afraid to touch it." They then discussed the issues of "not in my backyard movements" and how halfway houses were mostly built in neighborhoods where "they [could] just walk out of the house and start using."

The discussion turned to aftercare for the Women's Diversion Program. Denise and Anne saw a real need to get grant funding that would allow them to provide such services. Nick responded, "Well, if we have an aftercare program, they'll probably have to do weekly urines. And if they're out three, four, six months, and have a dirty urine [sample], they'll be re-arrested. Or we'd have to keep their case open while they get after-care, and if they get arrested, they'd be facing a harsher sentence." Denise and Anne admitted that they had not thought of that and changed their thinking about an aftercare program.

Nick ended the meeting by offering his congratulations to Denise and mentioning that she was "a good addition to the team" and was "doing a very good job." Denise said, "I just lost it the other day with Tanisha. I was really upset that we put her in jail. She was doing so well, and I know why she used that weekend. It was just really rough." Anne advised, "That will happen. You were working really closely with her, and she was doing so well." Nick agreed, "It's a hard thing. And I know [the judge] felt torn about doing it."

The meeting between Anne, Denise, and Nick shows the internal strug-gles within a criminal justice organization that simultaneously offered treatment. Other studies of specialized courts have explored how punish-ment and treatment are negotiated and constructed by court actors. Paik relates how weekly staff meetings in a juvenile drug court are less about a minor's charges or treatment reports and more about the staff's under-standings of a minor's "long-term . . . workability" (2011: 16). Kimberly Baker (2013) finds that judges and case managers at a drug court disagreed about the use of punishment as motivation. My data offer a new insight into the study of specialized courts: decisions about whether to impose a punitive sanction are also about organizational legitimacy (Zozula 2018). Increased leniency and discretion were seen as threats to Greenville Com-munity Court's legitimacy as a punishing agency. Providing aftercare would threaten the court's legitimacy as an effective therapeutic agent, as doing so would increase the likelihood of jail sentences.

This discussion also reveals court actors' frustration with infrastruc-tures beyond the community court. Two distinct ideas of community were presented in this discussion. There was the community in which many of the women lived or at least stayed during their outpatient treatment. This community was criminogenic; the networks the women had in the com-munity and the ease of procuring and using drugs there made it easy to revert to bad habits. The community that would provide a good environ-ment for these women while undergoing treatment and trying to change their lives did not want them. The people who lived in the part of the city that arguably would have led to better treatment outcomes did not want halfway houses in their neighborhoods. In both cases, "the community" was a hindrance to the provision of successful outcomes for offenders in treatment.

Blaming the System Backstage

It may have been expected that the opinions of the people who worked in the treatment branch of Greenville Community Court were sometimes at odds with the criminal justice aspects of their work. But both judges at Greenville Community Court also expressed frustration with rehabilitative infrastructures and other factors that allowed for people to engage in low-level offenses.

Mr. Farrell's case illustrates how courtroom interaction precluded any discussion of treatment that wasn't focused on individual accountability. Mr. Farrell was a sixteen-year-old multiracial offender with substance-abuse issues. He was charged with a breach of peace and an FTA at Greenville Community Court and assault and an FTA in another jurisdiction. He was a runaway who had stayed in a shelter about an hour away from home for approximately three weeks. He had turned himself in and been transported back to Greenville. Mr. Farrell had had no record until a few months earlier, when his substance-abuse problem had become apparent. His parents insisted that their son needed an inpatient drug-treatment program for teenagers, and the judge agreed. The defendant's parents attended every court date, armed with as many suggestions for programs as they could muster. Judge Rodriguez had previously called Mr. Farrell's parents "exceptional" and told the young man, "If you ever have a kid, and you can be only half the parent to your child as your parents are to you, you will be outstanding." This young man had previously told the court that his "life [was] threatened six times [in jail]," yet the judge had merely noted it on the "mitt" and sent him back to jail.[6]

Mr. Farrell had been in protective custody for a number of months. The judge was waiting for a bed to open up at a facility with forty-nine people on the waiting list ahead of Mr. Farrell. As the young man stood before court on this particular day, the judge said to him, "You're looking at someone who has to decide if you're worth saving. You are the only person who can make that decision—not your dad, not your mom, *you*. You have some serious, serious choices to make." When the young man's mother mentioned the treatment facility as an option, the judge curtly replied, "There is a forty-nine-person waiting list, and I'm not going to be inclined toward that until he pays me.[7] If he's not compliant, he comes back to me."

Watching the discussion between the judge, the defendant, and his family, I was quite surprised that the judge did not mention his frustration with the limited options he had to offer. That very morning, the judge (with help from the court manager and me) had composed a letter grieving the limited inpatient treatment options for minors in the state. A panel of judges in the area had ruled against funding the construction of a juvenile inpatient treatment facility because "there [wa]s no clear and compelling need." This comment infuriated the judge. We co-wrote two letters to these judges, arguing that such a place was definitely needed. We explained that when minors came to Greenville Community Court with substance-abuse issues, the court had to choose between jail and a five-hour-per-day teen diversionary program. Regrettably, the court had no middle option for young adults. The letters explicitly laid out the details of Mr. Farrell's case, with the judge arguing that he had someone in court *that very day* whom he was unable to place in an appropriate juvenile program.

Yet in the courtroom, the judge mentioned none of these issues. His frustration was aimed squarely at Mr. Farrell, and his discussion of the case at hand was framed in terms of individual accountability. The young man had a personal "choice" to show the judge whether he was "worth saving." The judge never let on that his hands were tied on this issue. Instead, he framed the case discussion in terms of individual responsibility and accountability. He discussed the lack of infrastructure and treatment options with Mr. Farrell's mother as though they were nonissues and unrelated to the issue of personal transformation. Yet behind the scenes, he felt so deeply that the lack of available treatment options affected his ability to work that he had written two letters to the judges who had voted against funding a juvenile treatment center.

Judge Corbett also exhibited this disconnect between emphasizing individual responsibility in courtroom interactions and acknowledging structural problems in the justice system. She had an overwhelming number of underage drinking cases in the span of three months. She sentenced those offenders to read books about underage drinking, to complete community service with the Boys and Girls Club, and to attend an event put on by Mothers against Drunk Driving (MADD). And yet despite all of this outward focus on individual rehabilitation and reformation, behind the scenes, she was actively working to fix what she saw as the primary cause of many of these underage drinking cases—the existence of "Seven," a bar that made underage drinking easy. Seven admitted eighteen- to twenty-year-olds in one door, and twenty-one-plus-year-olds in the other door but did not have a barrier between the drinking side and the nondrinking side inside the establishment. Young patrons often swapped wrist bands inside so that those who were under twenty-one could order drinks. Judge

Corbett wrote letters, had meetings with law enforcement, and made calls to politically active citizens in an attempt to close down Seven, or at least to revoke its liquor license.

Discomfort with Jail

While jail time was conceptualized as punitive and necessary, it made the people who worked in the court uncomfortable. While I was conducting fieldwork, the judge arranged for court staff to visit the women's prison a little less than an hour away from the court. While people were excited about the visit, they also expressed some discomfort. Tom, a court marshal who was nearing retirement during my fieldwork, discussed his unease with the trip to the women's prison in the days leading up to it:

> Yeah, I don't know about this trip. Seeing human beings locked up like that. Even here, it has an effect. Yesterday, they all stunk. And there's that heat energy that hits you in the face when you open the door. Ugh.

When we toured the prison, we visited some of the areas that were designated for more serious offenders. The conversations we had among ourselves emphasized how uncomfortable many of the court staff felt in the prison. When we viewed a cell that housed violent offenders, Tom said, "If I were in there, I'd just bang my head against the wall to end it all." The toilet in the cell we viewed looked particularly dirty, and one of the court reporters summed up the group's feelings by commenting how "gross [it is that prisoners] eat and shit in the same place." When learning that prisoners spent all but five hours a day in this cell, Pam, a court reporter, whispered to me, "Nick [the court manager] looks like he is going to throw up."

Conclusion

The previous chapter demonstrates how Greenville Community Court gains legitimacy by getting defendants to successfully complete their court orders. This chapter describes how the court deals with failure—noncompliance with court orders, misbehaving in court, re-arrests, and relapses. These failures could be cast as organizational failures: noncompliance could be seen as a mark of an unsuccessful problem-solving court. However, these cases do not present a threat to organizational legitimacy because they are narratively recast as individual moral failings and not failures of the court or the treatment programs. While many women repeat the Women's Diversion Program because they relapse, the program is not the problem: it is the women who fail the program. By casting failure as an individual moral defect, the court avoids institutional and organizational blame.

An interesting point of comparison comes from the sociology of education. Schools have been described as "sorting machines" (Kerckhoff 1995; Spring 1976) that train children for labor-market positions. Students are sorted in schools on the seemingly egalitarian basis of academic performance, yet we know that schools reproduce racial, gendered, and classed inequality. A child's eventual status attainment is far more reliant on the characteristics "inherited" from his or her family than on academic performance. Annette Lareau's (2003) classic study *Unequal Childhoods* describes how classed socialization influences how children and parents interact with school systems, ultimately limiting intergenerational mobility.

Schools are often held to certain performance standards, as many states require public schools to participate in mandatory testing to ensure that educational standards are met. Jennifer Booher-Jennings's (2005) study of an elementary school in Texas illustrates how organizations sort people to meet performance standards and preserve legitimacy. She finds that teachers and the school perceive students as falling into one of three informal categories: "safe cases" are certain to meet testing standards, "bubble kids" are on the cusp of being able to meet standards, and "hopeless cases" are thought to be unlikely to meet standards. Teachers, under pressure from the school, divert energy and resources away from the hopeless cases, instead pouring effort into the bubble kids in the hope that they can be converted from "nonpassers" to "passers."

I see Greenville Community Court as engaging in a similar process. It is a type of "sorting mechanism," by which offenders are processed into particular categories. As the previous chapter shows, defendants who comply with court orders have their cases nolled, so that they are not officially labeled as offenders. Defendants who successfully complete treatment are ceremoniously welcomed back into the community; the court performs "praising ceremonies" that reaffirm the defendants as noncriminals, transformed individuals who are ready to participate in the community. This chapter shows how the court sorts noncompliant cases and defines certain defendants as untreatable and inherently criminal.

Just as schools sort students into categories based on their ability to pass standardized tests, Greenville Community Court sorts defendants based on their compliance. We can consider all defendants at their first appearance as "on the bubble"; the court issues its sanctions, and it is up to the defendants to "pass," so to speak, vis-à-vis compliance. When defendants fail to meet court obligations, they are converted from "bubble cases" to "hopeless cases." Booher-Jennings observes teachers pouring resources into "bubble kids," hoping that with additional tutoring and effort, these students can pass the standardized test. Converting nonpassers to passers is desirable, as students' passing rates officially mark their teachers as effective or ineffective. Greenville Community Court does not pour resources into defendants; instead, it engages in ambivalent justice.

While teachers and schools are pressured to achieve certain passing rates, and students who do not pass can be considered failures of the teacher or the school, Greenville Community Court does not have that pressure. When defendants "fail," the fault is considered their own. The blame is not placed on the lack of treatment options or availability, the ethics of court-ordered treatment, or the community court model. Community courts' organizational flexibility allows them to provide "treatment for those who want it, and punishment for those who don't."

Greenville Community Court sends people to jail for noncompliance with court orders, not because of the crimes that they committed. Jail time is discursively framed as punishment for defendants' inability to take personal responsibility for their actions. Richard Sennett's (2007) discussion of identity in new organizations describes a relationship between "potential" and the "specter of uselessness" in occupational and educational settings. In these flexible organizations, individuals are expected to adapt to their whims and learn new tasks easily and with little training. When individuals fail to adapt, they are rendered useless. Sennett writes, "The statement 'you lack potential' is much more devastating than 'you messed up.' It makes a more fundamental claim about who you are. It conveys uselessness in a more profound sense" (2007: 123). At Greenville Community Court, this lack of potential is manifested in a lack of accountability. This focus on accountability allows the court to maintain its position that rehabilitation does and can work. When an offender is sentenced to jail time for failing to comply with the court's treatment orders, the perception of the individual is narratively shifted from someone who needs treatment and is not wholly responsible for his or her criminal actions to someone who is personally responsible for failing to meet the court's rational, reasonable, and achievable expectations.

But these expectations are actually harder to meet than they would appear, and the court actors are quite aware of the institutional obstacles and barriers to a defendant's successful completion of expectations. People who work at the court are frustrated with the lack of treatment options available and the lack of support from the community to help reintegrate and support offenders as they attempt to transition to more productive lifestyles. However, the language of the court privileges rational choice and individual accountability and therefore does not allow for a discussion of the social-structural forces that exacerbate addiction, criminal behavior, and marginalization.

Ambivalent justice, then, is a manifestation of the court's processes and procedures rather than of individual-level phenomena. The people who work at the court recognize and respond to myriad structural inequalities that they perceive as antithetical to the goals of rehabilitation. They point out that people may be relapsing or reoffending because of limited resources, criminogenic networks, and dysfunctional relationships and homes. Even the court's judges actively work behind the scenes to ameliorate structural issues that they see as contributing to low-level offending and/or hindering people from accessing needed treatment. And although threats of jail are frequently used in the courtroom, the people who work there are uncomfortable with jails and with incarcerating the offenders they process. Yet the acknowledgment of these issues backstage does not translate to frontstage interactions. The court's legalistic functions preclude any discussion of structural issues that may hinder some offenders from successfully complying with court orders.

This tension is well explored by other scholars of problem-solving courts, including drug courts and juvenile courts. Leslie Paik (2011) argues that the blending of therapeutic and legalistic discourses may water down both frameworks to such an extent that neither is particularly powerful or useful. Victoria Malkin (2003) argues that insofar as criminal justice institutions attempt to embrace therapeutic discourses, their main function will remain punishment. James Nolan (2001) and Rebecca Tiger (2013) are even more critical of the problem-solving court enterprise, as they caution that the therapeutic goals of problem-solving courts justify criminal justice supervision and regulation of private and formerly extralegal aspects of individuals' lives under the banner of rehabilitation.

This tension between the court's rehabilitative and punitive functions, between its role in treating and punishing offenders, is experienced not only within the court but also in the court's interactions with organizations, agencies, and other stakeholders. The need for jail time is connected to the organizational need to maintain community courts as criminal justice institutions and not merely social-service providers. Yet different stakeholder groups feel forcefully in favor of or uncomfortable with community courts' punitive practices.

6

Justice for All?

Marketing Justice to a Contested Community

The Center for Court Innovation's website boasts flashy graphics and a menu of topics regarding problem-solving justice. The organization seems to publish a new pamphlet or research report every month. The website serves multiple audiences: people who are curious about problem-solving justice, stakeholders, and criminal justice practitioners.

One document, titled "Building Support for Justice Initiatives: A Communications Toolkit," instructs problem-solving courts on effective public-relations tactics. It cautions, "An unwillingness or inability to build broad political support for an initiative is one of the leading causes of failure among criminal justice reforms" (Martinez 2010: 1). The brochure recommends that courts cultivate relationships with the local media, even suggesting that they pitch stories to local reporters and submit meaningful photographs with proposed captions. It encourages courts to "harness the power of the internet" by starting podcasts and using Facebook or Twitter to stay connected to relevant audiences. It also recommends that courts develop print media, as "there are still likely to be segments of your target audience that do not feel comfortable with the internet as their primary vehicle for information. Many high-ranking officials are not web-savvy" (Martinez 2010: 13).

Because stakeholder support for justice initiatives is so important, the brochure suggests that problem-solving courts develop a core message. However, this core message should be flexible enough to adapt for different audiences:

A one-size-fits-all model is rarely as effective as a message that is individually tailored to different audiences. Think about why different stakeholders would support your program. What are the benefits to them? For example, retail establishments might be interested in cleaner, more orderly streets; the local homelessness advocacy group might be interested in more effective service linkages for defendants; and neighborhood residents might want to know that their local park will be safer. Make sure you've thought through your core message and tailored it, as appropriate, to individual groups so that their interests are highlighted. (Martinez 2010: 3)

This brochure raises a few questions. The first is why problem-solving courts need to engage in marketing strategies. Criminal justice is, of course, "a growth industry," in that there will not be a shortage of criminals to punish anytime soon. Why, then, do community courts need to appeal to different stakeholders? The second question involves how marketing strategies are tailored and deployed to different audiences. How, then, is the community court's message crafted and disseminated to different audiences? Finally, it raises the question of what consequences result from operating with such a flexible message.

Greenville Community Court marketed itself for several reasons. First, it marketed itself to promote community involvement in justice, a central piece of its mission. Also, as it was a relatively new institution, it needed to make claims to legitimacy that would link it to the attendant social, symbolic, and economic resources. Finally, the court acted agentically to try to socialize people into accepting its particular brand of justice. Marketing tactics were about not only conforming to patterns of symbolic meaning but also creating new understandings about crime and justice.

In marketing itself, Greenville Community Court tailored its message to different audiences. The court drew from different meaningful tropes to appeal to the audience at hand. It highlighted community-service beautification efforts and punitive measures to appeal to residents and business owners. In meetings with social-service providers, it highlighted how the court wanted defendants to access and succeed at treatment. I use the term "organizational ambivalence" to describe how the court kept its message flexible and adaptable: it was punitive and rehabilitative; it cared about the community but marked some community members as criminals. The organizational ambivalence of the court allowed it to be flexible and adaptive, characteristics that will likely aid its mission of becoming an enduring criminal justice institution. While organizational ambivalence had positive implications for the court's legitimacy and continued existence, it may have had negative impacts on the more innovative justice practices available and on the community more broadly. In attempting to be all things to all people, the court's ability to mete justice in the way it deemed most appropriate may have been compromised. Greenville Community Court's unique approach to criminal justice may have been subsumed into more staunch and established ways of viewing the criminal justice system. Some stakeholders were resistant to hearing about court practices that did not align with their ideas about offenders, the community, and the goals of justice. The community, then—composed of vocal residents who rallied against quality-of-life crimes, politicians who wanted to save money but also did not want to appear "soft on crime," and treatment facilities that sometimes distrusted a legal system that punished so many of their clients—was not united in its approach to crime and justice. As Greenville Community Court bid for legitimacy by appealing to stakeholder group values, the "community" in "community courts" was, at times, dictated by the ideas of the most powerful and useful stakeholder groups. The quest for legitimacy left Greenville Community Court more beholden to particular interest groups and less so to others. Ultimately, the court's marketing practices disguised exclusionary practices involved in the creation of community.

Legitimacy

New organizations need to create legitimacy. "Organizational legitimacy refers to . . . the extent to which the array of established cultural accounts provide explanations for [an organization's] existence" (Meyer and Scott 1983: 201). Legitimacy is necessary for organizational functioning because it makes organizations stable and comprehensible, and with legitimacy comes resources. Legitimized institutions are perceived as meaningful and trustworthy, characteristics that can protect them against challenges, critiques, and competition with other organizations. Over time, organizational legitimacy may become naturalized and taken for granted.

Community courts must engage in legitimacy-creating activities because they are a relatively new institution. Community courts' ideas about justice and the community distinguish them from other criminal justice institutions, and some work is required to help people understand why they focus on only low-level crimes. Finally, community courts must create legitimacy to garner symbolic and nonsymbolic resources to help them accomplish their goals.

In Greenville Community Court's early days, it actually lacked a sufficient number of cases. This was surprising: one might think that Greenville Community Court would not need to "recruit" defendants because the quality-of-life offenders who were processed at the superior court would just be moved across the street to the community court. It might seem like a simple matter of putting a new address on court summonses and tickets, but this was not the case. Gary, the prosecutor at Greenville Community Court, commented:

> At first we were actually able to offer a defendant the option to do community service on their *very first appearance date*. And, we routinely had difficulty filling the 25-person capacity.
>
> . . . [W]e regularly had visitors from afar come to court to observe our operations. When planning ahead for such a visit, we would make an effort to "beef up" the dockets in order to show the full range of our activities and available services.[1]

This problem of filling the seats was not due to any lack of law-breaking activity. Instead, it was due to a lack of enforcement of minor law-breaking. Even after the initial startup issues of persuading police to ticket low-level offenders, the court faced legitimacy problems. During my fieldwork, I was struck by how the court perceived itself to be the underdog in almost every fight. The residents were too gung-ho about crime. The people who worked in social-service organizations thought the court was "the enemy." The superior court viewed the community court as a "circus."

The court's underdog status was not completely imagined, for it was embroiled in quite a few scandals. During my fieldwork, some public officials were charged with accepting bribes. The local newspapers claimed that they were "four community court officials," when, in fact, only one had worked in Greenville Community Court's social-services department, and that had been years earlier. Nick, the court manager, was incredibly upset about the news story. He contacted the reporter, insisting that "the article . . . reflect the allegations of the crimes" and that the newspaper retract their connection to community court. Nick told me that what truly concerned him was "the repercussions on the court. I'm not involved, the judge isn't [involved], Gary isn't [involved], but still . . . [*long pause*] three of them never worked here."

Judge Corbett, who had famously instituted anti–underage drinking programs at Greenville Community Court, hit a state trooper's parked vehicle and was arrested for driving under the influence. The local news had a field day with the irony of a judge who pursued anti-drinking dockets being arrested for driving while under the influence, stating, "The accident happened almost exactly a year after Corbett talked to students at [suburban high school] in [suburban jurisdiction] about the consequences of illegal drug and alcohol use. As a community court judge, Corbett deals with young people cited for underaged drinking, driving under the influence, and other infractions."[2] Furthermore, Judge Corbett's language during processing was considered offensive, which made the local newspaper even happier to report on the case. Corbett, who is black, called the arresting officer the "head n—— in charge" and protested that she was "sick of being treated like a negro from the hood." This incident did not reflect well on Greenville Community Court.

Greenville Community Court sometimes faced blame for some of the more serious crimes in the city. After a gang-related shooting left one young man dead and several others injured, politicians and lawyers quickly pointed a finger at the police and at the community court. The twenty-one–year-old man who died was the target of the shooting. He was out on probation in connection with a stabbing-related death. Oddly enough, politicians blamed the police and the community court for failing to incarcerate the young man who *died* in the shootout; he had been arrested four times in the months prior for criminal trespass, possession of marijuana, and a violation of probation. Interestingly, the mayor and the police chief claimed that if the young man had been incarcerated, he might still be alive. The state's attorney acknowledged that the young man had paid bail, so he technically *had* been incarcerated, but she still critiqued the police and the community court:

> Then there's the larger problem. Violent criminals are often being arrested on nonviolent charges that wind up in community court.
> If you know this is a person known to carry firearms, if you know this is a person who is suspected of shooting someone else, why don't you build that case and then send that case over to us [at the superior court] that establishes that the person is a violent individual?[3]

Greenville Community Court was a convenient scapegoat for a murder because it was too soft on crime, even though the crime in its purview was that of the homicide victim rather than the perpetrator. Although Greenville Community Court has been operational for more than a decade as of this writing, it is still not wholly embraced. Scandals associated with people who worked there decreased its legitimacy, especially in the case of Judge Corbett's charges. As the court handles only low-level offenses, when it fails to lock up someone involved in serious crimes, it risks becoming a scapegoat for politicians looking to place blame. These moments of bad press matter. While the court is funded through the state, it is entirely possible that the court could be defunded. Maintaining a public face for the court, then, is incredibly important to creating and maintaining legitimacy.

Culture and Legitimacy

While established organizations often have taken for granted legitimacy, new organizations must build this legitimacy. New organizations must convince other institutions, structures, and individuals that they should exist. To create and build legitimacy, new organizations must maintain a tricky balance between the established ways of doing things and the new way of doing things (Ashforth and Gibbs 1990; Suchman 1995). New organizations must be able to explain what makes them important and innovative while still deploying meaningful, recognizable justifications for their existence. New organizations must recruit or create new stakeholders and retain entrenched stakeholders. In short, new organizations must simultaneously distinguish themselves and conform to preexisting structures or institutions.

Scholars use Pierre Bourdieu's concept of the field to describe how organizations create, maintain, and pursue legitimacy. Fields are "structured spaces of positions . . . whose properties depend on their position within these spaces and which can be analyzed independently of the characteristics of their occupants (which are partially determined by them)" (1977: 72). Fields are organized structured positions, in which organizations (in this case) compete for resources on the basis of the rules, values, and norms of that particular field. Paul DiMaggio and Walter Powell argue that an "organizational field" is used to describe groups of organizations that actively participate in "a recognized area of institutional life" (1991: 64). They do not all need to be the same kind of organization; the criminal justice field, for instance, includes not only prisons but also courts and law enforcement. The concept of an organizational field emphasizes relationships between organizational actors. It also conceptualizes the field as a place for contestation and struggle, in which organizations compete for symbolic capital (such as esteem, prestige, and positive recognition). Different organizational fields may have their own rules and regulations, but more powerful organizations within those fields may be better able to define their goals and attributes (Bourdieu 1993; Emirbayer and Johnson 2008). Therefore, new organizations must offer "legitimating accounts" (Douglas Creed, Scully, and Austin 2002) that link their logic and practice to existing cultural views (Meyer and Rowan 1977).

Greenville Community Court's position within the criminal justice field conformed with some expectations of a court and introduced other new ideas and values. The court's power rested with the state, and it used state resources to punish offenders. It conformed to state law and state sentencing guidelines. It sentenced people to jail like a typical court but also offered them treatment. It employed a judge, a prosecutor, and a public defender, but the relationships between those positions were different. Greenville Community Court differed from other courts that merely executed the law by taking the position that courts should aim to solve problems related to crime. Greenville Community Court, then, attempted not only to conform to expectations of courts but also to gain prestige within the field by expanding the goals and values of criminal justice. Organizational legitimacy can come through effective symbolic association and distinction:

> Organizational actors distinguish themselves from others within their field by means of symbolically meaningful *position-takings*—e.g., works, services, acts, arguments, products—which derive their semiotic significance in relational fashion from their difference vis-à-vis other such position-takings within a *space of position-takings*. (Emirbayer and Johnson 2008: 14; emphasis in original)

Community courts make legitimacy claims through position-takings that are connected to (1) the courts, (2) therapeutic discourses, (3) economic cost benefits, (4) safety and security, (5) the community, and (6) quality-of-life discourses. Organizations derive legitimacy through symbolic oppositions or similarities to other relevant fields/organizations. Creating legitimacy, then, involves making culturally relevant choices. These choices are not made in a vacuum; organizations and audiences are responding to similar forces and are, in turn, productive of such forces. Simultaneously, audiences interpret what organizations do according to their own understandings and expectations.

Since community courts are relatively new institutions, they need to create legitimacy. They need to position themselves as distinct from traditional courts but still be understandable as a court. The qualities that make community courts distinct must be easily digestible and understandable. They must show that what they do is different from what traditional courts do. They must convince people who care about traditional courts to also care about community courts, including the media, politicians, and police officers. Community courts must also earn support from business owners, families who live in their neighborhoods, homeless shelters, and people who have not been particularly closely tied to courts.

Organizational Ambivalence

It would seem that the need to build legitimacy on symbolic distinctions would necessitate a clear purpose. The organization's position-taking must be precise and easily categorized, with lines and boundaries neatly and enduringly drawn. Much of the literature on organizations reflects this understanding and argues that to create and maintain legitimacy, organizations must have a clear logic (Baron, Hannan, and Burton 2001). Indeed, many studies of organizational success or failure point to the importance of a clear message and position from the outset (Baron, Hannan, and Burton 2001; Lawrence and Suddaby 2006).

Yet some studies argue the opposite: that organizations with dynamic or mutable identities may have more endurance. Organizations that have dynamic identities may be better suited to foster innovation (Friedland and Alford 1991; Jackson 2005). They may also be better equipped to take advantage of opportunities and to withstand constraints over a long period of time (Sgourev 2011), unlike organizations with rigid identities. This literature recognizes that culture is dynamic and mutually constitutive, that organizations may influence broader ideas, and that innovations and new discourses may shape organizationally legitimacy—it balances cultural reproduction with agency.

These strategies may be important for garnering resources. Mark Peyrot (1991) finds that community-based drug-treatment organizations use a "chameleon organizational strategy." He suggests that by adopting a generalist approach to drug treatment, these organizations have greater access to funding sources because they can link services that are not specifically drug-related to drug-related behaviors. Stoyan Sgourev (2011) finds that the "institutional heterogeneity" of the Metropolitan Opera allowed it to survive and thrive as it courted multiple audiences, adopted new technologies, and regularly changed its repertoire. The possibilities

142 | Chapter 6

were wide open, and the lack of a clear mission or purpose allowed the opera to remain aesthetically and commercially viable.

While Greenville Community Court certainly has clearly outlined practices, they are still organizationally ambivalent toward the fate of the offender. Indeed, its mission to punish *and* treat allows for so much flexibility that the court can emphasize or downplay either approach according to an audience's perceived preferences. As the previous chapters show, the court's primary aim is to rehabilitate offenders who need treatment and to nolle cases that can be nolled. The ambivalent-justice model helps the court internally embrace dualistic notions of the offender. Defendants who succeed at complying with the court conditions are people who deserved a break and showed through compliance that they are responsible people who have reformed. Those who fail at treatment are irresponsible people who do not want to change their criminal behavior and therefore deserve traditional punishment in the form of jail time. The dual model of punishment—treatment as punishment for those who want it, and jail as punishment for those who don't want it—is justified and causes little organizational conflict. This dualistic notion of crime and criminals serves community courts well as they market themselves to a wide variety of stakeholders. They can emphasize the treatment or punitive aspects of their daily case processing according to how they read the audience at hand.

An organization with contradictory attitudes or organizational ambivalence toward its outcomes and goals is necessarily riddled with problems. These organizations have and practice a great degree of agency. The ambiguity or heterogeneity of their organizational goals and practices affords organizations multiple trajectories and paths that may be capitalized in a variety of settings. Sgourev describes such agency as "active and artful exploitation[s] of institutional contradictions" (2011: 388). Organizations can then operate in different contexts that privilege certain actions and ideas over others and ably move between them (Greenwood et al. 2008). This idea of agentic organizational action is particularly interesting when applied to organizations engaged in competition for legitimacy.

These ideas also point us to the concept that appeals for legitimacy are linked to agendas to push the boundaries of the field and that outside structural and cultural forces continue to change and shape organizational actors. While traditional organizations may have achieved staid legitimacy, it does not necessarily mean that their legitimacy will never be called into question. Chapter 2 demonstrates this circumstance in its account of the criminal justice system's legitimacy crisis of the 1970s, which led to policy changes, and its legitimacy crisis of the late 1980s to early 1990s, which led to additional criminal justice strategies, including the creation of community courts. Community courts continually engage in marketing strategies because they have new ideas about justice that do not wholly conform to traditional ideas about justice. The justice process at community courts is not traditional. This desire to socialize and convert people and institutions to cultural ideas about crime, justice, the community, and criminals drives community courts to engage in marketing strategies. These are new ideas, but they do conform to other ways of understanding that make them palatable and appealing to a broad audience with divergent interests, opinions, and connections to the criminal justice system.

Punishment and Payback in Resident Meetings

Greenville Community Court understood itself as a "court for the community." It formed partnerships with local businesses and nonprofit organizations and ran donation drives for needy children during the holidays. Greenville Community Court worked diligently to listen to the concerns of the community it sought to serve and to address those concerns to the best of its ability. A representative from the court (and sometimes the judge) always attended the monthly Applewood Block Association (pseudonym) meetings. The Greenville Community Court representative(s) updated residents on the court's work and encouraged residents and business owners to contact the court with any concerns. I present data from one of these meetings to illustrate how a court representative downplayed the therapeutic goals of Greenville Community Court and emphasized the work that it did to enhance the community's quality of life.

This meeting shows how crime was very much an issue that concerned residents. However, talk about crime during this meeting operated to draw moral distinctions between the people at the community meeting and those who committed crimes. The community as a whole was conceptualized as the victim of serious criminals who robbed, raped, and murdered and of low-level criminals, such as sex workers who stood on corners and hot dog vendors who attracted too much foot traffic. Greenville Community Court was initially lauded for its community-service efforts and for improving the cleanliness of the neighborhood.[4] Then a very verbose and persuasive police lieutenant began to speak about issues of public safety. He talked about offenders on early release from prison who were recidivating at high rates. To address this issue, he and other political members of the community were working on getting global positioning system (GPS) tracking devices for these people. Vocal members of the Applewood Block Association supported the lieutenant's rousing speech advocating increased surveillance. Nick, the Greenville Community Court manager, spoke after the lieutenant, emphasizing the court's punitive aspects and its community-service crews who cleaned up the neighborhood. This meeting showed the flexibility and adaptability of Greenville Community Court's presentation. Nick understood the discourses that were pertinent to this audience in this meeting—namely, quality-of-life issues and tough-on-crime measures—and emphasized those while downplaying the court's therapeutic aspects.

The Applewood Block Association meeting was held in a church basement. The attendees were black, white, Latinx, and Italian American, and most appeared to be in their forties or older. The tables were arranged in a large, empty square with people sitting around it. Nick and I sat in a row of seats behind the square. Isabelle was the president of the Applewood Block Association. She was black, appeared to be in her forties, and spoke with an accent. She ran the meeting very strictly, shushing people engaged in side conversations. At one point, a group at the other end of the church basement began praying loudly, and, as Nick put it, Isabelle "[told] people to stop praying in a church."

The meeting began with introductions and a review of the previous meeting's minutes. Then Isabelle asked, "Who's got good news?" The good news started with a discussion of crime and quality-of-life issues. One man said, "Well, we'd been having some problems on Applewood Avenue. And in the last two to three months, it's really calmed down. There's still prostitution, but really much, much less. They're really doing a great job over there," nodding his head toward the police officers in attendance. Someone else said, "South Green Street has drastically improved. Crime's down; property damage is down. So good work on that one." Next, an elderly woman said, "Broad Street is much, much cleaner. I saw the boys cleaning the other day in the blue vests," referring to the vests worn by community-service crews. "And I rolled down the window and said, 'Thank you. Hallelujah.'" Nick, acknowledged the compliment, and the woman continued, "It makes such a difference. We could go out hourly and just pick up junk. . . . Oh, thank you so much."

The meeting moved toward a discussion of public safety after a quick review of education issues, pending construction, and farmers' markets. Isabelle asked the police lieutenant whether he would like to speak. The lieutenant then launched into a long speech, resembling that of a conservative politician. He first advocated for a GPS tracking device for offenders who were released from prison early, which he claimed would help with recidivism. Then the lieutenant and residents discussed local quality-of-life crimes and recent incidents in the city. I present this discussion at length to show how the discourses of community, criminals, and justice were deployed in the Applewood Block Association meeting. Greenville Community Court did not entirely share these same notions, but during the meeting, Nick conformed the court's message to fit these discourses.

The lieutenant, a superior court judge, and a conservative radio personality were advocating for a GPS tracking device for people on early release from prison. The lieutenant said that the device would "keep our streets safer." The device he described was intended to solve the "real problem" of recidivism in the city. He added that most of the crime in the city was committed by recidivists and that the justice system was not working: "Justice is like a revolving door, and [offenders] know how to play the game. They know what lawyers to get and how to get out early. . . . They know how to play the system, and that's devastating to you." But the problem of recidivism could be "solved . . . through technology." The GPS tracking device would monitor people for the full duration of their prison sentences, until they had "paid their debt to society." The device, the lieutenant boasted, would allow the police to track people within six feet of their actual locations. He urged, "We need to collectively act. . . . And there are those people who will say that this is an invasion of liberty and freedom; well, I say BS to that." The meeting attendees shouted, "Yes!" and I felt as though I had unwillingly stumbled into a political rally. The lieutenant assured the group, "These are not people that get a parking ticket. These are individuals who have been convicted in a court of law. I'll rest a lot easier with the watchful eye of Big Brother up there in the sky."

He stated that city residents and business owners should be particularly concerned with the problem of recidivism because of Greenville's shelter and social-service networks. He said, "When they're released from prison, the vast majority of them are brought to the city. I look at the paperwork every day. That's not supposed to happen, but it does, with all of our shelters and places like, as you all know, what we opened next to the music hall [referring to a shelter for men with HIV and AIDS]. Big surprise there." The lieutenant said that cars were broken into whenever there was a concert at that venue. One offender had told the lieutenant that concerts were "like Christmas" because of all the things thieves got while burglarizing cars. Later in his talk, the lieutenant explained how the homeless shelter contributed to crime: "You have people landing down on a shelter on Hoosier, and they don't have five cents in their pocket, and they can't get into the shelter until 4:00 P.M. What are they gonna do? They see the opportunity, [and] they take it. Now they have ten bucks in their pocket. Now they're gonna eat today."

The lieutenant's speech conceptualized crime as stemming from two sources: prisons and homeless shelters. The community was something to be protected from the criminals. While he talked a lot about recidivism, there was no discussion of how to solve recidivism itself. Rather, recidivism could either be deterred by electronic monitoring or it was inevitable—but at least the offender would be swiftly apprehended, thanks to GPS devices. There was little talk about rehabilitation efforts. The closest thing to a discussion of rehabilitation was when someone suggested that people released from prison be electronically monitored for longer periods of time and be forced to get jobs. The lieutenant responded, "I would suggest that you pose that question to your social-service agency. It's not my job. I know what you're saying, but it's not my job." This attitude was very different from the form of justice advocated by Greenville Community Court, in which the community as a whole would work to solve issues of crime. The revolving door of justice the lieutenant so clearly advocated against was one that sought to break the cycle of offending through indefinite incarceration. This view was quite different from that held by Greenville Community Court, which sought to break the revolving door of justice by introducing low-level offenders to treatment programs.

The recidivism problem was then described in more serious terms. The lieutenant again reiterated that justice was "just a revolving door. There was someone we let out, and he raped four women. Two young ladies are dead right now because of Jaquan Roberts. They call him "Country" on the street because he moved up from Georgia. . . . When he was eight years old, and I saw him on the corner, and I knew he'd be trouble. I just knew it. And now he's twenty-eight years, and he's the number-one crime wave in the north part of the city. We have pictures of this guy with Colt 45s with his buddies, because they think it's their turf. . . .We have pictures, but we should have his whereabouts."[5]

I was incredibly shocked at how positively the attendees responded to the lieutenant's discussion of the monitoring devices. Most were intently listening. I heard only one person grumble a snarky comment about the devices' being a way to avoid paperwork. I had assumed that the attendees would be political liberals who would disapprove of monitoring devices. However, I had forgotten how crime and the fear of crime can unite a group against actions, values, and even people that they perceive as threatening. Of course, the lieutenant also ratcheted up the ante; he first described car burglaries and then moved to rape and murder. But really, this issue of crime and fear of crime was about building community. The problem with crime was even framed as a problem of freedom and of good versus evil. The lieutenant described the monitoring device as being about "people's freedom to walk out of their house. It's about the quality of life. Like my mother always says, good will conquer evil." The theme of community and solidarity building continued as the discussion turned to quality-of-life crimes and then crimes more broadly. Through this discussion ran the notion that certain people were problematic. It also built notions of the community as based on morality and abiding by the law.

The lieutenant said that the police would place "emphasis on the quality-of-life crimes," reminding the residents that "public drinking will start up again when the weather's warmer." While the lieutenant said that the police were "really going to enforce [the problematic] areas," his examples were not about areas but about people. He mentioned "that man in the Jeep, over in front of the video store," and everyone in attendance groaned. A resident mentioned a hot dog vendor, which elicited yet another groan. The lieutenant said, "We need them there like we need a hole in the head. There are rumors that they serve alcohol from there." Someone joked, "Well, that's why they're so popular," and everyone laughed.

Catching the wave of levity, another resident offered "just an example of a dumb criminal story, but there's a lesson to it." He said that someone had left a phone in his car, and someone else had smashed the window and grabbed it. The owner of the stolen phone had called the number and offered to meet the person to buy it. He had then called the police and had them meet the man instead. Throughout the story, everyone chuckled, and the lieutenant said, "They're not in jail because they're smart." The man who told the story then offered the lesson: "But you know, don't leave anything valuable in your car, because they'll just smash your window and take it." The discussion among the meeting attendees built community through shared victimization and by contrasting the "responsible citizens" with "dumb" criminals.

This theme continued with a discussion of two serious incidents that had recently taken place in the neighborhood: a "riot" at the middle school and a carjacking. The residents did not perceive themselves as victims of either of these incidents, especially after the lieutenant clarified the details of the carjacking. Instead, the meeting participants discussed these incidents to commiserate about crime in the neighborhood, drawing moral, geographic, and temporal boundaries between the community of people who came to the neighborhood block association meeting and the people whose children got involved in riots or were victims of carjacking.

When a resident asked about the riot at the middle school, the lieutenant assuaged her concern: "You know, fifteen years ago, their parents were like this, running around, and they got their girlfriends pregnant at fifteen. You know, really, it's a generational problem here. Some of them are dead, incarcerated, or God knows where. It's the offspring repeating the cycle. We have a police officer in every school. We issued twenty-three violations and held a meeting for parents after the incidents. Do you know how many parents showed up? Three." Everyone moaned and groaned. Another resident asked, "What about the South End? Do you see as many problems there?" (The South End was a predominantly white and Latinx neighborhood. As such, I regarded this question as a coded way to ask about race and crime.) The lieutenant said, "There are little hellions everywhere." The resident asked this question again, and the lieutenant reiterated that he did not want to say that children behaved better or worse in certain neighborhoods.

Someone else brought up a recent carjacking, which was met with murmurs of "It's a shame," "Oh yeah," and "What about that?" The lieutenant responded, "Yeah, well that happened at 4:30 in the morning. And nothing good happens after 2:00 A.M. Everything is sensationalized in the media. A lot of these folks are doing things they shouldn't be doing. Some are true victims, and we give them our heart and soul, but, really, you wouldn't believe some of the calls we get. 'I was trying to buy drugs, and someone robbed me' or "I was trying to buy liquor on Sunday.'" Everyone at the meeting laughed. He continued, "You can't make this up. One day, I wonder what it would be like to have a normal day at work, but I've never had one."

These conversations in the Applewood Block Association meeting showed how the notion of community operated for residents and (at least) for this particular police officer. The discussion revealed that the group created a moral distinction between people who lived in the community and committed crimes and those who did not commit crimes. Even people who had been victimized were thought to have deserved it. People who had been robbed while trying to buy drugs or people who had been trying to buy alcohol on a day when it was illegal to do so were discussed as stupid and deserving of their victimization. Even victims of a carjacking were not "true victims" and did not get the police officers' "heart[s] and soul[s]" if they were "doing things that they shouldn't be doing."

At this point in the meeting, Nick, the court manager, began to speak about Greenville Community Court. Organizational theorists would point us to the discourses that were privileged in this discussion—primarily those regarding quality of life and community victimization. To gain, retain, or create legitimacy, Greenville Community Court had to frame its own work within the discourses that were set up in this meeting. It could have also distinguished itself by drawing on other salient discourses. In this presentation of Greenville Community Court's work, Nick framed its treatment programs as another potential solution to the revolving door of justice (a theme that had previously been developed by the lieutenant's discussion of the GPS monitoring device). Nick also emphasized the incarceration of repeat offenders. He presented the court's work by drawing on residents' concerns about the cleanliness of their neighborhood, concerns that had been brought up in the very beginning of the meeting but had since lost steam.

The lieutenant was not the only police officer at the meeting, although he was certainly the most verbose. Getting the meeting back on track, another police officer began to dispassionately detail recent arrests, including arrests of prostitutes in the neighborhood. A man who lived in the neighborhood said, "Thank you. It really makes a big difference. We do see the difference. I leave the house every morning at 4, and I always see that girl, but she wasn't around this week, so she either got arrested or moved on. Thank you." Nick then asserted himself into the conversation: "Yeah, we've seen them down at the Greenville Community Court. One person got six months, and there are some others that are on continuances. We're gonna try and get them into some of the programs that we have at the court. But, you know, tonight they're all in jail."

After receiving a permissive nod from Isabelle, Nick stood to deliver updates for Greenville Community Court: "Well, we've taken a visit to [the women's prison], which some of you may know is the only women's prison in the state. Christine, myself, the judge, and some other courtroom staff. We were pretty impressed with some of the programs that they have in place for the women there. You know, we're all about putting a stop to the revolving door." He also noted, "Oh, and they have a library there at the prison with about a thousand books, and only like fifty are in Spanish, so we're going to try to get some donations of Spanish books for the library." One of the residents asked about donating and seemed very excited.

A particularly vocal resident asked Nick what the court was doing and how many people it put in jail. Nick responded, "Well, I'd say about 80 percent of our caseload is one-time offenders, who we'll never see again. They come in, do their community service, and then they're done. But the other 20 percent are the repeat offenders. Some want help, and we give it to them. Some want help but can't, and they'd prefer to serve a life sentence three months at a time." The resident pushed: "So, do you force them into these programs?" Nick responded, "Judge really tries to make it about the individual. It depends on the person. He really tries to base it on the individual person. Uh . . . sometimes, we really do use that hammer."

Then Nick quickly changed the subject and ended his talk. He added something about the community-service crews, directing his comment first to the elderly woman who had spoken about the vacant lot in the beginning of the meeting. "Oh! And we're happy that you saw a difference on your street! If anyone has any community-service suggestions, you can call our hotline, and we'll check it out. If we can do it, we will." Nick sat down, and the meeting then turned to a discussion of general neighborhood cleanliness and improvement: lighting, trees, parking, and recycling.

Greenville Community Court's message in this meeting was shaped by the earlier discussions of quality of life, recidivism, and the community. Because the interaction was grounded in what Nick called a "John Wayne" approach to crime and justice, the message the court privileged was incapacitation rather than treatment. Nick quickly jumped on the opportunity to take some credit for the prostitutes who had been arrested and assured residents that "tonight they're all in jail," which downplayed the treatment component of Greenville Community Court's mission. He then further downplayed its therapeutic programming by framing treatment as wholly about the individual: those who "want help" get help; others "serve a life sentence three months at a time." The other discourse that Nick could successfully draw on was about improving quality of life through beautification efforts. He then reframed the discussion of the court's work away from executing punishment to emphasize the positive aspects of the court's programs, which involved clean-up and beautification projects.

The court attempted to gain legitimacy in the residents' meeting by conforming to the discourses that were relevant in that setting. The court's flexible mission to punish as well as to treat served it well here. Nick was able to read the room and downplay the court's therapeutic aspects. His presentation focused on the incarceration of prostitutes and individualized justice. The court's flexibility allowed him to highlight aspects of its mission that would best play to the residents and to downplay those aspects that might not play as well.

The flexibility and adaptability of the court's message was advantageous to its legitimacy and survival as a new criminal justice institution. But that flexibility and adaptability could also hinder its ability to recruit stakeholders to the parts of its mission that did not entirely conform to the stakeholders' own understandings, attitudes, and values. The Applewood Block Association meeting showed that understandings of crime, even low-level crimes, were powerful tools for creating solidarity and the idea of a community. The community that operated in the meeting was exclusionary, based on legal and moral boundaries. While Greenville Community Court also sorted people into community members or criminals through case processing, its idea of community as rehabilitative, welcoming, and inclusive for reformed offenders was not shared by many people who were part of that community.

Emphasizing Treatment with Social-Service Providers

While Greenville Community Court downplayed its treatment-oriented sanctions in meetings with residents and business owners, in meetings with social-service groups, representatives from the court emphasized this part of its work. Nick made an effort to attend the interorganizational meetings held by local domestic-violence and homeless shelters, although he did not attend the shelter directors' meetings as frequently as he did the Applewood Block Association meetings. I accompanied Nick to one of these meetings at the Salvation Army. The discussion was almost entirely focused on the concerns of people who ran homeless shelters and domestic-violence shelters, such as grants for transitional housing, where to buy cheap furniture, and how to make do with limited resources. Nick did little talking beyond asking questions to better get a sense of how the shelters operated. At the end of the meeting, he said briefly, "As you know, I'm from Greenville Community Court, and I just want to let you know that you can call us when you need anything. If one of your guys is coming in to see us, and there's anything that we should know, or anything we can do to help, don't hesitate to give us a call." He passed out business cards, chatted a little with the shelter directors, and then left the meeting.

As we walked back to the court, I asked Nick why he attended shelter directors' meetings. He explained:

> The first couple of times I went there, it was like they thought we were the enemy. We are a court, an enforcement agency, who tries to just lock up their guys. But after a while, I kept telling them that we have good social programs at the court, and if there is a way to keep them out of jail and put them in a program instead, that is what our goal is, really. And I tell them they should call me so we can try to work something out.

He also said that it was important to go to shelter meetings because "[we] need to let them know [we're] on their side."

Greenville Community Court had to actively maintain relationships with social-service providers, as they had valuable knowledge about resources that Greenville Community Court could utilize. I was surprised to discover that it was through contacts made at the shelter directors' meeting that Greenville Community Court had initially heard about an outpatient drug-treatment program to which the court had referred many defendants. One of the shelter directors had also told the court that if a female defendant really needed a bed, he would find a way to get her one, even though the shelter he ran was for men only. In addition to viewing itself as a court for the community, Greenville Community Court viewed itself as an organization that gave people second chances and opportunities to make positive changes in their lives. When representatives from the court met with people in the social-services sector, they emphasized treatment over punishment. We see above that Nick did not discuss enforcement, incarceration, and community-service work imposed by Greenville Community Court. Instead, Nick focused on actively listening to shelter directors' concerns to portray Greenville Community Court as an ally. He barely mentioned the court at all, except to encourage staff at homeless and domestic-violence shelters to perceive it as a partner that privileged helping people in need.

In presenting itself in homeless shelters, the court downplayed its punitive aspects and highlighted its therapeutic programming. Yet as previous chapters show, many defendants failed to fulfill the conditions of therapeutic sanctions. Getting people into treatment was certainly an organizational goal, but success in treatment was organizationally conceptualized as the defendants' own responsibility and duty. Although Nick emphasized rehabilitation and camaraderie in these meetings with shelter directors, the connection was based more on their symbolic knowledge of treatment rather than on how treatment actually worked in practice.

Other therapeutic agencies were more familiar with how treatment worked in practice. The following discussion showed how during a visit to an inpatient drug-treatment facility, the judge learned valuable information from the treatment director while also building trust and communication between the two organizations. The judge carefully listened to the director's descriptions and concerns and was excited to hear about the successes the facility was having. The center's director used this meeting to state that she would like to ask the court to put people in jail for short periods of time to motivate compliance.

The drug-treatment center, Haven House, was a really big house. As the judge and I entered, we noticed a large fish tank and a huge whiteboard on the wall marked with people's names, how long they had been there, and little check marks. The place was clean, although it smelled a bit stuffy. The judge, looking around, repeated, "It's nice in here" and "It's *really* nice in here" multiple times, bobbing his head in approval. Within a minute, Sharon, the director of Haven House, entered. She was tall, thin, and middle-aged. Sharon seemed a bit frazzled, but she also seemed to like talking about her work. For the fifth time, the judge said, "It's nice in here," and she responded that the facility had recently gotten a grant, so it redid the floors, painted, and remodeled the kitchen to improve the "flow."

Sharon walked us through the enormous house, telling us nice things about her job and sharing more frustrating aspects: a "crack house" across the street and residents sneaking pornographic contraband. The judge asked basic questions throughout the tour—"How many men and women are here?" "What is a contraband item?"—and commented, "It must get very hot up here!"

The judge was tremendously excited to see whether any of "our people" were currently at the house. As we walked by the carriage house, where clients of Haven House were in a group therapy meeting, a Latinx woman spotted us, gasped, and smiled. She waved to the judge and said, "Hi!!" Sharon told us that the woman, Wanda, was almost done with treatment. She had just gotten a job and would be moving to a sober house, but she would come back to help run some of the therapy sessions.

We sat at a picnic table to conclude the meeting. The judge asked, "What can I do to make your job easier?" Sharon responded, "That's a good question!" and thought about her answer. She said that sometimes they had a hard time with compliance and that she would like to be able to send clients who relapsed to jail, because when that *had* happened, they had returned more willing to cooperate: "After that, they are usually not a problem." The judge was excited to hear this, responding, "I would not mind that at all! I would love to do that; I want to do that *more*." He added, "There are very few judges in this area who would *not* be willing to do that for you." Then Sharon said, "Yeah, you know, just a weekend or a few days." She then told the judge that they could do that for only patients whose treatment was paid for by court insurance rather than by general social-service low-income benefits. She told him that with court insurance they could keep the bed reserved for that person but that with the other kind of insurance, "if that bed is not occupied for one night, even if they are in jail and we know it, we have to open the bed to someone else." Surprised by this, the judge said that he would be sure to keep that in mind when arranging treatment.

Although this meeting was about a thirty-minute drive for the judge, it was worth the time spent for the connection and the information that he got out of the meeting. He learned that court insurance allowed inpatient facilities to retain a patient's bed, whereas public health insurance did not. He also learned that Haven House's director would be happy if the judge put its clients in jail for short stints. In turn, Sharon also learned that she could make this request of Greenville Community Court and that she could find out whether anyone else had a pending court case.

The judge's discussion of Greenville Community Court's work with Haven House was quite different from Nick's discussion of the court with the shelter directors, even though both groups are social-service providers. In shelter meetings, Greenville Community Court claimed that it would do whatever it could to keep people out of jail and that the court really wanted to get people into treatment. At Haven House, the judge said that he would "love" to send people to jail for short stints, if that would help motivate compliance. Even groups within the social-service community had different needs and different values. Organizationally, the court did all of these things. But rather than sharing the variety of services, goals, and processes involved in Greenville Community Court's work, court representatives first learned what message would appeal to each group. By hanging back and reading the room in residents' meetings, shelter directors' meetings, and drug treatment centers' meetings, court representatives gleaned which parts of the court's mission would best appeal to the audience at hand and selectively emphasized those qualities.

Unifying Punishment and Treatment with Underage Drinkers

When Greenville Community Court representatives attended meetings of external organizations, they tailored the court's identity to the interests of each particular audience. They aimed to form alliances with groups whose interests, solely in relationship to the court, preferred either punitive or rehabilitative sanctions. Within the daily work in the courtroom, Greenville Community Court simultaneously performed its identities of being "tough on crime," showing concern about the community at large, and encouraging personal transformation. Here, we also see a move from "narrating the self" (Gubrium and Holstein 1997) to the performance and construction of identity in action. The following example of the "anti–underage drinking docket" shows how Greenville Community Court improvised within interactions to convey both messages to a carefully recruited audience of members who held political clout.

Across a two-month period, police officers charged sixty students from local universities with underage drinking. Greenville Community Court processed each case with a continuance, meaning that all students would return to court. Greenville Community Court specifically set aside one court session (the "underage drinking docket" or the "anti–underage drinking protocol") for all the students to return to court having completed some work between their initial court dates and the day of the underage drinking docket. The students' initial sanction was to read a book about drinking (either *Smashed: The Story of a Drunken Girlhood* or *From Binge to Blackout: A Mother and Son Struggle with Teen Drinking*) and to write an essay relating the book to their own lives. They brought these essays with them to court on the date of the anti–underage drinking docket. On this day, Greenville Community Court had arranged various speakers to address the students: a representative from Mothers against Drunk Driving (MADD), a forensic pathologist, the dean of a university, and several community representatives. Greenville Community Court officials had also invited a journalist from Greenville's main newspaper to cover the event.

When I arrived at the court the morning of the underage drinking docket, the room was filled to capacity. Nick sat down next to me and whispered, "We're gonna put one guy in jail. He was drunk off his ass, not with this group. He'll be example number one. He deserves it, though." As court began, the prosecutor started the day with opening comments about this "example number one":

> Before we start with the protocol, I'd like to call one case before the court. He has a new case as well as a case pending for next month. They appear to be the same charges: he was so intoxicated, he broke his neighbor's window because he was convinced it was his house.

The defendant, a white man who appeared to be in his mid-thirties, was escorted from lockup by two marshals and stood before the court in handcuffs and shackles. The prosecutor read from the police report—a woman said that a man had been banging on her door, demanding to be let inside. The man had then smashed the window to her living room and attempted to crawl inside, thinking that it was his house. The judge matter-of-factly stated that the defendant would go to jail. Greenville Community Court continued the matter for two weeks, the judge set a $50,000 bond, and the marshals escorted the defendant back into lockup.

Next, the judge proceeded with the college drinking cases. She stated, "This is the official docket of the court's anti–underage drinking protocol. The message should be that Greenville takes underage drinking very seriously." Gary, the prosecutor, then took the reins and explained the various consequences that the students could have faced had the police officers pursued different charges:

> What most of you have been charged with is loitering on permitted premises: you were underage in an establishment that is permitted for those of the legal drinking age. You could have been charged with constructed possession of alcohol by a minor. For constructed possession, you don't even need to have a drink in your hand; if you are sitting at a table where someone has a drink, and you could feasibly reach across the table and grab it, that is constructed possession. For the first offense, you could face a monetary fine of up to $500, and for the second charge, if you are convicted, you could lose your motor vehicle license for up to four months. This applies to out-of-state licenses as well. The state has a deal with all other states that if you have your licenses revoked, you cannot return to another state and drive as well.

Some of the students had fake IDs. The prosecutor explained, "Being in possession of a fake ID is punishable by one to five years in jail, and it is a felony offense. You could lose many of your civil rights as a citizen, such as voting rights in some states."

When the court had first encountered these cases, the judge had had many of the students "drop a urine" to see whether they would test positive for drugs. At the anti–underage drinking docket session, the prosecutor explained the consequences for being convicted of a drug crime:

> Many of you tested positive for drugs or admitted that you would have tested positive for drugs. Under the new Patriot Act, if you are found in possession of a small amount of marijuana, a small drug offense, you are no longer eligible for any federal financial aid or student loans. You would revoke any scholarships, so unless you are independently wealthy, you would not be able to continue college. This applies even for possession of paraphernalia, even for a small amount of marijuana.

This docket was the only time in the course of my fieldwork when I heard court personnel discuss someone's future as being jeopardized by drugs or alcohol within the framework of federal civil liberties, voting rights, or rights as a citizen. The court did not officially sanction students with these charges; instead, it threatened them with the potential consequences of "constructed possession" of alcohol and/or possession of a small amount of marijuana.

Greenville Community Court next opened the floor up to the speakers. The speaker from MADD spoke to the gathered audience about the time she drove drunk and killed one of her best friends, who was a passenger in her car. The forensic pathologist talked about how he frequently saw young people dead from alcohol- and drug-related accidents. The president of the Applewood Block Association, Isabelle, addressed the students last. She said to the courtroom, "I see you all, [and] I see my kids. You are important. You are valuable. . . . [When you are drinking,] you're not only hurting yourself; you are hurting everyone in the community. . . . Zero tolerance for every crime in the city [is about] wanting better for the people of Greenville."

By strategically calling the drunk man who had broken into his neighbor's house "example number one" and inviting the speaker from MADD and the forensic pathologist to detail severe consequences of drug and alcohol consumption, Greenville Community Court publicly presented itself as tough on crime. The docket opened with the explicit announcement that the city took "underage drinking very seriously." Greenville Community Court used an opportunity from its routine proceedings—the man who had broken into his neighbor's house—and strategically placed his case immediately before the start of the anti–underage drinking docket. He was explicitly used as "example number one" to show that the court was "tough on crime." Indeed, the judge issued him a punitive sanction (jail time) rather than a rehabilitative sanction, as the college students had received. This presentation of "toughness" was strategic in that it conveyed to key community members and defendants that Greenville Community Court could and did sentence people to jail for alcohol-related charges. Yet Greenville Community Court tempered this toughness with an emphasis on "paying back the community," which recalled its interactions in block association meetings. The prosecutor announced that the students had not completed their sentences by simply attending the court docket and turning in their essays; by order of the court, they also had to complete twenty hours of community service at the Boys and Girls Club to pay back the community.

Next, the judge invited several students to come to the front of the court to read their essays. The judge asked the dean of students from a local university to pick the first speaker. He chose a young woman who cried the entire time she read her paper. She said:

> We have opportunities many would kill for, and now I know all of my accomplishments can mean nothing in one instant. I do not completely regret everything because it has shown me that I need to focus on my future and my education. I am a good person. I am on the Dean's list. I am family oriented, and I've done community service since I was six years old. I apologize to you, Your Honor, and to the court. I hope you can regain faith in young adults and our future.

When she finished reading, the judge told her to approach the bench and "give [her] a hug." People in the audience clapped. Court staff wiped tears from their eyes or smiled broadly. Her essay so astutely conveyed the court's message that the prosecutor joked aloud, "That was a setup. You didn't just randomly pick that young lady."

This interaction set the tone for the rest of the docket. Other students were called up, none of whom spoke as succinctly and emotionally as the first student. One young woman, talking about how she felt, commented, "It is time . . . to grow up. Partying is not worth it." She ended her statement with the assertion that she was "a good person" and that this was not the path that she wished to go down. When the girl finished, the judge said to her, "You read the book, and you are a good person. You come up here and give me a hug, too." One young man spoke about how he could not imagine how his mother felt about his court case, and the judge told him, "You are a good son. You can come up here and give me a hug, too." Each time the judge invited the speakers to give her a hug, the entire courtroom clapped and smiled.

Here, we see how Greenville Community Court's message of rehabilitation and personal transformation stood out. The judge, in dialogue with individual students, remembered bits and pieces about the students' cases before she called them and personalized her message to each. In having the students testify that they had changed and had learned their lesson, Greenville Community Court affirmed that treatment in a court setting could work. The students were effectively characterized as having "learned a lesson" and as being "good," thereby allowing them to be rewarded with praise and reintegrated into the community.

Organizationally speaking, if Greenville Community Court operated without the need to constantly build legitimacy, it would not have organized a specialized docket for underage drinkers. Given the caseload, it would have been easier for Greenville Community Court to hold the cases on separate days. The court did not need to alter its sessions to accommodate such a large number of cases. It did not need to call in representatives and a member of the press from the community. These cases could have been handled like every other recurring offense at the court (for instance, Greenville Community Court never held special "substance-abuse" or "crimes by minors" dockets). Because Greenville Community Court saw this circumstance as an opportunity to convey an image to the public and to garner support from community leaders, it had specifically arranged this day as a public and publicized event.

Yet the anti–underage drinking docket, a legitimacy-creating event, focused on white college students, a group of offenders who were seen as good candidates for reform. When I asked about this situation, the court actors insisted that the social class or race of defendants did not matter in terms of the planning and execution of the anti–underage drinking docket. They merely saw the situation as "an opportunity" to bring similar cases together. The presentation of justice itself conveyed the varied and nuanced ways in which Greenville Community Court enacted justice. It combined punitive measures, rehabilitative measures, education, praise, and shame. It directly involved community members in the justice process and in the sanction of community service. However, the anti–underage drinking docket included a sympathetic offender group and community members who were experts or community members with some local power. The court clearly promoted particularly classed and racialized notions of treatment, justice, and the community that it justified in the name of appealing to stakeholders.

Conclusion

Law professor Timothy Casey (2005) argues that problem-solving courts are headed for a crisis of legitimacy. Currently, he says, the legitimacy of problem-solving courts stems from charismatic leaders and "borrowed" legitimacy from traditional courts. When the first generation of leaders ages out and when problem-solving courts act in ways that are openly counter to traditional courts, then they will lose legitimacy. He writes, "As soon as the smoke clears, however, the problem-solving courts will have to justify their exercise of authority. . . . This will be a difficult, perhaps impossible, task" (2005: 1503–1504).

I agree with much of Casey's discussion of the problematic nature of problem-solving courts. Yet my data do not support Casey's claim that problem-solving courts will face a crisis of legitimacy. My study of Greenville Community Court shows that it already is participating in legitimacy-creating behaviors that are not based on charismatic leadership or traditional court legitimacy. The very flexible nature of community courts allows them to draw from various culturally resonant resources. Greenville Community Court gains legitimacy by claiming that it punishes people who truly deserve it. It draws on ideas about culpability, which state that some people are not wholly responsible for their crimes and that those people may change their behaviors through therapeutic interventions. It draws from quality-of-life discourses that define and demark the idea of the community. It engages in marketing strategies by publicizing such events as the anti–underage drinking program, which highlights the court's rehabilitative practices by compiling a sympathetic offender group and presenting the court's serious position on low-level crimes. The court meets with residents and tells them that it is helping make their neighborhood more beautiful and that it is putting the bad guys in jail. It meets with therapeutic organizations to argue that it really cares about helping people and will do whatever it can to make the organizations' jobs easier.

This campaigning does not indicate that community courts are already in a crisis of legitimacy. Instead, the marketing of justice points toward a unique kind of organizational agency that allows for Greenville Community Court to continually adapt its message to the audiences from whom it can garner support. Indeed, the model of problem-solving courts more broadly aims to be flexible and adaptable from its very inception. In his book on the global adoption of problem-solving courts, James Nolan (2009) finds that different nations enact the problem-solving model, not only vis-à-vis their current legal structures but also, more importantly, through their cultural understandings. For instance, problem-solving courts in some nations readily adopt therapeutic jurisprudence, whereas courts in other nations adopt it with caution or eschew it altogether. That is, the model of problem-solving courts is mutable and adaptable to particularly nationalistic and local cultural contexts that allow it to grow and change in different locations.

Organizational theorists argue that successful organizations situate themselves within cultural logics that make them readily interpretable. Greenville Community Court does this by drawing on logics that are not limited to the field of criminal justice; it draws on notions of the community, the criminal, therapy, and punishment that exist in a broader cultural space beyond the simple framework of "the courts." The very hybrid nature of community courts allows them to agentically garner these resources that leave issues for the identity and legitimacy of community courts.

While Greenville Community Court works alongside social-service organizations, as it gains legitimacy, it may not be competing with the traditional courts for resources; it may indeed be competing with the social-service organizations. Victoria Malkin cautions that community courts' claims to legitimacy through incorporating therapeutic and social-service tropes may push out other, more grassroots organizations:

> Community groups and local organizations which focus on community programs compete for declining public and private resources. Groups are thus forced to monitor their programs as they legitimize them for further funding. Some argue that this competition for resources engenders an accountable system as the "best man" wins.
>
> While this is ideal in a level playing field, when community courts compete for these resources, they have advantages over smaller grassroots organizations in terms of their political and cultural capital. (2003: 1590)

As community courts become more entrenched in therapeutic discourses, and as they are better able to show how their offender populations are in need of these services, they may alienate or harm other organizations that aim to execute similar programs.

The contested notion of a community could also undermine community courts. The mission to involve the community in community courts may reproduce social inequalities. The "community" may mean those people and organizations with the time, resources, and political voices to participate. Other individuals and groups who are alienated by the legal system and/or who do not have similar access to the collective efficacy may become further alienated despite the courts' best efforts. Through the courts' efforts to promote community inclusion in the justice process, they may empower particular groups and further marginalize other groups that feel less entitled or are less able to participate. The process of targeting and excluding certain groups from the rights and security of "community" is excellently illustrated in two areas deeply connected to community courts: the politicization of quality-of-life discourses and community policing tactics. Alex Vitale's *City of Disorder* (2008) documents how residents in distinct New York City neighborhoods mobilized around quality-of-life discourses and empowered politicians who promised to combat urban disorder. Vitale finds that even residents with long-standing liberal activism and personal economic insecurity resorted to punitive, law-and-order enforcement around homeless populations. Community policing tactics are consistently shown to breed distrust between racial minorities, law enforcement, and the criminal justice system more broadly (Fratello, Rengifo, and Trone 2013).[6] Despite Greenville Community Court's commitment to the community, and the work of its actors behind the scenes to mobilize more structural solutions to the problems brought before the court, it is clear that some groups are able to make claims on the court and effectively use its resources more than others.

Conclusion

Courting the Community

Greg Berman, the director of the Center of Court Innovation, opened the 2016 International Conference of Community Courts with the following remarks:

> It's pretty clear that we're living through a moment of both great crisis and great opportunity when it comes to criminal justice. When we last gathered, . . . the storm clouds were still coming together. Since that time, almost every week has brought grim news about the state of criminal justice in our country: unwarranted uses of force, fees and fines being used to balance municipal budgets, dire statistics about mass incarceration, protests in the streets. Alongside these developments we've also seen, drip by drip by drip, the continued erosion of public trust in justice, particularly in low-income neighborhoods and among communities of color. So I would argue that the sense of crisis is very real, but I would also argue that the sense of opportunity is equally real. . . .
>
> The question for those of us who have gathered here today is simple: "How does community justice fit into this new world order? What can community courts . . . do to advance the cause of justice reform?" (Center for Court Innovation 2016)

Community courts promise to reform the criminal justice process in ways that address individual and community needs. Through the practice of therapeutic jurisprudence, community courts claim that they enact individualized justice in a manner that rehabilitates and deters individual offenders. Through restorative justice and broken windows theory orientations, community courts seek to address quality-of-life issues, promote community investment, and cultivate collective efficacy. In practicing this hybridized form of justice, community courts additionally seek to alleviate pressures on traditional courts, restore judicial discretion, and handle misdemeanor cases efficiently. They "court the community" by seductively promising residents and business owners safer streets, quieter neighbors, and clean vacant lots. They shower social-service providers with additional judicial resources to aid in offenders' compliance. They pledge to other court systems that they will ease their burdensome caseloads. In this concluding chapter, I reflect on Berman's statements on the crises and opportunities in contemporary criminal justice in light of the lessons herein. I also answer where community courts "fit into this new world order," with regard to the criminal justice landscape and to theoretical considerations in sociology.

The Questionable Impact of Community Courts

Community courts certainly aim to address the erosion of trust in the criminal justice system, and this ethnographic study reveals that much of community courts' daily work centers around legitimacy-building practices. Community courts are deeply committed to procedural justice, scheduling community service at times that are convenient for defendants, motivating judicial compliance with praising ceremonies and "tough-love" talks, treating defendants as individuals, and so forth. This attention to procedural justice is equally concerned with "producing" good defendants and creating an organizational identity that conveys efficiency and humane treatment. Community courts actively construct their legitimacy with a wide variety of stakeholders, forging positive relationships with residents, business owners, and other community members outside the courtroom. This study's organizational focus illustrates how criminal justice organizations act agentically and strategically to garner resources, produce desired outcomes, and cultivate beneficial partnerships across agencies.

Courting the Community demonstrates that the key to community courts' legitimacy stems from their identity as flexible organizations that embrace multiple goals. The ethnographic data compiled in this book illustrate how Greenville Community Court incorporates "seemingly disparate logics . . . into a coherent project" (Werth 2013: 237) under the umbrella of problem-solving justice. Defendants deserve punishment or treatment (and sometimes both). The court is rational and strict in one instance while understanding and lenient in the next. Greenville Community Court believes that "the community" can promote and assuage criminological tendencies. This book illustrates the salience of discourses about punitiveness, rehabilitation, zero tolerance, quality of life, and community in contemporary criminal justice. Furthermore, it shows how community courts can use these discourses to garner legitimacy.

Noticeably absent from community courts' legitimacy claims are basic numeric data, gleaned from rigorous assessments of community courts that document their cost-effectiveness and impact on recidivism and crime rates. This absence can be accounted for in two distinct ways. As James Nolan (2001) observes in *Reinventing Justice*, officials engaged in the drug court movement expressed caution at using traditional evaluation rubrics when making claims about the vitality and successes of drug courts. Instead, these officials "[viewed] stories . . . as more persuasive and credible than traditional empirical measurements" (Nolan 2009: 128). Since community courts and drug courts are problem-solving courts, one would expect officials in both systems to share a preference for narrative over quantification. Second, only a small number of studies measure community courts' impact on standard outcomes. While community courts do not use these studies as a source of legitimacy, it is worth a short detour to consider the results of such evaluations.

Evidence of community courts' impacts on recidivism, crime rates, and cost-effectiveness tells an inconclusive story. Michele Sviridoff et al.'s (2002) study on Midtown Community Court shows that the court had no effect on recidivism rates and that declines in selected quality-of-life crimes in Midtown's catchment area were not attributable to it. Evaluations of community courts in Liverpool and Seattle also lack compelling evidence of their impact on re-offending (Jolliffe and Farrington 2009; Nugent-Borakove 2009). However, some studies find in favor of community courts' impact on recidivism rates (Kilmer and Sussell 2014; Lee et al. 2013; Ross et al. 2009). Studies on the cost-effectiveness of community courts yield similarly mixed results: while some studies show that community courts save money (Lee et al. 2013; Ross et al. 2009), another study finds that community courts increase spending (Weidner and Davis 2000). The handful of evaluation studies that assess the promised benefits of community courts does not provide reliable evidence that community courts deliver on these promised outcomes.

These studies *do* find consistent and compelling evidence that community courts are perceived as legitimate by defendants and community members. In an evaluation of Hartford Community Court, a majority of defendants perceive their sentences to be fair and report being treated with respect (Justice Education Center 2002). Community members and other stakeholders overwhelmingly report that they believe that community courts reduce quality-of-life crimes, express appreciation for community courts' concerns for residents, and display support for the stated goals of community courts (Berman and Feinblatt 2005; Justice Education Center 2002; Lee et al. 2013; Malkin 2003). While these studies often rely on convenience or purposive samples, taken alongside my findings in this book, it is clear that community courts are effective in achieving procedural-justice outcomes and legitimacy in the eyes of stakeholders.

Courting the Community's ethnographic data are uniquely situated to explain how community courts are deemed legitimate, despite their unclear positive impacts on criminal justice outcomes. In all public-facing interactions, whether in the courtroom with defendants, meetings with the Applewood Block Association, or discussions with community leaders, Greenville Community Court officials strategically "read" the audience at hand and selectively present the court's identity according to whatever style, substance, or presentation is most appealing. Community courts are organizationally ambivalent—because they encompass such a variety of logics, goals, and discursive tactics, community courts do not need to commit to one clear strategy or outcome. As Chapters 4 and 5 argue, Greenville Community Court demonstrates organizational ambivalence toward offenders and the sources of their culpability. The court acknowledges "underlying social issues" that fuel criminal behavior, yet the solution to those "social issues" is configured as an individual accountability project. Through the practice of ambivalent justice, the court places responsibility for compliance on the individual, thereby enabling the court to rehabilitate and incarcerate with little internal conflict. This ambivalence allows community courts to frame offenders' compliance *and* noncompliance as success stories; compliance illustrates the court's ability to reform those who "want and need help," and noncompliance illustrates the court's ability to punish low-level offenders who "want to serve a life sentence three months at a time." With organizational ambivalence, all roads lead to community courts' legitimacy.

Putting aside concerns about how community courts achieve the favor and trust of their constituents, let us return to Berman's metaphor and consider whether community courts can repair the leaky faucet eroding trust in the criminal justice system. To weigh this possibility, it is necessary to view community courts in a broad context. Empirical studies on the effects of quality-of-life and community policing (the law enforcement arm that accompanies community courts) routinely fail to demonstrate that these policing practices influence overall crime rates. Instead, these studies overwhelmingly find that these policing practices discriminate against communities of color and engender distrust in the criminal justice system (see Fratello, Rengifo, and Trone 2013; Gelman, Fagan, and Kiss 2007; Rosenfeld, Terry, and Chauhan 2014). In fact, respondents in assessments of community courts—defendants and residents alike—report feelings of frustration and injustice around the enforcement of quality-of-life crimes (Lee et al. 2013). Interestingly, the legitimacy bestowed upon community courts is not even granted to law-enforcement teams who send people to community courts, let alone to the criminal justice system at large. Historical context provides another consideration. As detailed in Chapter 2, 1993 witnessed the opening of the first community court, in no small part with the express purpose of addressing a crisis of legitimacy in the criminal justice system fueled by "revolving-door justice," mass incarceration, and the lack of judicial discretion. Twenty-five years later, as I write this Conclusion, the faucet continues to leak, and the sink basin continues to erode.

Flexible Specialization and the Competition for Legitimacy

An overarching concern of this book is to describe how organizations embrace and enact multiple logics to create and maintain legitimacy. Institutional theorists have shown us that organizations compete for legitimacy. C. Everett Hughes describes institutions as "enterprising" and competitive, arguing that "the survival of an institution . . . represents the persistence of particular definitions of wants and of corporate ways of satisfying them" (1936: 181). More contemporary institutional scholars use Pierre Bourdieu's concepts of fields and position-taking to describe how organizations delineate boundaries, construct relationships, and compete for symbolic capital (DiMaggio and Powell 1991). Community courts add to the study of organizations by showing how organizations with flexible missions engage in performative action for instrumental goals, such as efficient case processing and offender compliance, and symbolic goals, such as recognition as a legitimate and morally upright organization.

Considering community courts from an organizational perspective allows us to draw connections to larger trends in how culture shapes organizations. As David Harvey argues, post-Fordism is marked by a "flexible system production with [an] emphasis on problem-solving, rapid and often highly specialized responses, and adaptability of skills to special purposes" (1990: 155). As traditional institutions fail to accommodate new cultural logics and structural realities of postmodernity, new organizational forms are constructed to serve subpopulations of the public, like flying buttresses built to support a structurally unstable building. Richard Sennett (2007) explains that under "the new capitalism," this "delayering of institutions" is central to the rise of flexible organizational forms. Community courts are but one example of how we have moved to more niche, individualized, and flexible social formations to address societal needs. Education has gone flexible with the "school-choice" movement, which advocates for additional education options, such as charter schools, magnet schools, homeschooling, and voucher programs, inter alia (Wells et al. 1999). We see this flexibility in higher education, with degree programs and entire universities built online for students who work full-time in the labor market or as caregivers at home. Political actors and insurance companies are currently advocating for healthcare flexibility, pushing policies that would allow people to pick their healthcare benefits à la carte. Work has become flexible, with telecommuting, flex-time, and other adaptations that have blurred the lines between home and the office (Hochschild 1997). Our own bodies have "gone flexible," as anthropologist Emily Martin (1994) explains in her riveting study of immunology and health.[1] The criminal justice system is yet another area in which specialized "markets" are created to supplement already existing structures.

There is an inherent morality in the narrative of flexibility (Martin 1994). Flexible corporations are better adapted to the market than traditional corporations, flexible bodies are healthy and modern, and flexible workers possess greater potential and are not useless. While this flexibility appears liberating, for organizations that must compete for legitimacy, the flexibility is much more rigid than it seems. "Novel organizational forms are most likely to become legitimated when they fit into the preexisting cultural beliefs, meanings, and typifications of an organizational community" (Ruef 2000: 661). Chapter 2 discusses the fact that the idea of community courts is not novel but instead reproduces existing ideas about the criminal justice system and repackages them as "innovative."[2]

We can think of how other hybrid organizational configurations organize their claims for legitimacy. Magnus Gulbrandsen (2011) finds that academic research institutes are often engaged in legitimacy battles as they negotiate different between "pure" and "applied" research and public and private sectors. Linda Renzulli (2005) discusses charter schools' emergence in the context of discourses about student performance, student need, and the desire for autonomy. Legitimacy practices of novel organizations often benefit from the fact that cultural tropes that we consider to be static are themselves dynamic and contested (see, for instance, Howard Becker's [1982] work on art and Thomas Gieryn's [1999] analysis of what constitutes "science").

While these cultural structures are limiting in the practice of "innovative" organizations, an organizational perspective affords us the ability to conceptualize criminal justice institutions as agentic actors, actively negotiating meaning. The sociological study of punishment in the contemporary United States is primarily concerned with macrolevel questions about the punitive turn and long-term effects of mass incarceration. Indeed, these questions are extraordinarily important. However, this book asks readers to reconsider punishment as a "cultural agent" (Garland 1990) that shapes patterns of meaning beyond the courtroom walls. Greenville Community Court is an active cultural agent that strategically cultivates its image as an organization and its understanding of offenders.

Considering how criminal justice organizations engage in meaning making "on the ground" can illuminate how macrolevel patterns are interpreted, enacted, and resisted in everyday interactions.

Disciplinary Social Control

Recent scholarship in criminal justice has pointed toward the rise in administrative social control (Feeley and Simon 1992). This form of criminal justice supervision is particularly experienced outside prisons. Michelle Phelps (2013, 2017) develops the concept of "mass probation" to describe the explosion of community supervision of misdemeanor offenses in the United States, alongside the more heavily documented phenomenon of mass incarceration. Issa Kohler-Hausmann's (2018) work on misdemeanor processing in New York City illustrates the extensive resources required of court actors and defendants to handle low-level offenses. Forrest Stuart's (2016) ethnography *Down, Out, and Under Arrest* describes how the "therapeutic policing" of poor residents of Skid Row serves as a responsibilization strategy aimed at keeping people out of prison. The sociology of punishment has only begun to interrogate the various ways that penal logics are enacted on people who commit low-level crimes.

Community courts provide yet another entrance point to help us understand the expanded social control of low-level offenders in the criminal justice system. It is clear that social control of low-level offenders is part of a larger project of disciplinary social control. Foucauldian techniques of surveillance and examination through a diffuse network of social-service providers and criminal justice experts inform our understanding of this growing aspect of criminal social control. Rehabilitative strategies aimed at creating self-regulating subjects are juxtaposed against seemingly more punitive sanctions. As others have articulated, this contrast between therapeutic and punitive strategies is not binary and oppositional but instead leaky and mutually constitutive (Hannah-Moffat 2005; Hutchinson 2006; Stuart 2016). These tactics around low-level offenders are part of a larger neoliberal project of self-governance.

This ethnography of one community court illustrates how this disciplinary process operates a performatively moral sorting system. Greenville Community Court engages in a moral construction of criminals that is not based on their crimes but instead on their willingness (or presentation of willingness) to become responsible citizens. People are sentenced to jail not because of their crimes but because of their failures to take advantage of opportunities to better themselves. We can see how similar institutional and discursive boundary work is constructed in other areas of social life. Discourses about "deserving" and "undeserving poor" shape social-welfare benefits, constructions of women as victims or criminals informs how we handle domestic-violence survivors (Richie 1996), and labeling struggling students as "hopeless cases" or learning-disabled structures educational resources (Booher-Jennings 2005).

The punishment process embodies a neoliberal logic of individual responsibility, self-governance, and unfettered ability to engage in free choice. This logic enables a punishment process that assigns community membership and valuable citizenship. The moral sorting at community courts decides who deserves jail time or treatment. To paraphrase Susan Starr Sered and Maureen Norton-Hawk (2014: 159), "it is a short hop" from treating individual character flaws to criminalizing them. This added moral component further justifies people as really deserving jail time, people who, in the grand scheme of things, have committed very minor crimes. Bernard Harcourt writes:

> The practices of punishment that we choose may participate in creating the categories of law-abider and disorderly. But if, in fact, the processes of punishment not only create the social solidarity among honest people, but also simultaneously create the very category of honest people, then the legitimating effect on society is fabricated and artificial. (2001: 141)

We should reflect on the idea that punishment creates social constructed categories of people. We should also, in turn, acknowledge that rehabilitative and punitive "solutions" to criminal offending are strictly rooted in ideas of individual responsibility that preclude more structural, complex understandings of criminal behavior.

If the criminal justice system has only two modalities of social control available—punish or treat—one wonders how to break the categories open to present some alternative consideration for offenders. Is there some other cultural framework that could provide a "legitimating account" (Douglas Creed, Scully, and Austin 2002)? This question becomes even more complicated when we recognize arms of "the carceral" as reaching far beyond the walls of prisons and jail cells and touching people's lives at home, work, and school. I don't dare presume a solution here, but recent scholarship proposes that a human-rights framework could be a powerful new direction (Sered and Norton-Hawk 2014). This larger conversation, however, warrants far more attention than a few paragraphs assigned to this concluding chapter.

Criminalizing Incivility and the Meaning of Community

Émile Durkheim, a founding scholar of sociological thought, elucidates how crime contributes to the formation and maintenance of society. He argues that punishment makes communities cohesive, defining the boundaries around proper ways of being and promoting community solidarity. Durkheim asks readers to

> imagine a society of saints, a perfect cloister of exemplary individuals. Crimes will there be unknown; but faults which appear tolerable to the layman will create there the same scandal that the ordinary offense does in ordinary consciousness. If, then, the society of saints has the power to judge and punish, it will define these lesser acts as criminal and will treat them as such. ([1895] 1982: 100)

Despite recent decreases in violent crime in the United States, we are not "a society of saints." Yet we have expanded criminal justice supervision to very low-level, quality-of-life crimes and use them as a rubric for defining community membership.

I once asked Nick what Greenville would be like without the court. He told me a story about an affluent woman who had visited the courtroom and said to Judge Balick, "I shudder to think what the city would be like without the community court here. What you guys kind of do is keep a lid on the civility." Quality-of-life discourses have permeated official and commonsense understandings of how neighborhoods can maintain order. The quality-of-life discourse is apocalyptic and exclusive. As the woman's comment illustrates, neighborhoods are constructed as insecure and about to boil over with criminal behavior. Broken windows theory and community courts have crystalized and legitimated these modern urban tensions and embedded them with actual resources.

Community courts are often found in rapidly gentrifying urban areas, such as San Francisco's Tenderloin district; Santa Ana, California; and Red

Hook in Brooklyn, New York. These urban spaces are contested as newer and often wealthier residents change the landscape and culture scape of urban areas, sometimes unconsciously. Quality-of-life discourses promise to alleviate tensions around contested urban space; they appear to be common ground across racial and socioeconomic boundaries. Who wouldn't want a safer and cleaner neighborhood? Yet as Andrew Deener argues, quality-of-life issues are a "political mirage" (2012: 246) that pits neighbors against one another instead of promoting shared values.

At the very heart of the idea of community is the relationship between individual and community rights. To have meaningful membership in a community, each member must actively negotiate his or her rights as an individual with the rights of the group. It is quite easy to advocate for community rights for those whose individual rights align with those of the community; it is quite another matter to reorient community rights to service individual rights for those who are most vulnerable. While community courts work for "the community," their focus on individual accountability and therapeutic jurisprudence aims to make deviant individuals reorient their own individual trajectories and behaviors with community interests and do not call into question the basis of claims for these community rights. In an empirical test of broken windows theory, Robert Sampson and Stephen Raudenbush (1999) find that the relationship between crime and disorder is largely spurious; instead, what aligns these two concepts is collectivity efficacy—a system of informal trust and social control among residents of the same geographic area. Community courts take this notion of collective efficacy and formally build it into the criminal justice system. But by formalizing an informal activity and giving it administrative, bureaucratic, and punitive "teeth," they have transformed collective efficacy into a criminal justice practice instead of a neighborly practice. Community courts enable a "hollow tolerance" (Vitale 2008: 190–191) of undesirable behaviors and people that abruptly becomes a punitive intolerance when defendants fail to accommodate the processual goals of the court.

Community is a precious and desirable goal, and we should look to forge stronger relationships between individuals who share the same geographic space. But the criminal justice system is not the appropriate tool with which to build such a cherished structure. The criminal justice system constructs a defensive community with a series of moralized moats and barriers rather than engineer an inclusive community with bridges and pathways. Instead of broken windows and pots about to boil over, we should seek a new metaphor to guide how we enact and shape community.

Methodological Appendix

This project investigates how community courts enact meanings around crime, criminals, and community through case processing and how community courts strategically use these meanings to create organizational legitimacy. To meet these ends, I conducted ethnographic fieldwork in one community court for an eleven-month period. Ethnographic research is an ideal methodology to uncover "law in action" (Nelken 1984; Pound 1910; Travers and Manzo 1997), as it allows researchers to observe what community members do and say in their daily work. I observed official court sessions, which revealed how Greenville Community Court enacted justice designed to motivate offender compliance and affirm organizational legitimacy. I also observed court officials' meetings with shelter directors, social-service providers, and residents to understand how Greenville Community Court translated its flexible punishment logics to a variety of stakeholders. Ethnographic methods were especially well-suited to this field site, as specialized courts themselves construct meaning through narrative, "therapeutic theater," and storytelling (Nolan 2001). Greenville Community Court, as documented throughout this book, viewed courtroom interaction as central to its organizational identity. Because specialized courts so centrally use performance and narrative as legitimacy-building strategies, ethnographic analysis was necessary to account for the functions and processes of this court. In this Methodological Appendix, I further elaborate my methods of data collection and analysis. While ethnography was most suitable to answer the questions that I ask in this study, I also note its general limitations.

GAINING ACCESS AND NEGOTIATING POSITIONALITY

To conduct ethnographic research at a community court, I first needed to obtain approval from a community court and from my university's Institutional Review Board (IRB), which is designed to enforce ethical research and protect human subjects. I approached Greenville Community Court officials with the prospect of my research, vouched by contacts and experiences from working at another community court in another city.[1] My research had to be cleared by bureaucratic structures in Greenville Community Court's system, and the decision makers agreed to my research, provided that I use a pseudonym for the court and its actors. Officials from my university IRB office kindly helped me navigate the thorough approval process. However, even with Greenville Community Court's approval in place, the IRB approved my research only under the condition that I would not interact with defendants, as the IRB considered them to be a special protected class.

I was initially disappointed that the IRB blocked my access to defendants at Greenville Community Court, but ultimately this limitation was beneficial to my work. The IRB insisted on this stipulation before I engaged in data collection, allowing me to narrow my focus to Greenville Community Court as an organization. This substantive focus also helped me better navigate ethical considerations that arise around positionality in ethnographic research. In a widely influential article, anthropologist Laura Nader (1972) describes the relationship between the researcher and his or her community as "studying down" or "studying up." When studying down, the researcher has greater power than community members involved in the study; studying up is when the researcher investigates institutions, organizations, or people with greater power than the researcher. Historically, ethnographers studied down, both in early anthropology, in which the white, Western anthropologist traveled to "primitive" communities to extract insights about cultural formations, and in the Chicago school of sociology, in which ethnographers sought to explain the lives of poor or working-class immigrants and racial minorities in urban communities. Studying down is laden with ethical issues around positionality. Ethnographers often exoticize the practices of marginalized people, following the "jungle book trope" (Rios 2011) or engaging in "imperialist nostalgia" (Rosaldo 1993). Theorizing about the practices of marginalized communities can naturalize and reify their marginalization; inequality, poverty, and other social problems seem inevitable or unimportant when an ethnographer omits them from investigation. In studying up, ethnographers retrain their focus on people and organizations that enact official power on others, thereby claiming that the exercise of power is itself worthy of critical interrogation. In studying up at Greenville Community Court, I investigated how legal power is enacted, constructed, and legitimized through interaction with defendants, social-service providers, and community members. I did not ask, "Why do defendants conform to or reject community court orders?" Instead, I asked, "How does the community court interact with different categories of Greenville community members and why?" This approach afforded important insights into ways that specialized courts interpret and process defendants and how they translate meanings around case processing to generate legitimacy to a wider audience of a variety of stakeholders.

I sought to conduct my research in a manner that allowed reciprocity between Greenville Community Court and me. To this end, I asked Greenville Community Court whether I could conduct research on its inner workings, and in exchange, I offered my labor as an unpaid intern. As an intern, I was eager to aid the court in any way I could, offering to run statistical analyses on their datasets, coding and analyzing data, and so forth. However, Greenville Community Court was uninterested in my methodological skills and planned limited work for my internship.[2] Each day started with friendly chats with court marshals, stenographers, and other staff. Once court started, I was released to "go watch court."

My duties as an intern at Greenville Community Court revealed two key insights early in the data-collection process. First, systematic data collection and analysis toward traditional evaluative measurements were unimportant at Greenville Community Court. I state this observation not because Greenville officials did not use my methodological training to their advantage but because the rare data collected by Greenville Community Court were not systematically analyzed with regard to these outcomes. The court tracked the number of cases it processed each month along with basic information around dispensation but did little to analyze that data. It also compiled a dataset on prostitution cases, but that dataset contained demographic data on offenders; the person who showed me that information pointed my attention to the ages of sex workers with cases at the court, commenting how sad it was that a sixteen-year-old was involved in prostitution and that a fifty-four-year-old was *still* involved in prostitution. I also learned that "watching court" was central to court actors' understanding of their work at Greenville Community Court. When court actors who worked outside the courtroom had "downtime," they would come "watch court." When an interesting case was on the docket, people made sure they were in the courtroom to witness it. This fascinating and peculiar practice directed my questions toward constructions of meaning in the courtroom.

My identity as a young-looking, white woman interning at Greenville Community Court certainly influenced aspects of my data collection. When I initially entered the field, it was very much a "boys club," and I had to actively negotiate my status as a woman in the field. I quickly learned to dress professionally but frumpily and to laugh at jokes that I might have scoffed at in my everyday life. During my fieldwork, whenever I met someone new, I introduced myself as an intern who was conducting research on community courts for a dissertation. Despite their knowledge that I was engaged in data collection (along with repeated reminders), I did not get the impression that court actors were cautious around me—no one joked about my being an interloper, and fewer than a handful of comments over the course of eleven months were explicitly "off the record." I believe that the court actors were not concerned with my position as a researcher because they were incredibly generous people who strongly believed in community courts and their mission, and because I look(ed) like a nonthreatening white teenager and not an authoritative scholar. Over time, I found my place in the organizational culture at Greenville Community Court; to many, I was a wall fixture or the intern who drank black coffee, and to others, I became a friend.

After eight months, I had exhausted the time period that the state allotted for a court intern. At this point, I embarked on a three-month period of data collection wherein I observed court as a "member of the public," watching from the benches with defendants and their loved ones. Court staff and I remained friendly, so during this period, I continued to have access to meetings that I wanted to attend, and I continued to help court staff with grunt work.

CODING AND ANALYZING

My data come from detailed field notes, following the guidance of Robert Emerson, Rachel Fretz, and Linda Shaw's *Writing Ethnographic Fieldnotes* (1995). I took copious notes during court cases and during meetings (another benefit of being an intern—my furious note-taking was never questioned). People in my "real life" have told me that I am easy to talk to and a good listener, a skill that I am sure translated to my fieldwork. I was friendly and eager to listen in interactions with court actors, and I kept this self-presentation even in moments of discomfort, laughing and smiling along during conversations about stupid defendants and good-looking women. Like all good ethnographers, I used the bathroom (luckily it was a single-stall room) to write field notes when I knew I couldn't otherwise or to let down my guard (Goffman 1959). I sometimes left myself voicemails on my phone on the drive home, to be sure I remembered a specific conversation or to remind myself to pursue a certain point of inquiry. In the evenings, I typed field notes that I filled with detail; Clinton Sanders and Gaye Tuchman mentored me, emphasizing thick description and inductive reasoning. I coded and analyzed my data using a grounded-theory approach (Charmaz 2006; Lofland and Lofland 1995; Strauss and Corbin 1994), which "consist[s] of simultaneous data collection and analysis, with each informing and focusing the other throughout the research process[,] . . . [resulting] in an analytic interpretation of participants' worlds and of the processes constituting how these worlds are constructed" (Charmaz 2006: 508).

VALIDITY, RELIABILITY, AND GENERALIZABILITY

Validity of measurement is a central concern in scientific research. How do I know that what I am measuring is real? In the social sciences, this concern is acutely felt; as social scientists measure concepts instead of physical realities, our measurements are subject to criticism.

While concerns regarding validity abound in the social sciences, they are not method-specific. Human beings create all methodological tools, and all involve multiple subjective decisions about measurement and research design.

Several features of ethnography in general and of my research design specifically address concerns regarding validity. In the grounded-theory method, participants' understandings of their own worlds guide the researcher's data collection and analysis. As Kathy Charmaz writes, "The hallmark of grounded theory . . . consists of the researcher deriving his or her analytic categories directly from the data, not from preconceived concepts or hypotheses" (1995: 32). As such, my analysis emerged not from my own expectations about community courts but from deep engagement with my field notes. Unlike cross-sectional designs, which measure a phenomenon at one point in time, ethnography is a longitudinal data-collection process that allows researchers to repeatedly measure concepts over a long period of time. Because I was in the field for eleven months, I am confident that the patterns that I describe throughout the book are indeed patterns. Two examples illustrate this claim. I observed two judges (and sometimes substitute judges) preside over Greenville Community Court. This "natural" change in my field site allowed me to understand that accountability in the courtroom is not the result of an individual judge's personality but an organizing feature of the court. Consistent measurement of cases involving minors and other young people allowed me to understand the "anti–underage drinking docket" (described in Chapter 6) as exceptional in its form and routine in the court's embrace of flexible punishment. Aside from consistent measurement, ethnographers employ intra-method triangulation to shore up their claims. I triangulated my findings by co-constructing field interviews often and with most actors whom I met over the course of my research. About four months into my fieldwork, Greenville Community Court hired another intern, whom I call Becca in this text. By the time I met Becca, I had already made my methodological blunders and had a decent working idea of what was happening in this court. Becca was another "insider/outsider," and I often talked to her to triangulate my analyses with someone who was not "native" to the court. Finally, existing research provided another point of triangulation.

There is also the question of generalizability: how can one's findings from a specific field site apply to other field sites? The generalizability of ethnographic work is not about confidence intervals and sampling techniques, as it is in quantitative work. Instead, the concern for generalizability of ethnographic work relies on the generalizability of the process and findings rather than the generalizability of the sample. As such, we look to existing literature to help us understand whether what "we see" is in fact what is "really there." Court ethnographies by Malcolm Feeley, Carla Barrett, and Leslie Paik grounded my work, as did other scholarship on specialized courts. Studies done by Rebecca Tiger, James Nolan, and Jennifer Murphy helped me adjudicate between broader patterns of specialized courts and unique features of Greenville Community Court.

PRESENTATION OF DATA

Stylistically, in this book, I err on the side of Clifford Geertz's (1973) call for "thick description" and have worked diligently to make my writing clear and somewhat artful (or at least not terribly boring). I aim to present my data with fairness and kindness toward my respondents. Greenville Community Court's mission to address often-overlooked community concerns and to treat defendants fairly is decent. While this book is ultimately critical of community courts' missions and practices, I do not judge my respondents for their service therein. The people who work at Greenville Community Court are kind, intelligent, and hardworking, and they are doing their best to repair a broken system.

Notes

INTRODUCTION

1. Cases that are successfully disposed of through community service or treatment are "nolled." A nolle is a *nolle prosequi*, a legal term that translates to "unwilling to pursue." This means the case will be "erased" from the defendant's record after a stipulated period of time. In the state in which I did my fieldwork, a case remains on the defendant's record for thirteen months. This waiting period ensures that the case may be reopened should new evidence be found. Furthermore, if the defendant is re-arrested within that thirteen-month period, the prosecutor may use the charges that were nolled to argue for a longer sentence. The kinds of cases at Greenville Community Court would not be affected by an accumulation of new evidence, but they are affected by the accumulation of charges. That is, if a defendant successfully completes community service on a larceny charge and is re-arrested for another larceny charge within thirteen months, he or she may be charged as a persistent larceny offender. If the defendant does not accumulate any new charges during those thirteen months, the case is "erased" from some official records. Police reports and inquiries about criminal conduct would not have access to the nolled case. Records would turn up clean. However, internal judicial records would still show the case.

2. In addition to pseudonyms, I have also altered some identifiable characteristics of personnel, and some people in this book are composites created from more than one person. These practices are all typical in ethnographic research, although scholarly debates around these issues continue. See Jerolmack and Murphy 2017.

3. Senate confirmation hearings, September 13, 2005.

CHAPTER 1

1. In this book, I refer to judges by their title and last names and all other court staff members by their first names. I do so to preserve how court staff referred to

one another; no one called judges by their first names, and court staffers were only referred to by their last names when interacting with defendants. Defendants were always referred to by their last names along with their honorifics (i.e., Mr. or Ms.) in official court proceedings and usually by last name only when court staff discussed a case outside the official docket. I preserve these naming conventions in this book because they convey information about status at Greenville Community Court.

2. A quick note on language around sex work and prostitution: when I discuss criminal charges or the kind of case related to sex work, I use the word "prostitution." When I refer to the people engaged in sex work, I use the term "sex worker." When other people at Greenville Community Court referred to people engaged in sex work, in this book I preserve the respondents' language. Additionally, I understand that defendants who may have pled guilty on prostitution charges may not have been engaged in sex work.

3. I borrow this metaphor from Bradley E. Wright's undergraduate criminology class at the University of Connecticut.

4. While James Wilson and George Kelling provide examples of visible signs of disorder, their definition allows for a great deal of flexibility. Perceptions of and thresholds for disorderliness may vary by neighborhood (Wilson and Kelling 1982; Skogan 1990). Wilson and Kelling view the vagueness of their concept of disorder as necessary and integral to broken-windows policing; they argue that officers must develop contextual knowledge to practice discretion wisely. Bernard Harcourt (2001) argues that Wilson and Kelling's category of disorganization is tenuously held together by the notion of "irregularity." For Harcourt, the vagueness of the category of "disorder" is indicative of the new juridical power structures described in Michel Foucault's writing. The conflation of "the abnormal" or "the disorderly" with "criminal" justifies penal intervention, criminalization, and surveillance.

5. Therapeutic jurisprudence may also be situated in arguments for and against indeterminate sentencing (Winick 1999).

6. Defendants may hire private attorneys, but most do not.

7. It should be noted that the interpretation of community policing and zero-tolerance policing may substantially vary by neighborhood. Specifically, neighborhoods in which community members distrust the police and/or believe that their rights are being infringed through zero-tolerance tactics do not experience an increase in collective agency, nor do they develop positive associations with law enforcement (Harcourt 2001).

8. Formerly, the Times Square Business Improvement District.

9. James Nolan's excellent book *The Therapeutic State* (1998) thoroughly traces how the state used therapeutic narratives as a source of legitimation for its power and reach in the late twentieth century.

10. Robert Sampson and Stephen Raudenbush define *collective efficacy* as "the linkage of cohesion and mutual trust with shared expectations for intervening in support of neighborhood social control" (1999: 612–613).

11. The studies summarized in this paragraph are by no means an exhaustive review of empirical tests of broken windows theory. I describe these particular studies because they are important and frequently referenced in scholarship.

12. "Net widening" refers to an increase in criminal justice control and supervision.

13. In 1991 and 1992, federal courts overturned these laws in New York and California. In Greenville, aggressive panhandlers can be fined up to $90 and face up to thirty days in jail. Additionally, I should note that panhandling ordinances are fre-

quently proposed and passed in local governments throughout the United States, and the American Civil Liberties Union (ACLU) is often involved in legal actions aimed at repealing these ordinances.

14. Wilson and Kelling advocate for police officers' use of discretion in enforcement.

15. While many contend that net widening comes from enforcement (Harcourt 2001; McArdle and Erzen 2001), empirical studies do not find evidence in support of this assertion. See Golub et al. 2003.

CHAPTER 2

1. A small but significant prisoners' rights movement existed at this time. See Friedman 1994: 312–316 and Thompson 2017.

2. Neo-Marxist theories argue that rehabilitation is a tool of social-class control. Rehabilitative punishments take marginalized and poor groups and socialize them into roles that are conducive to capitalist interests. If they are unable to conform, then they are removed from the labor pool. Labeling theories claim that when social-control agents/criminal justice actors define someone as needing rehabilitation, the label is so pervasive that the individual's chance to prove him- or herself as no longer criminal is nearly impossible. A compelling critique in this vein was levied by David Rosenhan's (1973) experiment, in which experimenters who were not mentally ill gained admission to mental hospitals and provided honest information aside from the claimed condition of "hearing voices." After admittance, the "pseudopatients" acted as they normally would, but mental-health professionals interpreted their behavior as symptomatic of their mental illnesses.

3. This quote is from the introduction of James Q. Wilson's revised edition of *Thinking about Crime* (1983). The original edition was published in 1975.

4. Although Robert Martinson's article contains some caveats for the lack of programmatic success in his review, and he would later retract his position that programs have no effect on recidivism (Martinson 1979), the phrase "nothing works" became a catch-all for the futility of rehabilitation.

5. Franklin Zimring and David Johnson (2006) argue that the movement against rehabilitation and indeterminate sentencing was also motivated by "a decline in trust of government" that began in the 1970s and continues to the present.

6. Violent-crime rates continued to increase nationally until peaking in 1991 at a rate of 758.2 per 100,000 people.

7. Increasing crime rates were not the only reason that crime became politicized. For a more in-depth discussion, see Zimring and Johnson 2006 and Cullen and Gilbert 1982.

8. For offenders who had mental-health issues or drug problems, Midtown Community Court connected them to treatment programs, such as programs for male, female, and transgender prostitutes; in-house drug-abuse counseling; and anti-shoplifting programming. Offenders without medicalized issues could enroll in Times Square Ink, an in-house optional program that provided job training and a minimal stipend. This program allowed offenders to build their résumés, which was intended to help them gain employment.

9. Midtown Community Court did not actually end up using the Longacre Theatre space. Instead, it is housed in a building that used to be a magistrate court on Fifty-Fourth Street.

10. I revisit this concept in Chapter 6, where I identify community courts' flexibility in both procedure and mission as their fundamental strength as an organization.

CHAPTER 3

1. This list is adapted from an internal document at Greenville Community Court.

2. The placement of the toilet for defendants in the holding cell posed problems when women were in lockup; many of the marshals who monitored defendants in lockup were men because it was rare for *only* female defendants to be in lockup.

3. Treatment options varied by a defendant's criminal record, perception of the severity of the substance-abuse issue, perception of the needs of the defendant, and the availability of funding and space in programs. The notable exception to this type of exploration of treatment options (although limited) occurred when the defendant was a sex worker. Greenville Community Court had its own internal program—called Women's Diversion Program—that handled defendants in almost every prostitution case. This outpatient program ran for two consecutive weeks every three months.

4. During the stage in my fieldwork where I only sat and watched court as if I were waiting to be called, if a marshal did not know me, he or she would come over to me and ask me to stop taking notes. I often explained that I had permission to do so, and with a glance from the judge, I was allowed to continue.

5. During my fieldwork, laws for cases involving minors changed: the court instituted a separate docket for minors, which required the courtroom to be closed to the public. The judges kindly allowed me to remain in the courtroom during these cases.

6. I am unable to comment on Greenville Community Court's recidivism rate. I asked for it on multiple occasions, but it does not keep internal records of repeat offenders. The only way to examine recidivism would have been to obtain permission from the state judicial office, which I did not pursue.

7. The court cannot release a minor without the presence of a legal guardian or family member over the age of eighteen.

CHAPTER 4

1. It was fairly rare for Gary, the prosecutor, to decide that he did not want to pursue the charges listed on the police report. In some instances, he would make this decision based on the lack of information in the police report. In other cases, he would simply decide that it was not worth pursuing. Once, Gary dismissed a case in which the defendant was selling ice cream without a license. With mock outrage, he exclaimed, "Oh, God! Selling ice cream in a parking lot without a license! Oh, God! [*siren noise*]" He then added that the defendant was too old for him to pursue charges.

2. I cannot state the compliance rates of community service through Greenville Community Court in contrast with those of the superior court. However, other studies of Midtown Community Court and Hennepin County Community Court in Minneapolis find that community courts have a higher compliance rate than do traditional courts. That being said, Michele Sviridoff et al.'s analysis does not control for offense type (Eckberg 2001; Sviridoff et al. 2000, 2002).

3. Certainly there were people who were processed at Greenville Community Court for minor offenses but had more serious pending issues at the superior court. In those cases, the serious charge always took precedence, and so the case was transferred "across

the street." It is unclear and unimportant here whether any of these defendants pled not guilty to any or all of their charges.

4. Pretrial hearings are a common practice at traditional courts. They are held before a judge to determine whether a prosecutor has sufficient evidence to bring a case to trial. Such hearings are standard procedures. They also tend to include last-ditch attempts to resolve the issues without going to trial, as trials are expensive and time-consuming for the state. I never witnessed a pretrial hearing at Greenville Community Court.

5. Marc Galanter's primary point is about large parties, such as insurance companies and corporations, but his insights regarding institutional knowledge apply to individuals with repeated contact with the justice system as well.

6. Nick explained the program to me: "It is really tough. Developed in Puerto Rico, so it usually caters to that population. It's not exclusive, but there are some cultural aspects to the program. It's independent of state money, and sometimes they raise money by going door to door, like a salesman-type thing. It's a two-year program, and usually people who go through it become counselors. There was actually some legal battle about it in Pennsylvania, because they aren't funded by state money, and yet these people without licenses are basically drug counselors, so now it's illegal there. It's loosely organized, so it varies from state to state."

7. For confidentiality reasons, I cannot cite the exact source of these quotations.

CHAPTER 5

1. If someone suffered from a mental illness and killed another person, it would be reasonable to sentence that defendant to jail despite concerns about culpability, as he or she would pose a threat to others.

2. Greenville Community Court avoided labeling prostitution charges in court as such, as doing so was thought to be further stigmatizing to the defendants.

3. The judge referenced nine months here instead of eighteen, which Gary advocated for, because Ms. Torres had two soliciting charges that could be served consecutively (hence the eighteen months) or concurrently (hence the nine months).

4. I do not know of any late-night libraries.

5. The Women's Diversion Program was funded through an external grant.

6. The "mitt" was the remittance document that a defendant would take back to jail. It noted the progress of the case and the sentence or the continuance dates. It could also contain notes on the defendant him- or herself. Common notes on the mitt included "place in medical detox" if a defendant was being sent to jail with serious substance-abuse issues, "place on suicide watch" if the court believed the defendant may commit suicide, or "defendant is pregnant" for defendants who were pregnant, signaling a need for prenatal care.

7. By "pays," the judge meant "pays me the time he owes" (i.e., repays his debt to society).

CHAPTER 6

1. For confidentiality reasons, I cannot cite the exact source of this quotation from Gary.

2. Per IRB guidance regarding confidentiality, I cannot cite the exact source of this quotation.

3. For confidentiality reasons, I cannot cite the exact source of this quotation from the state's attorney.

4. Residents in this meeting understood quality of life, disorder, and neighborhood cleanliness in a manner consistent with broken windows theory. In broken windows theory, disorder includes both physical disorder (which Sampson and Raudenbush define as "the deterioration of urban landscapes, for example, graffiti on buildings, abandoned cars, broken windows, and garbage in the streets" [1999: 603–604]) and social disorder (which they define as "behavior usually involving strangers and considered threatening such as verbal harassment on the street, open solicitation for prostitution, public intoxication, and rowdy groups of young males in public" [1999: 604]). The demarcation of physical and social disorder, the operationalization of these concepts, and the moral and political ramifications of categorizing certain people as disorderly have provoked much debate, which I cover in some detail in Chapter 1.

5. Jaquan Roberts did not kill two women. Two women were killed when other people were shooting, aiming to kill Roberts. I don't know whether the attendees were aware of that.

6. A notable exception is the Boston Police Department's partnership with the Ten Point Coalition (a group of black clergy and laypeople) under Operation Ceasefire (Brunson et al. 2015). However, even with the success of that program, there remains unease, as evidenced by the title of Rod Brunson et al.'s article, "We Trust You, but Not That Much: Examining Police–Black Clergy Partnerships to Reduce Youth Violence."

CONCLUSION

1. Emily Martin's *Flexible Bodies* (1994) tackles far more than immunology and the body. Chapter 7, in particular, traces the idea of flexible systems across a wide variety of venues, such as religious thought, feminism, and product markets, that are not otherwise addressed in this book.

2. Rebecca Tiger (2013) discovers a similar pattern in her study of drug courts. She argues that drug courts recycle and rebrand the logic of rehabilitation from the Progressive Era with updated medicalized "knowledge."

METHODOLOGICAL APPENDIX

1. In the interest of confidentiality, I cannot describe my specific reasons for selecting Greenville Community Court.

2. This is not to say that I was completely derelict in these duties; there were certainly times when I helped court actors. I worked in social services once when the department was understaffed. I compiled a binder with readings that included information about broken windows theory, David Wexler's writings on therapeutic jurisprudence, informational pamphlets and data from the Center for Court Innovation, and writings from the court staff itself, among other things. After our visit to the women's prison, I helped the judge spearhead a book drive for Spanish-language books. As a part of that drive, I solicited donations from my friends, colleagues, and Greenville's Latinx community organizations.

References

Allen, Francis A. 1981. *The Decline of the Rehabilitative Ideal: Penal Policy and Social Purpose*. New Haven, CT: Yale University Press.

Almore, Mary G. 1977. "Rehabilitation: The 'Fudge Factor' of Corrections." *Criminology* 15 (2): 147–148.

American Friends Service Committee. 1971. *Struggle for Justice*. New York: Hill and Wang.

Anderson, David C. 1996. "In New York City, a 'Community Court' and a New Legal Culture." National Institute of Justice Program Focus.

Ashforth, Blake E., and Barrie W. Gibbs. 1990. "The Double-Edge of Organizational Legitimation." *Organization Science* 1 (2): 177–194.

Bailey, Walter C. 1966. "Correctional Outcome: An Evaluation of 100 Reports." *Journal of Criminal Law, Criminology and Police Science* 57 (2): 153–160.

Baker, Kimberly M. 2013. "Decision Making in a Hybrid Organization: A Case Study of a Southwestern Drug Court Treatment Program." *Law and Social Inquiry* 38 (1): 27–54.

Baron, James N., Michael T. Hannan, and M. Diane Burton. 2001. "Labor Pains: Change in Organizational Models and Employee Turnover in Young, High-Tech Firms." *American Journal of Sociology* 106 (4): 960–1012.

Barrett, Carla J. 2012. *Courting Kids: Inside an Experimental Youth Court*. New York: New York University Press.

Bauman, Zygmunt. 2001. *Community: Seeking Safety in an Insecure World*. Cambridge, UK: Polity.

———. 2013. *Liquid Modernity*. Cambridge, UK: John Wiley and Sons.

Beck, Allen J., and Bernard E. Shipley. 1989. *Recidivism of Prisoners Released in 1983*. Washington, DC: U.S. Bureau of Justice Statistics.

Becker, Howard S. 1982. *Art Worlds*. Berkeley: University of California Press.

Belknap, Joanne. 2001. *The Invisible Woman: Gender, Crime, and Justice*. Belmont, CA: Wadsworth.

Bell, Colin, and Howard Newby. 1971. *Community Studies: An Introduction to the Sociology of the Local Community*. London: George Allen and Unwin.

Berger, Dan. 2007. "Regarding the Imprisonment of Others: Prison Abuse Photographs and Social Change." *International Journal of Communication* 1:210–237.

Berman, Greg, and John Feinblatt. 2005. *Good Courts: The Case for Problem-Solving Justice*. New York: New Press.

Bibas, Stephanos. 2004. "Plea Bargaining outside the Shadow of Trial." *Harvard Law Review* 117 (8): 2463–2547.

Blomberg, Thomas G., William Bales, and Karen Reed. 1993. "Intermediate Punishment: Redistributing or Extending Social Control?" *Crime, Law and Social Change* 19:187–201.

Blomberg, Thomas, and Karol Lucken. 1994. "Stacking the Deck by Piling Up Sanctions: Is Intermediate Punishment Destined to Fail?" *Howard Journal of Criminal Justice* 33:62–80.

Blumberg, Abraham S. 1966. "The Practice of Law as a Confidence Game: Organizational Cooperation of a Profession." *Law and Society Review* 1 (2): 15–40.

———. 1967. *Criminal Justice*. Chicago: Quadrangle Books.

Booher-Jennings, Jennifer. 2005. "Below the Bubble: 'Educational Triage' and the Texas Accountability System." *American Educational Research Journal* 42 (2): 231–268.

Bourdieu, Pierre. 1977. *Outline of a Theory of Practice*. Translated by Richard Nice. New York: Cambridge University Press.

Braithwaite, John. 1989. *Crime, Shame, and Reintegration*. Cambridge: Cambridge University Press.

Brunson, Rod K., Anthony A. Braga, David M. Hureau, and Kashea Pegram. 2015. "We Trust You, but Not That Much: Examining Police–Black Clergy Partnerships to Reduce Youth Violence." *Justice Quarterly* 32 (6): 1006–1036.

Burns, Stacy Lee, and Mark Peyrot. 2003. "Tough Love: Nurturing and Coercing Responsibility and Recovery in California Drug Courts." *Social Problems* 50 (3): 416–438.

Casey, Timothy. 2005. "When Good Intentions Are Not Enough: Problem-Solving Courts and the Impending Crisis of Legitimacy." *Southern Methodist University Law Review* 57 (4): 1459–1518.

Center for Court Innovation. 2012. "Community Justice 2012: The International Conference of Community Courts." Accessed January 18, 2019. https://www.courtinnovation.org/articles/community-justice-2012-international-conference-community-courts.

———. 2016. "Community Justice 2016: The International Conference of Community Courts." Accessed January 18, 2019. https://www.courtinnovation.org/articles/community-justice-2016.

———. n.d. Accessed 2013. https://www.courtinnovation.org/topic/community-court.

Chan, Janet B. L., and Richard Victor Ericson. 1981. *Decarceration and the Economy of Penal Reform*. Toronto: Centre of Criminology, University of Toronto.

Charmaz, Kathy. 1995. "Grounded Theory." In *Rethinking Methods in Psychology*, ed. Jonathan A. Smith, Rom Harré, and Luk Van Langenhove, 27–65. London: Sage.

———. 2006. *Constructing Grounded Theory: A Practical Guide through Qualitative Analysis*. London: Sage Publications.

Chesluk, Benjamin. 2007. *Money Jungle: Imagining the New Times Square*. New Brunswick, NJ: Rutgers University Press.

Chesney-Lind, Meda. 1989. "Girls' Crime and Woman's Place: Toward a Feminist Model of Female Delinquency." *Crime and Delinquency* 35:5–29.

Clegg, Stewart, and Carmen Baumeler. 2010. "Essai: From Iron Cages to Liquid Modernity in Organization Analysis." *Organization Studies* 31 (12): 1713–1733.

Collins, Patricia Hill. 2004. *Black Sexual Politics: African Americans, Gender, and the New Racism*. New York: Routledge.

Conrad, Peter. 2007. *The Medicalization of Society: On the Transformation of Human Conditions into Treatable Disorders*. Baltimore, MD: John Hopkins University Press.

Cooper, Davina. 1995. "Local Government Legal Consciousness in the Shadow of Juridification." *Journal of Law and Society* 22 (4): 506–526.

Crawford, Adam. 1999. *The Local Governance of Crime Control: Appeals to Community and Partnerships*. New York: Oxford University Press.

Cullen, Francis T., and K. E. Gilbert. 1982. *Reaffirming Rehabilitation*. Cincinnati: Anderson Press.

Deener, Andrew. 2012. *Venice: A Contested Bohemia in Los Angeles*. Chicago: University of Chicago Press.

Denzin, Norman K. 1987. *The Recovering Alcoholic*. Newbury Park, CA: Sage Publications.

DiMaggio, Paul J., and Walter W. Powell. 1991. "The Iron Cage Revisited." In *The New Institutionalism in Organizational Analysis*, ed. Walter W. Powell and Paul J. DiMaggio, 63–82. Chicago: University of Chicago Press.

Dixon, Jo. 1995. "The Organizational Context of Criminal Sentencing." *American Journal of Sociology* 100 (5): 1157–1198.

Douglas Creed, W. E., Maureen A. Scully, and John R. Austin. 2002. "Clothes Make the Person? The Tailoring of Legitimating Accounts and the Social Construction of Identity." *Organization Science* 13 (5): 475–496.

Duneier, Mitchell. 1999. *Sidewalk*. New York: Farrar, Strauss and Giroux.

Durkheim, Émile. (1895) 1982. *The Rules of Sociological Method*. Translated by W. D. Halls. New York: Free Press.

Eck, John E., and Edward R. Maguire. 2000. "Have Changes in Policing Reduced Violent Crime? An Assessment of the Evidence." In *The Crime Drop in America*, ed. Alfred Blumstein and Joel Wallman, 207–265. Cambridge: Cambridge University Press.

Eckberg, Deborah A. 2001. "Hennepin County Community Justice Project: Summary Report of Short-Term Evaluation." Hennepin County, MN: Hennepin County District Court Research Department.

Eisenstein, James, Roy B. Flemming, and Peter Nardulli. 1988. *The Contours of Justice: Communities and Their Courts*. Boston: Little Brown.

Eisenstein, James, and Herbert Jacob. 1977. *Felony Justice: An Organizational Analysis of Criminal Courts*. Boston: Little, Brown.

Elias, Norbert. (1939) 1978. *The Civilizing Process: The History of Manners*. Oxford, UK: Blackwell Publishing.

Emerson, Robert M. 1969. *Judging Juveniles: Context and Process in a Juvenile Court*. Chicago: Adeline Publishing.

Emerson, Robert M., Rachel I. Fretz, and Linda L. Shaw. 1995. *Writing Ethnographic Fieldnotes*. Chicago: University of Chicago Press.

Emirbayer, Mustafa, and Victoria Johnson. 2008. "Bourdieu and Organizational Analysis." *Theory and Society* 37 (1): 1–44.

Engen, Rodney L., and Sara Steen. 2000. "The Power to Punish: Discretion and Sentencing Reform in the War on Drugs." *American Journal of Sociology* 105 (5): 1357–1395.

Ewick, Patricia, and Susan S. Silbey. 1998. *The Common Place of Law: Stories from Everyday Life*. Chicago: University of Chicago Press.

Fagan, Jeffrey, and Victoria Malkin. 2002. "Theorizing Community Justice through Community Courts." *Fordham Urban Law Journal* 30 (3): 897–953.

Federal Bureau of Investigation. n.d. Uniform Crime Report. Accessed 2017. https://www.ucrdatatool.gov/Search/Crime/Local/JurisbyJuris.cfm.

Feeley, Malcolm M. 1992. *The Process Is the Punishment: Handling Cases in a Lower Criminal Court*. New York: Russell Sage Foundation Publications.

Feeley, Malcolm M., and Jonathan Simon. 1992. "The New Penology: Notes on the Emerging Strategy of Corrections and Its Implications." *Criminology* 30 (4): 449–474.

Feinblatt, John, Greg Berman, and Michele Sviridoff. 1997. "Neighborhood Justice at the Midtown Community Court." *Crime and Place Plenary Papers of the 1997 Conference*. Washington, DC: National Institute of Justice.

Ferretti, Fred. 1971a. "Autopsies Show Shots Killed 9 Attica Hostages, Not Knives; State Official Admits Mistake." *New York Times*, September 15, p. 1.

———. 1971b. "'Like a War Zone': Air and Ground Attack Follows Refusal of Convicts to Yield." *New York Times*, September 14, p. 1.

Fine, Gary. 1995. "Public Narration and Group Culture: Discerning Discourse in Social Movements." In *Social Movements and Culture*, ed. Hank Johnston and Bert Klandermas, 127–143. Minneapolis: University of Minnesota Press.

Flemming, Roy B., Peter F. Nardulli, and James Eisenstein. 1992. *The Craft of Justice: Politics and Work in Criminal Court Communities*. Philadelphia: University of Pennsylvania Press.

Foucault, Michel. 1979. *Discipline and Punish: The Birth of the Prison*. New York: Vintage.

Fratello, Jennifer, Andres F. Rengifo, and Jennifer Trone. 2013. *Coming of Age with Stop and Frisk: Experiences, Self-Perceptions, and Public Safety Implications*. New York: Vera Institute of Justice.

Friedland, Roger, and Robert R. Alford. 1991. "Bringing Society Back In: Symbols, Practices and Institutional Contradictions." In *The New Institutionalism in Organizational Analysis*, ed. Walter W. Powell and Paul J. DiMaggio, 232–263. Chicago: University of Chicago Press.

Friedman, Lawrence. 1994. *Crime and Punishment in American History*. New York: Basic Books.

Galanter, Marc. 1974. "Why the Haves Come Out Ahead: Speculations on the Limits of Legal Change." *Law and Society Review* 9 (1): 95–160.

Garland, David. 1990. *Punishment and Modern Society: A Study in Social Theory*. Chicago: University of Chicago Press.

———. 2001. *The Culture of Control: Crime and Social Order and Contemporary Society*. Chicago: University of Chicago Press.

Geertz, Clifford. 1973. *The Interpretation of Cultures: Selected Essays*. New York: Basic Books.

Gelman, Andrew, Jeffrey Fagan, and Alex Kiss. 2007. "An Analysis of the New York City Police Department's 'Stop-and-Frisk' Policy in the Context of Claims of Racial Bias." *Journal of the American Statistical Association* 102 (479): 813–823.

Gieryn, Thomas F. 1999. *Cultural Boundaries of Science: Credibility on the Line.* Chicago: University of Chicago Press.

Giuliani, Rudolph W., and William J. Bratton. 1994. *Police Strategy No. 5: Reclaiming the Public Spaces of New York.* New York: New York City Police Department.

Goffman, Erving. 1959. *The Presentation of Self in Everyday Life.* New York: Doubleday.

Golub, Andrew, Bruce D. Johnson, Angela Taylor, and John Eterno. 2003. "Quality-of-Life Policing: Do Offenders Get the Message?" *Policing: An International Journal of Police Strategies and Management* 26 (4): 690–707.

Greenwood, Royston, Christine Oliver, Kerstin Sahlin, and Roy Suddaby, eds. 2008. "Introduction." In *The Sage Handbook of Organizational Institutionalism*, 1–71. New York: Sage Publications.

Gubrium, Jaber F., and James A. Holstein. 1997. *The New Language of Qualitative Method.* New York: Oxford University Press.

———. 2001. *Handbook of Interview Research: Context and Method.* London: Sage Publications.

Gulbrandsen, Magnus. 2011. "Research Institutes as Hybrid Organizations: Central Challenges to Their Legitimacy." *Policy Sciences* 44 (3): 215–230.

Hannah-Moffat, Kelly. 2005. "Criminogenic Needs and the Transformative Risk Subject." *Punishment and Society* 7 (1): 29–51.

Hannah-Moffat, Kelly, and Paula Maurutto. 2012. "Shifting Targeted Forms of Penal Governance: Bail, Punishment and Specialized Courts." *Theoretical Criminology* 16 (2): 201–219.

Harcourt, Bernard E. 2001. *The Illusion of Order: The False Promise of Broken Windows Policing.* Cambridge, MA: Harvard University Press.

Harvey, David. 1990. *The Condition of Postmodernity: An Enquiry into the Origins of Cultural Change.* Malden, MA: Blackwell Publishers.

Herbert, Steve. 2009. *Citizens, Cops, and Power: Recognizing the Limits of Community.* Chicago: University of Chicago Press.

Herbert, Steve, and Elizabeth Brown. 2006. "Conceptions of Space and Crime in the Punitive Neoliberal City." *Antipode* 38 (4): 755–777.

Hochschild, Arlie Russell. 1997. *The Time Bind: When Home Becomes Work and Work Becomes Home.* New York: Henry Holt.

Howe, Adrian. 1994. *Punish and Critique: Towards a Feminist Analysis of Penality.* New York: Routledge.

Hughes, Everett C. 1936. "The Ecological Aspect of Institutions." *American Sociological Review* 1 (2): 180–189.

Hutchinson, Steven. 2006. "Countering Catastrophic Criminology: Reform, Punishment and the Modern Liberal Compromise." *Punishment and Society* 8 (4): 443–467.

Hylton, John H. 1981. "Community Corrections and Social Control: The Case of Saskatchewan, Canada." *Crime, Law and Social Change* 5 (2): 193–215.

Jackson, Bruce. 1968. "Our Prisons Are Criminal." *New York Times Magazine*, September 22, pp. 45–47, 54–60.

Jackson, Gregory. 2005. "Contested Boundaries: Ambiguity and Creativity in the Evolution of German Codetermination." In *Beyond Continuity: Institutional Change in*

Advanced Political Economies, ed. Wolfgang Streeck and Kathleen Thelen, 229–252. New York: Oxford University Press.

Jeffery, C. Ray. 1969. "Comments of the Editor." *Criminologica* 7 (1): 2–4.

Jerolmack, Colin, and Alexandra K. Murphy. 2017. "The Ethical Dilemmas and Social Scientific Trade-offs of Masking in Ethnography." *Sociological Methods and Research*, doi: 10.1177/0049124117701483.

Jolliffe, Darrick, and David Farrington. 2009. *Initial Evaluation of Reconviction Rates in Community Justice Initiatives*. London: Ministry of Justice UK.

Jones-Brown, Delores. 2007. "Forever the Symbolic Assailant: The More Things Change, the More They Remain the Same." *Criminology and Public Policy* 6 (1): 103–121.

Justice Education Center. 2002. *Evaluation of the Hartford Community Court*. Hartford, CT: Justice Education Center.

Kaplan, Fred. 1997. "Looks Count." *Boston Globe*, January 19, p. E1.

Katz, Charles M., Vincent J. Webb, and David R. Schaefer. 2001. "An Assessment of the Impact of Quality-of-Life Policing on Crime and Disorder." *Justice Quarterly* 18 (4): 825–876.

Kaye, Kerwin. 2013. "Rehabilitating the 'Drugs Lifestyle': Criminal Justice, Social Control, and the Cultivation of Agency." *Ethnography* 14 (2): 207–232.

Kelling, George L., and Catherine M. Coles. 1997. *Fixing Broken Windows: Restoring Order and Reducing Crime in our Communities*. New York: Simon and Schuster.

Kelling, George L., Mona R. Hochberg, Sandra Lee Kaminska, Ann Marie Rocheleau, Dennis P. Rosenbaum, Jeffrey A. Roth, and Wesley G. Skogan. 1998. *The Bureau of Justice Assistance Comprehensive Communities Program: A Preliminary Report*. Washington, DC: National Institute of Justice.

Kerckhoff, Alan C. 1995. "Institutional Arrangements and Stratification Processes in Industrial Societies." *Annual Review of Sociology* 21 (1): 323–347.

Kilmer, Beau, and Jesse Sussell. 2014. "Does San Francisco's Community Justice Center Reduce Criminal Recidivism?" San Francisco: RAND Corporation and the Superior Court of California.

Kohler-Hausmann, Issa. 2018. *Misdemeanorland: Criminal Courts and Social Control in an Age of Broken Windows Policing*. Princeton, NJ: Princeton University Press.

Kupchik, Aaron. 2006. *Judging Juveniles: Prosecuting Adolescents in Adult and Juvenile Courts*. New York: New York University Press.

Kupers, Terry A. 1999. *Prison Madness: The Mental Health Crisis behind Bars and What We Must Do about It*. New York: Jossey-Bass Publishers.

Lane, Eric. 2002. "Due Process and Problem-Solving Courts." *Fordham Urban Law Journal* 30 (3): 955–1026.

Lang, Julius. 2011. "What Is a Community Court? How the Model Is Being Adapted across the United States." Washington, DC: U.S. Bureau of Justice Assistance.

Langan, Patrick A., and David J. Levin. 2002. "Recidivism of Prisoners Released in 1994." Washington, DC: Bureau of Justice Statistics.

Lareau, Annette. 2003. *Unequal Childhoods: Class, Race, and Family Life*. Los Angeles: University of California Press.

Lawrence, Thomas B., and Roy Suddaby. 2006. "Institutions and Institutional Work." In *Handbook of Organizational Studies*, 2nd ed., ed. Stewart R. Clegg, Cynthia Hardy, Thomas Lawrence, and Walter R. Nord, 215–254. London: Sage Publications.

Lee, Cynthia G., Fred L. Cheesman II, David Rottman, Rachel Swaner, Suvi Hynynen

Lambson, Michael Rempel, and Ric Curtis. 2013. *A Community Court Grows in Brooklyn: A Comprehensive Evaluation of the Red Hook Community Justice Center*. Williamsburg, VA: National Center for State Courts.

Lipton, Douglas, Robert L. Martinson, and Judith Wilks. 1975. *Effectiveness of Correctional Treatment: A Survey of Treatment Evaluation Studies*. Westport, CT: Praeger Publishers.

Lofland, John, and Lyn Lofland. 1995. *Analyzing Social Settings*. Belmont, CA: Wadsworth.

Logan, Charles H. 1972. "Evaluation Research in Crime and Delinquency: A Reappraisal." *Journal of Criminal Law, Criminology, and Police Science* 63 (3): 378–387.

Lyons, Richard D. 1993. "1992 Unemployment Rate Hit a 15-Year High." *New York Times*, January 29.

Macleod, Gordon, and Craig Johnstone. 2012. "Stretching Urban Renaissance: Privatizing Space, Civilizing Place, Summoning 'Community.'" *International Journal of Urban and Regional Research* 36 (1): 1–28.

Malkin, Victoria. 2003. "Community Courts and the Process of Accountability: Consensus and Conflict at the Red Hook Community Justice Center." *American Criminal Law Review* 40 (4): 1573–1593.

Martin, Emily. 1994. *Flexible Bodies: Tracking Immunity in American Culture from the Days of Polio to the Age of AIDS*. Boston: Beacon Press.

Martinez, Jimena. 2010. "Building Support for Justice Initiatives: A Communications Toolkit." Washington, DC: U.S. Bureau of Justice Assistance.

Martinson, Robert. 1974. "What Works?—Questions and Answers about Prison Reform." *The Public Interest* 35:22–54.

———. 1979. "New Findings, New Views: A Note of Caution Regarding Sentencing Reform." *Hofstra Law Review* 7 (2): 243–258.

Matthews, Roger. 2005. "The Myth of Punitiveness." *Theoretical Criminology* 9 (2): 175–201.

McArdle, Andrea, and Tanya Erzen, eds. 2001. *Zero Tolerance: Quality of Life and the New Police Brutality in New York City*. New York: New York University Press.

Mechanic, David, and David A. Rochefort. 1990. "Deinstitutionalization: An Appraisal of Reform." *Annual Review of Sociology* 16 (1): 301–327.

Merry, Sally Engle. 1990. *Getting Justice and Getting Even: Legal Consciousness of Working-Class Americans*. Chicago: University of Chicago Press.

Meyer, John W., and Brian Rowan. 1977. "Institutionalized Organizations: Formal Structure as Myth and Ceremony." *American Journal of Sociology* 83 (2): 340–363.

Meyer, John W., and W. Richard Scott. 1983. "Centralization and the Legitimacy Problems of Local Government." In *Organizational Environments: Ritual and Rationality*, ed. John W. Meyer and W. Richard Scott, 199–215. Beverly Hills, CA: Sage.

Morris, Norval, and Michael Tonry. 1991. *Between Prison and Probation: Intermediate Punishments in a Rational Sentencing System*. New York: Oxford University Press.

Murphy, Jennifer. 2015. *Illness or Deviance? Drug Courts, Drug Treatment, and the Ambiguity of Addiction*. Philadelphia: Temple University Press.

Musto, David F. 1997. *The American Disease: Origins of Narcotic Control*. 3rd ed. New York: Oxford University Press.

Myers, Steven Lee. 1993. "Squeegees' Rank High on Next Police Commissioner's Priority List." *New York Times*, December 4, p. 23.

Nader, Laura. 1972. "Up the Anthropologist: Perspectives Gained from Studying Up." *Reinventing Anthropology*, ed. Dell Hymes, 284–311. New York: Pantheon Books.

Nagel, Stuart S., and Marian Neef. 1979. *Decision Theory and the Legal Process*. Lexington, MA: Lexington Books.

Nelken, David. 1984. "Law in Action or Living Law? Back to the Beginning in Sociology of Law." *Legal Studies* 4 (2): 157–174.

New York State Special Commission on Attica. 1972. *The Official Report of the New York State Commission on Attica*. New York: Praeger.

Nolan, James L. 1998. *The Therapeutic State: Justifying Government at Century's End*. New York: New York University Press.

———. 2001. *Reinventing Justice: The American Drug Court Movement*. Princeton, NJ: Princeton University Press.

———. 2009. *Legal Accents, Legal Borrowing: The International Problem-Solving Court Movement*. Princeton, NJ: Princeton University Press.

Nugent-Borakove, Elaine. 2009. *Seattle Municipal Community Court: Outcome Evaluation Final Report*. Denver, CO: Justice Management Institute.

O'Malley, Pat. 1999. "Volatile and Contradictory Punishment." *Theoretical Criminology* 3 (2): 175–196.

Paik, Leslie. 2011. *Discretionary Justice: Looking inside a Juvenile Drug Court*. Piscataway, NJ: Rutgers University Press.

Parenti, Christian. 2000. *Lockdown America: Police and Prisons in the Age of Crisis*. New York: Verso.

Peyrot, Mark. 1991. "Institutional and Organizational Dynamics in Community-Based Drug Abuse Treatment." *Social Problems* 38 (1): 20–33.

Phelps, Michelle S. 2013. "The Paradox of Probation: Community Supervision in the Age of Mass Incarceration." *Law and Policy* 35 (1): 51–80.

———. 2017. "Mass Probation: Toward a More Robust Theory of State Variation in Punishment." *Punishment and Society* 19 (1): 53–73.

Pound, Roscoe. 1910. "Law in Books and Law in Action." *American Law Review* 44:12–36.

Pratt, John. 2000. "Emotive and Ostentatious Punishment." *Punishment and Society* 2 (4): 417–439.

Rankin, Joseph H. 1979. "Changing Attitudes toward Capital Punishment." *Social Forces* 58 (1): 194–211.

Reinarman, Craig. 1994. "The Social Construction of Drug Scares." *Constructions of Deviance: Social Power, Context, and Interaction*, ed. Patricia A. Adler and Peter Adler, 92–105. Belmont, CA: Wadsworth.

Reinarman, Craig, and Harry G. Levine. 1997. *Crack in America: Demon Drugs and Social Justice*. Los Angeles: University of California Press.

Renzulli, Linda A. 2005. "Organizational Environments and the Emergence of Charter Schools in the United States." *Sociology of Education* 78 (1): 1–26.

Richie, Beth. 1996. *Compelled to Crime: The Gender Entrapment of Battered Black Women*. New York: Routledge.

Rios, Victor M. 2011. *Punished: Policing the Lives of Black and Latino Boys*. New York: New York University Press.

Roberts, Julian. 1992. "Public Opinion, Crime, and Criminal Justice." *Crime and Justice: A Review of Research* 16:99–180.

Robinson, Gwen. 2008. "Late-Modern Rehabilitation: The Evolution of a Penal Strategy." *Punishment and Society* 10 (4): 429–445.

Robison, James, and Gerald Smith. 1971. "The Effectiveness of Correctional Programs." *Crime and Delinquency* 17 (1): 67–80.

Rosaldo, Renato. 1993. *Culture and Truth: The Remaking of Social Analysis.* Boston: Beacon Press.

Rose, Nikolas. 2000. "Community, Citizenship, and the Third Way." *American Behavioral Scientist* 43 (9): 1395–1411.

Rosenfeld, Richard, Karen Terry, and Preeti Chauhan, eds. 2014. *Justice Quarterly: Special Issue on the New York Crime Drop* 31 (1): 1–192.

Rosenhan, D. L. 1973. "On Being Sane in Insane Places." *Science* 179 (4070): 250–258.

Ross, Stuart, Mark John Halsey, David Newton Bamford, Nadine Cameron, and Anthony King. 2009. *Evaluation of the Neighbourhood Justice Centre, City of Yarra: Final Report.* Melbourne, Australia: University of Melbourne.

Rouse, Timothy P. 1996. "Conditions for a Successful Status Elevation Ceremony." *Deviant Behavior* 17 (1): 21–42.

Ruef, Martin. 2000. "The Emergence of Organizational Forms: A Community Ecology Approach." *American Journal of Sociology* 106 (3): 658–714.

Ruef, Martin, and W. Richard Scott. 1998. "A Multidimensional Model of Organizational Legitimacy: Hospital Survival in Changing Environments." *Administrative Science Quarterly* 43 (4): 877–904.

Russell-Brown, Katheryn. 2009. *The Color of Crime.* New York: New York University Press.

Sampson, Robert J., and Stephen W. Raudenbush. 1999. "Systematic Social Observation of Public Spaces: A New Look at Disorder in Urban Neighborhoods." *American Journal of Sociology* 105 (3): 603–651.

Schulhofer, Stephen J. 1992. "Plea Bargaining as Disaster." *Yale Law Journal* 101 (8): 1979–2009.

Scott, Robert E., and William J. Stuntz. 1992. "Plea Bargaining as Contract." *Yale Law Journal* 101 (8): 1909–1968.

Seddon, Toby. 2007. "Coerced Drug Treatment in the Criminal Justice System: Conceptual, Ethical and Criminological Issues." *Criminology and Criminal Justice* 7 (3): 269–286.

Sennett, Richard. 2007. *The Culture of the New Capitalism.* New Haven, CT: Yale University Press.

Sered, Susan Starr, and Maureen Norton-Hawk. 2014. *Can't Catch a Break: Gender, Jail, Drugs, and the Limits of Personal Responsibility.* Chicago: University of Chicago Press.

Sgourev, Stoyan V. 2011. "'Wall Street' Meets Wagner: Harnessing Institutional Heterogeneity." *Theoretical Sociology* 40 (4): 385–416.

Simon, Jonathan. 1995. "They Died with Their Boots On: The Boot Camp and the Limits of Modern Penality." *Social Justice* 22 (1): 25–48.

Skogan, Wesley G. 1990. *Disorder and Decline: Crime and the Spiral Decay in American Neighborhoods.* Los Angeles: University of California Press.

Smith, Neil. 2002. "New Globalism, New Urbanism: Gentrification as a Global Urban Strategy." *Antipode* 34 (3): 427–450.

Snell, Tracy L. 1996. *Correctional Populations in the United States, 1993.* Rev. ed. Washington, DC: Bureau of Justice Statistics.

Spring, Joel. 1976. *The Sorting Machine: National Educational Policy since 1945*. New York: David McKay.

Strauss, Anselm, and Juliet Corbin. 1994. "Grounded Theory Methodology." *Handbook of Qualitative Research* 17:273–285.

Stuart, Forrest. 2016. *Down, Out, and Under Arrest: Policing and Everyday Life in Skid Row*. Chicago: University of Chicago Press.

Suchman, Mark C. 1995. "Managing Legitimacy: Strategic and Institutional Approaches." *Academy of Management Review* 20 (3): 571–610.

Suddaby, Roy, and Royston Greenwood. 2005. "Rhetorical Strategies of Legitimacy." *Administrative Science Quarterly* 50 (1): 35–67.

Sviridoff, Michele, David B. Rottman, Brian J. Ostrom, and Richard Curtis. 2000. *Dispensing Justice Locally: The Implementation and Effects of the Midtown Community Court*. Amsterdam, The Netherlands: Harwood Academic Publishers.

Sviridoff, Michele, David B. Rottman, Rob Weidner, Fred Cheesman, Richard Curtis, Randall Hansen, and Brian J. Ostrom. 2002. *Dispensing Justice Locally: The Impacts, Cost and Benefits of the Midtown Community Court*. New York: Center for Court Innovation.

Thompson, Heather Ann. 2010. "Blinded by a 'Barbaric South': Prison Horrors, Inmate Abuse and the Ironic History of the American Penal Reform." In *The Myth of Southern Exceptionalism*, ed. Matthew D. Lassiter and Joseph Crespino, 74–95. New York: Oxford University Press.

———. 2017. *Blood in the Water: The Attica Prison Uprising of 1971 and Its Legacy*. New York: Vintage Books.

Tierney, John. 1995. "The Holy Terror." *New York Times*, December 3, sec. 6, p. 60.

Tiger, Rebecca. 2013. *Judging Addicts: Drug Courts and Coercion in the Justice System*. New York: New York University Press.

Tonry, Michael, and Mary Lynch 1996. "Intermediate Sanctions." *Crime and Justice* 20:99–144.

Travers, Max, and John F. Manzo, eds. 1997. *Law in Action: Ethnomethodological and Conversation Analytic Approaches to Law*. Dartmouth, MA: Aldershot.

Trice, Harrison M., and Paul Michael Roman. 1970. "Delabeling, Relabeling, and Alcoholics Anonymous." *Social Problems* 17 (4): 538–546.

Tyler, Tom R. 1990. *Why People Obey the Law*. Princeton, NJ: Princeton University Press.

Ulmer, Jeffery T. 2005. "The Localized Uses of Federal Sentencing Guidelines in Four U.S. District Courts: Evidence of Processual Order." *Symbolic Interaction* 28:255–279.

Ulmer, Jeffery T., and John H. Kramer. 1996. "Court Communities under Sentencing Guidelines: Dilemmas of Formal Rationality and Sentencing Disparity." *Criminology* 34 (3): 306–332.

Van Cleve, Nicole Gonzalez. 2016. *Crook County: Racism and Injustice in America's Largest Criminal Court*. Stanford, CA: Stanford University Press.

Vitale, Alex S. 2008. *City of Disorder: How the Quality of Life Campaign Transformed New York Politics*. New York: New York University Press.

Waldram, James B. 2012. *Hound Pound Narrative: Sexual Offender Habilitation and the Anthropology of Therapeutic Intervention*. Los Angeles: University of California Press.

Weidner, Robert R., and Chuck Davis. 2000. *Benefits and Costs of the Hennepin County Community Court: A Preliminary Analysis.* Minneapolis: Institute on Criminal Justice, University of Minnesota Law School.

Wells, Amy Stuart, Alejandra Lopez, Janelle Scott, and Jennifer Jellison Holme. 1999. "Charter Schools as Postmodern Paradox: Rethinking Social Stratification in an Age of Deregulated School Choice." *Harvard Educational Review* 69 (2): 172–205.

Werth, Robert. 2013. "The Construction and Stewardship of Responsible Yet Precarious Subjects: Punitive Ideology, Rehabilitation and "Tough Love" among Parole Personnel." *Punishment and Society* 15 (3): 219–246.

Westat. 2012. *East of the River Community Court (ERCC) Evaluation: Final Report.* Rockville, MD: Westat.

Wexler, David B. 2000. "Therapeutic Jurisprudence: An Overview." *Thomas M. Cooley Law Review* 17:125–134.

Wexler, David B., and Bruce J. Winick. 1996. *Law in a Therapeutic Key: Developments in Therapeutic Jurisprudence.* Durham, NC: Carolina Academic Press.

Wilson, James Q. 1983. *Thinking about Crime.* 2nd ed. New York: Vintage Books.

Wilson, James Q., and George Kelling. 1982. "Broken Windows: The Police and Neighborhood Safety." *Atlantic Monthly*, March, pp. 29–38.

Winick, Bruce J. 1997. "The Jurisprudence of Therapeutic Jurisprudence." *Psychology, Public Policy and Law* 3 (1): 184–206.

———. 1999. "Redefining the Role of the Criminal Defense Lawyer at Plea Bargaining and Sentencing: A Therapeutic Jurisprudence/Preventative Law Model." *Psychology, Public Policy and Law* 5 (4): 1034–1083.

Zimring, Franklin E., and David T. Johnson. 2006. "Public Opinion and the Governance of Punishment in Democratic Political Systems." *Annals of the American Academy of Political and Social Science* 605:266–280.

Zozula, Christine. 2018. "Courting the Community: Organizational Flexibility and Community Courts." *Criminology and Criminal Justice* 18 (2): 226–244.

Index

The page number followed by the letter *t* refers to the table. The page number followed by the letter *f* refers to the figure.

CHRISTINE ZOZULA is an Assistant Professor of Sociology and of Criminology and Criminal Justice at the University of Rhode Island.